Guru Gobind Singh (1666–1708)

Master of the White Hawk

An equestrian portrait of Guru Gobind Singh

Courtesy: Government Museum and Art Gallery, Chandigarh.

Guru Gobind Singh
(1666–1708)

Master of the White Hawk

J. S. Grewal

OXFORD
UNIVERSITY PRESS

OXFORD
UNIVERSITY PRESS

Oxford University Press is a department of the University of Oxford.
It furthers the University's objective of excellence in research, scholarship,
and education by publishing worldwide. Oxford is a registered trademark of
Oxford University Press in the UK and in certain other countries.

Published in India by
Oxford University Press
22 Workspace, 2nd Floor, 1/22 Asaf Ali Road, New Delhi 110 002, India

First Edition published in 2019
Seventh impression 2024

ISBN-13 (print edition): 978-0-19-949494-1
ISBN-10 (print edition): 0-19-949494-0

ISBN-13 (eBook): 978-0-19-099038-1
ISBN-10 (eBook): 0-19-099038-4

Typeset in Trump Mediaeval LT Std 9.5/13
by Tranistics Data Technologies, Kolkata 700 091
Printed in India by Replika Press Pvt. Ltd

To Professor Indu Banga
who has been actively associated with all the books
I have published during the past half a century

Contents

Tables and Figures

Tables

Figures

Maps

Images

Appendices

Preface

In celebration of the tercentenary of Guru Gobind Singh's birth, I wrote (jointly with S. S. Bal) a biographical study of Guru Gobind Singh for the Panjab University. It was published in 1967, and reprinted in 1987. Three other biographies of Guru Gobind Singh were published in 1965–7. But none of them gave references to the sources used for the statements made in the text. Historians of a new generation have referred to our biographical study as an 'authoritative' and a 'seminal' work. The present study is distinguished by the use of contemporary and near contemporary sources in Gurmukhi, Persian, and English as much as its widened scope.

This study has 12 chapters placed in four parts. The first part has two chapters. The first relates in a way to historiographical context, highlighting new perspectives on issues and sources which have emerged in the past few decades. The second chapter outlines the context provided by the Mughal state for developments related to the Sikh Panth. Far from being an inert framework, the Mughal state was an active agency for shaping events.

The second part too has two chapters on the pre-Khalsa decades. Chapter 3 relates to the early life and the first decade of Guru Gobind Singh's Guruship and chapter 4 deals with his political activity from 1685 to 1698. The third part has three chapters. Chapters 5 and 6 relate to the literary activity at the court of

Guru Gobind Singh from 1685 to 1698, and the social and political import of courtly literature. The institution of the Khalsa, the most momentous event of Guru Gobind Singh's life, forms the subject of chapter 6.

The fourth part has 5 chapters. Escalation of conflict between the Mughal authorities and Guru Gobind Singh, resulting in the evacuation of Anandpur, is the subject of chapter 8. In chapters 9 and 10, Guru Gobind Singh negotiates a peaceful settlement with Aurangzeb and Bahadur Shah. On the failure of negotiations, Banda was commissioned as a Singh to lead the Khalsa Singhs in revolt against the Mughal state in a bid for Khalsa Raj. In chapter 11, Guru Gobind Singh enunciates the last commandment of his life, the vesting of Guruship in the Granth and the Panth. The political, social, and cultural legacies of Guru Gobind Singh are discussed in chapter 12.

A number of controversial themes have been discussed in short appendices: (a) Khalsa identity in a recent study of the Sikh warrior tradition; (b) Ani Rai's *Jangnama*; (c) Guru Gobind Singh's speech on the Baisakhi of 1699; (d) Koer Singh's *Gurbilas*; (e) Bhai Nand Lal's homage to the Sikh Gurus; (f) Signification of the term 'Khalsa'; (g) Perspectives on the *Zafarnama*; (h) How to account for Guru Gobind Singh's presence near Bahadur Shah (1707–8); (i) Mata Sundari, Mata Sahib Devi, and the Khalsa Panth; and (j) *Hanne Hanne Patshahi*.

The sub-title of the book, 'Master of the White Hawk', is added with deference to its association with Guru Gobind Singh in popular Sikh art and lore. Incidentally, the Mughal emperor Akbar was also fond of the white hawk.

Working on this book, I have become indebted to a number of institutions and individuals. I may mention in particular Bhai Kahn Singh Nabha Library, Punjabi University, Patiala; the Library of its Department of Punjab Historical Studies; A. C. Joshi Library, Panjab University, Chandigarh; Bhai Gurdas Library, Guru Nanak Dev University, Amritsar; and Sikh History Research Library, Khalsa College, Amritsar. Among the persons who have been helpful throughout this work, I would like to mention Professor Indu Banga, Dr Karamjit K. Malhotra, Professor Sheena Pall, and Professor Reeta Grewal (my daughter). Without their sustained interest and active support, the book would not have been completed. I am grateful to them.

I am thankful to Komal for typing out several drafts of the book with diligence and care.

It has been a pleasure to work with the OUP team. I appreciate their professional concern.

J. S. Grewal

Chandigarh
4 October 2018

I

Introductory

1

New Perspectives and Sources

In the past few decades, several new issues have been raised in Sikh studies, notably martyrdom in the Sikh tradition, Sikh iden-tity, and the question of equality, caste, and gender in the Sikh social order. At the same time, a number of historians have taken a lively interest in the making of the *Adi Granth* and the *Dasam Granth*, and in *Rahitnama* literature. The eighteenth-century Sikh literature has been explored by scholars from different disciplines. The Sikhs began to figure in Persian works in the early eighteenth century, and in English works in the late eighteenth century. All these sources have created the possibility of a fresh study of Guru Gobind Singh.

Martyrdom, Identity, and Gender Relations

'Of all the martyrs the Sikh faith has produced,' observes Louis E. Fenech, 'none has received the attention given to Guru Tegh Bahadur.' The verses on the martyrdom of Guru Tegh Bahadur in the *Bachittar Natak* are amongst 'the most celebrated in Sikh lit-erature'. The way Sikh martyrdom is understood today seems to be 'a direct result of this passage', which is the first in Sikh literature to state that sacrificing one's life for the sake of *dharam* ensured a spot in paradise. Never before had such courage been absorbed into 'a conceptual system which rewarded the heroic sacrifice of one's life for a righteous cause with liberation'.[1]

Fenech argues that the twentieth-century Tat Khalsa wrongly treated the martyrdom of Guru Tegh Bahadur as a sacrifice to save Hinduism. In his view, the *tilak* and *janju* in the passage under consideration refer to the frontal mark and the sacred thread of Guru Tegh Bahadur himself. In other words, Guru Tegh Bahadur sacrificed his life for the sake of his own faith. Indeed, the contemporary *Sri Gur Sobha* refers to dharam and the *dharamsal* for which Guru Tegh Bahadur gave his head.[2] It must be added, however, that in the *Bachittar Natak*, Guru Tegh Bahadur is referred to as 'the protective sheet of India (Hind)' and in the *Sri Gur Sobha*, the Guru is 'the protective sheet of the world' (*jagg chadar*).[3] This suggests a general principle for his sacrifice, such as the freedom of conscience.

Sikh identity has been debated over in the past three decades.[4] The institution of the Khalsa, in Harjot Oberoi's view, ended the ambiguities of Sikh religiosity. The first major signifier of the changing alignment and orientation was the coming of the term 'Khalsa'. This new personhood was confirmed through a novel ritual called *khande ki pahul*. To this new identity, Guru Gobind Singh gave further shape by commanding the Khalsa to carry arms on his person and by making *hukka*-smoking a taboo. Manuals of code-of-conduct, called Rahitnamas, were prepared, laying down the nature of piety for the Khalsa and covering all domains of human life.[5]

Paradoxically, as the Khalsa mode attained hegemony within the Sikh tradition, simultaneously it came to be accepted that there were alternative ways of being a Sikh. In other words, the Sikh *Panth* was not coterminous with the Khalsa and it was possible to be a Sikh without being a Khalsa. The term used for such non-Khalsa Sikhs was *Sahajdhari*. Included among them were the *Nanak-Panthi*s and the *Udasi*s. Their religious culture was conceded to be 'legitimate'. The *Dasam Granth*, as much as the *Adi Granth*, came to be regarded as a sacred text.[6]

Jeevan Deol looks upon the creation of the Khalsa as a seminal moment in the shaping of the Sikh consciousness. The Rahitnamas for Deol are closest to an exclusively Khalsa discourse. What is central to the definition of a member of the Khalsa in the *Tankhahnama* is the ideal of *nam*, *dan*, and *isnan* and obedience to the *bani*. At the centre of the Sikh identity, thus, is the community of believers, constituted through worship and commensality. The stress in the *Sakhi Rahit* is on the separateness of the Khalsa and the need to reinterpret the discourse of Indic life cycles. The *Sakhi Rahit* is particularly strong against popular piety and Brahmin-centered rituals. Instead, the ritual universe of the Khalsa is centered around the *shabad*; the Sikh sacred universe is centered around pilgrimages to sites associated with the Gurus. The Rahitnama attributed to Chaupa Singh embodies many of the central themes of the eighteenth-century discourses of community formation.[7]

The most prominent marker of the Khalsa distinctiveness is the duty of each Singh to bear arms and keep his hair long. The discourse is explicitly political. In the Chaupa Singh text, the ultimate meaning of the Khalsa is the pursuit of political sovereignty. The attainment of sovereignty forms the much-quoted climax of the *Tankhahnama*:

Raj karega Khalsa aki rahe na koi
Khwar hoe sabh milenge bachae saran jo hoi

[The *Khalsa* shall rule and none shall withstand them; shorn of honour, they shall all submit, and only they who take refuge with the *Khalsa* shall be saved.]

This stress on political sovereignty, rather unique in the north-Indian religious context of the period, forms an essential part of discourse on the formation of the Khalsa identity.[8]

Avtar Singh points to ethics as an important marker of the Sikh identity. This was in consonance with Guru Nanak's enunciation, 'Truth is higher than everything, but higher still is true conduct.' The echo of Guru Nanak's *'upar sach achar'* (higher still is true conduct) can be heard in Guru Gobind Singh's *'subh karman te kabhu na taru'* (May I never falter in doing good). Avtar Singh has rightly emphasized the importance of ethics in the Sikh ideology with the notion of equality built into its universality. This is one of the several features which link the pre-Khalsa with the Khalsa Panth.[9]

Purnima Dhavan is seriously concerned with the 'Khalsa identity' in her recent publication *When Sparrows Became Hawks:
The Making of the Sikh Warrior Tradition, 1699–1799*. In her view,
the *Bachittar Natak* and the *Sri Gur Sobha* present two opposing
concepts which influenced the nature and character of the Khalsa
identity during the eighteenth century, accommodating considerable
diversity within the Khalsa order. Another factor that influenced
the formation of the Khalsa identity was the increasing presence
of peasant communities among the Khalsa, especially the Jats.
Re-formed in 1708–48, the Khalsa identity crystallized in the late
eighteenth century when the 'peasant soldier' was transformed
into an 'elite warrior'. Dhavan raises a number of questions in
relation to the Khalsa identity, and provides plausible answers.
She uses Sikh literature of the eighteenth century, especially the
Rahitnama and *Gurbilas* literature. Her interpretation of this
evidence is open to debate.[10]

A number of historians have taken interest in the issues of caste
and gender in the Sikh social order.[11] A few works in the *Dasam
Granth* have been studied from the viewpoint of gender relations. Nikky-Guninder Kaur Singh talks of Durga becoming Guru
Gobind Singh's favourite literary subject. Durga is 'recalled' as a
figure of myth and not 'invoked' as a goddess. Nowhere does Guru
Gobind Singh profess himself to be a devotee of the Goddess. God
created Durga for the destruction of demons. The martial exploits
of Durga are celebrated, but she is not deified. The affirmation of
female power by Guru Gobind Singh illustrates the overall positive
attitude towards women in the Sikh speculation. Durga's qualities
could inspire men and women to positive action; they could
overcome their weakness and cowardice, overthrow the unjust
political authorities, abolish social inequalities, and ultimately
forge a new structure based on more just and egalitarian values.[12]
The case appears to have been much overstated.

Doris R. Jakobsh thinks that the heightened politicization of
the Panth would have relegated women to set positions more
in line with traditional female roles. In a military environ-
ment, the demotion of women was a certainty. The development of militancy among the Sikhs peaked with the ascendancy
of Guru Gobind Singh. The transformation from 'masculine to

hyper-masculine ethos' was now complete. Jakobsh supports her hypothesis with evidence from the *Charitaro Pakhyan* and the *Chaupa Singh Rahit-Nama*. Most of the tales relate to love, sexual intrigue, and violence, and women are often the seducers. Women in the *Charitaro Pakhyan* symbolize the ultimate antithesis of the warrior-saint norm that the Guru was attempting to construct. They had the power to turn the warrior-saint away from his true calling. Much impressed by the 'theology of difference' as a hypothesis, Jakobsh tends to oversimplify the issue of gender in the Order of the Khalsa.[13]

Gurinder Singh Mann does not attribute the texts in question to Guru Gobind Singh and points out that both Nikky Singh and Jakobsh are highly selective in what they cull from the *Dasam Granth*. Their interpretations of gender relations are consequently lopsided.[14]

Sikh Scripture, the *Dasam Granth*, and the Rahitnamas

In *The Making of Sikh Scripture*, Gurinder Singh Mann refers to the dominant Sikh view since the nineteenth century which places the making of the Sikh scripture, known as the *Adi Granth*, at Damdama (Talwandi Sabo) in 1705–6. However, the first manuscript of the *Adi Granth* was dated 1782, and it was followed by manuscripts inscribed in 1688, 1691, and 1692. The *Adi Granth*, evidently, was compiled in the early 1680s at Damdama in Anandpur.[15] In other words, the *Adi Granth* became a canonical text much before Guru Gobind Singh's stay in Talwandi Sabo (Damdama Sahib). There can be no doubt about Guru Gobind Singh's deep interest in the *Granth*.

The authorship of the *Dasam Granth* has been debated for over a century and a half. Many scholars attribute the creation of the whole of the *Dasam Granth* to Guru Gobind Singh, while others attribute only a very small part to him. The debate has been studied rather thoroughly by Ratan Singh Jaggi. He suggests three periods of controversy in which scholars were ranged on both sides, attributing all or only a few compositions of the

Dasam Granth to Guru Gobind Singh. Jaggi concluded that there were three categories of compositions: (*a*) the *Jap, Akal Ustat* (leaving out Chhands 201–30), *Savvayyae,* and the *Zafarnama* as the works of Guru Gobind Singh, (*b*) the *Shabad Hazare, Khalsa Mahima, and Gian Prabodh* as 'mixed' in terms of authorship, and (*c*) the remaining works composed by poets other than Guru Gobind Singh.[16] Among the eminent scholars who ascribed the entire *Dasam Granth* to Guru Gobind Singh were Trilochan Singh, D. P. Ashta, Bhai Randhir Singh, and Harbhajan Singh. In the opposing group were the scholars of Bhasaur, Shamsher Singh Ashok, and Giani Harnam Singh.[17]

C. H. Loehlin includes the *Jap, Akal Ustat, Bachittar Natak, Chandi Charitar I* and *II, Var Bhagauti ki, Gian Prabodh, Hazare Shabad, Savvayyae,* and *Zafarnama* in the compositions usually considered Guru Gobind Singh's own. The Guru's authentic compositions cover only about 168 of the total 1428 pages of the *Dasam Granth*. Compiled after Guru Gobind Singh's death, the *Dasam Granth* had a considerable influence on the lives of the Sikhs. The two *Granth*s together formed 'the Sikh ideal man, the soldier-saint'.[18]

W. H. McLeod looked upon the autobiographical *Bachittar Natak* and the *Zafarnama,* the *Jap, Akal Ustat, Gian Prabodh, Shabad Hazare,* and also 'perhaps' *Chandi di Var* as the works of Guru Gobind Singh. The remainder of the *Dasam Granth* was substantially the work of the court poets. This view, published in 1975, was modified in 1989, further reducing the number of works of Guru Gobind Singh.[19]

Gurinder Singh Mann points out, 'We know relatively little about the precise corpus of the Guru's writings, the circumstances of their entry into these texts, and the history as well as the position of the *Dasam Granth* within the Sikh community.' Guru Gobind Singh's compositions were there in the *Dasam Granth* and *Sri Sarab Loh Granth,* but were very few. Even the *Sarab Kal Ki Benati* (*Bachittar Natak*), composed around 1698, was the work of a court poet.[20]

Literary activity reached its peak during the time of Guru Gobind Singh in two phases. Poets from the Mathura region came to Paunta and the products of their literary activity were compiled as *Krishan Avtar* in 1688. Some of these poets followed Guru Gobind Singh to Anandpur and continued to write on Hindu deities. These compositions were added to the previous corpus in 1698 to compile the *Bachittar Natak Granth*. Some other poets came to the court at Anandpur and composed the tales of kings, warriors, uncouth men, and women of easy virtue. An assortment of such stories was compiled in the form of *Charitaro Pakhyan* in 1696. Yet another compilation was entitled *Sri Sarab Loh Granth* (1698). These texts were the 'markers of the aura of royalty that the Sikhs attempted to create at Anandpur'.[21] One of the fundamental dimensions of the compositions of the *Dasam Granth* and the works of the poets at Guru Gobind Singh's court was their 'performative' nature. Prepared to fulfil the needs of patrons, authors, Sikhs, or listeners, most of the works were not meant to be understood in the same way as the *Adi Granth*.[22]

'The Adi Granth is the Guru,' says W. H. McLeod. He goes on to add that the same respect was bestowed on the second Sikh scripture, the *Dasam Granth*, 'It too was regarded as the visibly present Guru and thus received the same veneration.' For the basis of this statement, McLeod refers to John Malcolm's *Sketch of the Sikhs*.[23] However, Malcolm does not use the word 'Guru', not even for the *Adi Granth*. What he says exactly is that the book of the 10th king was considered 'in every respect, as holy as' the Adi Granth of Guru Nanak.[24]

Next to the Sikh scripture and the *Dasam Granth* was the Rahitnama literature. Dating the Rahitnamas has been an important issue. W. H. McLeod asserted in his book *Sikhs of the Khalsa* that no Rahitnama was composed in the lifetime of Guru Gobind Singh. The *Tankhahnama*, the earliest Rahitnama for him, was written a few years after Guru Gobind Singh's death. He places the *Sakhi Rahit* and the *Rahitnama Prahilad Singh* in the mid-1730s, the *Chaupa Singh Rahit-Nama* between 1740 and 1765, and the Rahitnamas of Desa Singh and Daya Singh at the end of the eighteenth century.[25]

The rediscovery of a copy of the *Nasihatnama* of 1718–19 (which is actually the well-known Tankhahnama generally attributed to Bhai Nand Lal) has radically changed the perspective on Rahitnamas. Karamjit K. Malhotra has studied the *Nasihatnama* in detail and suggested that no element in this manuscript goes against the assumption that the original was composed in the life-time of Guru Gobind Singh, between 1699 and 1708.[26]

It has been argued recently that much of the *rahit* literature was produced during the lifetime of Guru Gobind Singh. The first statement of rahit created during Guru Gobind Singh's time is attributed to Bhai Nand Lal. Popularly known as *Prashan-Uttar*, it is placed in 1694. The Rahitnama of Prahilad Singh was com-posed in 1695. The Tankhahnama attributed to Nand Lal (the *Nasihatnama*) appears to have been created in the years that followed. The preface and the rahit part of the *Chaupa Singh Rahit-Nama* formed the original core to which other segments, the narrative and the *tankhah* (penance) parts, were added later. The core was approved by the Guru on 14th May 1700. The *Prem Sumarag Granth*, a comprehensive document, marked the peak among the rahit documents produced at Anandpur; it synchro-nizes well with the Sikh religious, social, and political aspira-tions of the rule of *deg* and *teg*.[27]

Six Rahitnamas are thus placed in the time of Guru Gobind Singh. This change, in perspective, may suggest a major modifica-tion in our understanding of the Khalsa way of life. In any case, the origin of all the important norms and ideals of rahit are to be traced to the time of Guru Gobind Singh.

Some other works may be added to the contemporary sources. The *Sri Gur Sobha* complements the *Bachittar Natak* with the earliest account of the institution of the Khalsa, the battles of the Khalsa, and the end of Guru Gobind Singh's life with the dec-laration of vesting of Guruship in the Granth and the Panth.[28] The *Parchian Patshahi Dasvin ki* tends to present episodes (*sakhi*s) of Guru Gobind Singh's life from the Udasi perspective, but with some significant pieces of factual information.[29] The *Amarnama* gives an eyewitness account of some incidents in the life of Guru Gobind Singh at Nanded (Abchalnagar).[30] Ani Rai's *Jangnama Guru Gobind Singh ji ka* is regarded as an impor-tant contemporary work, but no one has discussed its historical significance.[31]

Finally, there are the *hukamnama*s of Guru Gobind Singh, both dated and undated, which have a significance of their own. Seen in relation to the various aspects of his life, the hukamnamas of Guru Gobind Singh provide valuable insights.[32]

Eighteenth-Century Sources: Gurmukhi, Persian, and English

Gurbilas appeared as a new form of Sikh literature, narrating the glorious events of Guru Gobind Singh's life in a broad chronological sequence.[33] Koer Singh's *Gurbilas Patshahi 10* covers the entire life of Guru Gobind Singh, going far beyond the information from the *Bachittar Natak* and the *Sri Gur Sobha*, with the oral evidence provided by Bhai Mani Singh.[34] Sukha Singh's *Gurbilas Patsahi 10* follows the broad pattern of Koer Singh's work, but elaborates most of the episodes.[35] The *Guru Kian Sakhian* of Sarup Singh Kaushish, with 76 sakhis on Guru Gobind Singh, is remarkable for the information it provides on events, dates, persons, and places.[36]

The increasing concern of the eighteenth-century Sikhs with the 10 Gurus as a single entity is reflected in the *Bansavalinama* of Kesar Singh Chhibber and the *Mahima Prakash* of Sarup Das Bhalla. Chhibber's work has 14 chapters, one each on the 10 Gurus and one each on 'Banda Sahib', Ajit Singh, Mata Sahib Devi, and the contemporary Sikhs. In his own way, Chhibber tries to cover the whole of Sikh history from the time of Guru Nanak to his own.[37] Sarup Das Bhalla's work consists of sakhis of all the 10 Gurus, the maximum number of them on Guru Nanak, followed by Guru Gobind Singh. There is one sakhi on Banda. Sarup Das Bhalla represents a tradition different from the one represented by Kesar Singh.[38] Ratan Singh Bhangu's *Sri Gur Panth Prakash*, written in the second decade of the nineteenth century, was professedly meant to answer one question: 'How did the Sikhs become sovereign?' His main concern with the answer to this question makes his work eminently historical. Bhangu felt concerned with the past and the future of the Sikhs.[39]

Nearly the whole span of Sikh history up to the early nineteenth century is covered by extracts from Persian sources included in *Sikh History from Persian Sources*. However, only a small part of these extracts relate to Guru Gobind Singh.[40] By far the most valuable evidence on Guru Gobind Singh comes from the *Ahkam* (orders) and the *Akhbarat* (news reports). The Persian writers of the late eighteenth and the early nineteenth century, commissioned or encouraged by the servants of the East India Company, used oral evidence collected from their contemporaries.[41] Rarely do they use the early eighteenth-century works as their sources. Their works are more relevant for their own times rather than the time of Guru Gobind Singh. Therefore, it is necessary to assess their credibility before using them as authentic testimony.[42]

The most important sources in English were the works of Antoine Louis-Henri Polier, James Browne, and George Forster. They all wrote in the 1780s to serve the interests of the East India Company. But none of them produced a reliable account. John Malcolm's *Sketch of the Sikhs* was published in book form in 1812. The early phase of British historical writing on the Sikhs ended with J. D. Cunningham's *History of the Sikhs: From the Origin of the Nation to the Battles of the Sutlej* in 1845–6. Interested primarily in the Sikhs of their own time, the European writers generally traced the political activity of the Sikhs to the time of Guru Gobind Singh. Beginning with their own observation and oral evidence, the European writers began to use commissioned works from Persian and Sikh sources translated into English. They were distinguished from other writers by their concern for empirical evidence and rational interpretation.[43]

Malcolm was critical of both Sikh and Muslim writers; the former for their 'enthusiastic admiration' of the Gurus and the latter for misrepresenting them. Nevertheless, he gave preference to the Sikh writers because it was of 'the most essential importance to hear what a nation has to say of itself'. Guru Nanak wanted to reform and not destroy the religion of his ancestors. 'It was reserved for Guru Gobind to give a new character to the religion of his followers.' However, he did this not by making any material change in the tenets of Guru Nanak but by establishing institutions and usages which separated the Sikhs from Hindus and destroyed at one blow a system of civil polity that had withstood the shock of ages. Malcolm is emphatic that 'wherever the religion of Guru Gobind prevails, the institutions of Brahma must fall'.[44]

Malcolm's *Sketch of the Sikhs* is distinguished from the work of his predecessors by a considerable use of Sikh sources on the religion of the Sikhs. The scope of his work is also much larger. He emphasizes the difference between the Khalsa Singhs and the rest of the Sikhs. His account of the Sikh religion is more detailed than that of his predecessors, but his conceptualization of Sikh beliefs and practices is not clear. The evidence he cites in support of his view of Sikhism as a Hindu reform does not lead to this inference.[45]

Cunningham was different from his British predecessors in his appreciation of a non-Christian religion as a motivating force for social action. The motive of revenge on the part of Guru Gobind Singh was not enough to explain the rise of the Khalsa into political power.[46] Guru Gobind Singh declared that all the members of the Khalsa order were one: 'the lowest were equal with the highest' and 'the four races must eat as one out of one vessel'. He saw what was yet vital and 'relumed it with Promethean fire'. What the Khalsa achieved after his death was the result of the ground he had prepared. The achievement of the Khalsa was virtually an achievement of Guru Gobind Singh.[47]

Significantly, the bulk of the evidence on Guru Gobind Singh comes from Gurmukhi sources. Chronology is not a strong point of this evidence, but there is detailed information relayed apparently for its own sake. The Persian sources form only a small part of the sources, but they are strong in chronology and, therefore, useful out of all proportion to the bulk. In English, there are no contemporary sources on Guru Gobind Singh, but the European authors are more seriously concerned with factual accuracy and rational reconstruction of events. All the three categories of sources become more meaningful if seen in combination rather than in isolation.

In all, 10 works in Gurmukhi are consulted more than others. Chronologically, they are the *Bachittar Natak* (1698), *Sri Gur Sobha* (1708), the *Parchian* of Sewadas (1709), the Rahitnama associated with Chaupa Singh (1700, 1740–65), Koer Singh's *Gurbilas* (1751), Chhibber's *Bansavalinama* (1769), Bhalla's *Mahima Prakash* (1776), *Guru Kian Sakhian* of Kaushish (1790), Sukha Singh's *Gurbilas* (1797), and *Sri Gur Panth Prakash* of

Ratan Singh Bhangu (1810–14). Sukha Singh was familiar with Koer Singh's *Gurbilas*, while both of them were familiar with the first three works. Chhibber was familiar with the work of Chaupa Singh. Sarup Das Bhalla was familiar with the *Bachittar Natak*. Ratan Singh Bhangu refers to Sukha Singh's *Gurbilas* in several different situations. All these works support, supplement, and complement one another. They also differ, and it is not easy to resolve all the differences. It may be added that the evidence of these works becomes more useful when seen in combination with one another and with the sources in Persian and English.

Notes

1. Louis E. Fenech, *Martyrdom in the Sikh Tradition: Playing the 'Game of Love'* (New Delhi: Oxford University Press, 2002 [2nd impression]), pp. 82, 85–6, 124–5. J.S. Grewal, *The Sikhs: Ideology, Institutions, and Identity* (New Delhi: Oxford University Press, 2009), pp. 42–75.

2. Fenech, *Martyrdom in the Sikh Tradition*, p. 124.

3. Sainapat, *Sri Gur Sobha*, edited by Shamsher Singh Ashok (Amritsar: Shiromani Gurdwara Prabandhak Committee, 1967), p. 11.

4. J. S. Grewal, *Recent Debates in Sikh Studies: An Assessment* (New Delhi: Manohar, 2011), pp. 101–32.

5. Harjot Oberoi, *The Construction of Religious Boundaries: Culture, Identity and Diversity in the Sikh Tradition* (New Delhi: Oxford University Press, 1994), pp. 59–62.

6. Oberoi, *The Construction of Religious Boundaries*, pp. 65–82.

7. Jeevan Deol, 'Eighteenth Century Khalsa Identity: Discourse, Praxis and Narrative', in *Sikh Religion, Culture and Ethnicity*, edited by Christopher Shackle, Gurharpal Singh and Arvindpal Singh Mandair (Richmond: Curzon Press, 2001), pp. 25–38.

8. Deol, 'Eighteenth Century Khalsa Identity', pp. 38–40.

9. Avtar Singh, 'Sikh Identity and Continuity: A Perspective from Ethics', in *Philosophical Perspectives on Sikhism*, edited by Gurnam Kaur (Patiala: Punjabi University, 1998), pp. 75–80. For the controversy on Sikh identity, see J. S. Grewal, *Historical Perspectives on Sikh Identity* (Patiala: Punjabi University, 1997).

10. For a brief discussion of Dhavan's work, see Appendix 1.1.

11. W. H. McLeod, *The Evolution of the Sikh Community* (Delhi: Oxford University Press, 1975), pp. 83–104. Jagjit Singh, 'Caste System and the Sikhs', in *Perspectives on the Sikh Tradition*, edited by Gurdev

Singh (Patiala: Siddharth Publications, 1986), pp. 231–314. J. S. Grewal, *Guru Nanak and Patriarchy* (Shimla: Indian Institute of Advanced Study, 1993). J. S. Grewal, 'Caste and the Sikh Social Order', and 'Sikhism and Gender', in *The Sikhs: Ideology, Institutions, and Identity* (New Delhi: Oxford University Press, 2009), pp. 189–225. For caste and gender in the eighteenth-century Sikh social order, see Karamjit K. Malhotra, *The Eighteenth Century in Sikh History: Political Resurgence, Religious and Social Life, and Cultural Articulation* (New Delhi: Oxford University Press, 2016), pp. 203–21.

12. Nikky-Guninder Kaur Singh, *The Feminine Principle in the Sikh Vision of the Transcendent* (Cambridge: Cambridge University Press, 1993), pp. 121–31.

13. Doris R. Jakobsh, *Relocating Gender in Sikh History: Transformation, Meaning and Identity* (New Delhi: Oxford University Press, 2003), pp. 44–8.

14. Gurinder Singh Mann, 'Sources for the Study of Guru Gobind Singh's Life and Times', *Journal of Punjab Studies* (Special Issue on Guru Gobind Singh), 15, nos 1 and 2 (Spring–Fall 2008): 230–40, 251–2.

15. Gurinder Singh Mann, *The Making of Sikh Scripture* (New York: Oxford University Press, 2001), pp. 82–5, 121–2. See also Pashaura Singh, *The Guru Granth Sahib* (New Delhi: Oxford University Press, 2001), pp. 82–5. Mann clarifies that the addition of the bani of Guru Tegh Bahadur does not make a compilation, like MS 1192, the *Adi Granth*. Furthermore, a set of compositions in branch 2 of the earlier manuscripts appears to have been dropped. For a discussion of the early manuscripts of the *Adi Granth* compiled at Damdama in Anandpur, see Harbhajan Singh, *Gurbani Sampadan Nirnay* (Chandigarh: Satnam Prakashan, 1982), pp. 110–50.

16. Ratan Singh Jaggi, *Dasam Granth da Kartritav* (New Delhi: Punjabi Sahit Sabha, 1966), p. 195.

17. Jaggi, *Dasam Granth da Kartritav*, pp. 25–6.

18. C. H. Loehlin, *The Granth of Guru Gobind Singh and The Khalsa Brotherhood* (Lucknow: Lucknow Publishing House, 1971), pp. 7, 9, 10, 18, 57.

19. W. H. McLeod, *The Evolution of the Sikh Community*, pp. 79–81. W. H. McLeod, *The Sikhs: History, Religion and Society* (New York: Columbia University Press, 1989), pp. 90–1.

20. Mann, 'Sources for the Study of Guru Gobind Singh's Life and Times', pp. 251, 258.

21. Mann, 'Sources for the Study of Guru Gobind Singh's Life and Times', pp. 248–9, 275, n. 131.

22. Louis E. Fenech, *The Darbar of the Sikh Gurus: The Court of God in the World of Men* (New Delhi: Oxford University Press, 2008), pp. 10, 20–2, 25, 56–8, 60, 62, 64–6, 87–104, 136–45, 148–9, 154–6.

23. McLeod, *The Sikhs*, pp. 89–90.

24. Malcolm (John), *Sketch of the Sikhs* (New Delhi: Asian Educational Service, 1986 [1812]), p. 173.

25. W. H. McLeod, *Sikhs of the Khalsa: A History of the Khalsa Rahit* (New Delhi: Oxford University Press, 2003), pp. 70–2.

26. Karamjit K. Malhotra, 'The Earliest Manual on the Sikh Way of Life', in *Five Centuries of Sikh Tradition: Ideology, Society, Politics and Culture*, edited by Reeta Grewal and Sheena Pall (New Delhi: Manohar, 2005), pp. 55–81.

27. Mann, 'Sources for the Study of Guru Gobind Singh's Life and Times', 243–5.

28. Sainapat, *Sri Gur Sobha*, edited by Shamsher Singh Ashok.

29. *Episodes from Lives of the Gurus: Parchian Sewadas*, translated and edited by Kharak Singh and Gurtej Singh (Chandigarh: Institute of Sikh Studies, 1995). The Gurmukhi text published by the editors and referred to as the *Parchian Sewadas*, has been used in the present study.

30. Nath Mal, *Amarnama*, edited by Ganda Singh (Amritsar: Sikh History Society, 1953).

31. For a discussion of Ani Rai's work, see Appendix 1.2.

32. *Hukamname Guru Sahiban, Mata Sahiban, Banda Singh ate Khalsa Ji De*, edited by Ganda Singh (Patiala: Punjabi University, 1967). For a brief discussion of the hukamnamas of Guru Gobind Singh, see C. H. Loehlin, *The Granth of Guru Gobind Singh and the Khalsa Brotherhood*, pp. 60–7.

33. For a cogent statement on all the old and new forms of Sikh literature in the eighteenth century, see Malhotra, *The Eighteenth Century in Sikh History*, pp. 233–49.

34. Koer Singh, *Gurbilas Patshahi 10*, edited by Shamsher Singh Ashok (Patiala: Punjab University, 1968). See Appendix 1.3.

35. Sukha Singh, *Gurbilas Patsahi 10*, edited by Gursharan Kaur Jaggi (Patiala: Punjabi Languages Department, 1989). See Appendix 1.3.

36. Bhai Svarup Singh Kaushish, *Guru Kian Sakhian*, edited by Piara Singh Padam (Amritsar: Singh Brothers, 1999).

37. Kesar Singh Chhibber, 'Bansavalinama Dasan Patshahian Ka', edited by Ratan Singh Jaggi, in *Parkh*, vol. 2 (Chandigarh: Panjab University, 1972).

38. Sarup Das Bhalla, *Mahima Prakash*, Part I, edited by Shamsher Singh Ashok and Gobind Singh Lamba (Patiala: Punjab Languages Department,

1970); Part II, edited by Gobind Singh Lamba and Khazan Singh (Patiala: Punjab Languages Department, 1971).

39. Ratan Singh Bhangu, *Sri Gur Panth Prakash*, edited by Balwant Singh Dhillon (Amritsar: Singh Brothers, 2004).

40. J. S. Grewal, 'Introduction' to *Sikh History from Persian Sources*, edited by J. S. Grewal and Irfan Habib (New Delhi: Tulika/Indian History Congress, 2001).

41. J. S. Grewal, *Guru Tegh Bahadur and the Persian Chroniclers* (Amritsar: Guru Nanak Dev University, 1976), pp. 22, 25–6.

42. For a discussion of the Persian sources, see Appendix 1.4.

43. J. S. Grewal, *Historical Writings on the Sikhs (1784–2011): Western Enterprise and Indian Response* (New Delhi: Manohar, 2011), pp. 17–37.

44. Grewal, *Historical Writings on the Sikhs*, pp. 40–59.

45. Grewal, *Historical Writings on the Sikhs*, pp. 57–8.

46. Grewal, *Historical Writings on the Sikhs*, pp. 110–56.

47. Joseph Davey Cunningham, *History of the Sikhs: From the Origin of the Nation to the Battles of the Sutlej* (New Delhi: Rupa & Co, 2002 [1849]), pp. 65, 68, 70–3, 82–4.

Appendix 1A

Khalsa Identity in a Recent Study of the Sikh Warrior Tradition

The first three chapters of Purnima Dhavan's *When Sparrows Became Hawks: The Making of the Sikh Warrior Tradition, 1699–1799* are the most relevant for our present purpose: (*a*) 'Introduction: The Origins of the Khalsa', (*b*) 'Early Narratives of the Last Guru and the Creation of the Khalsa', and (*c*) '(Re)Making the Khalsa, 1708–1748'.

Dhavan states in the Introduction that the hagiographic narratives created in the eighteenth century dominate the modern understanding of how and when the Khalsa was created. Recent scholarship suggests, however, that the characteristic rites, texts, and the visible markers of the Khalsa identity changed considerably in the century after 1699 and the Khalsa identity crystallized before the end of the century. Dhavan's study was meant to interrogate how the hagiographic accounts of the Khalsa's history shaped and extended the Khalsa identity during the eighteenth century. The vision and teachings of Guru Gobind Singh are presumed to have been the central motivational factors in mobilizing Punjabi peasants, but a new research suggests that the participation of the peasants in martial activities of the Khalsa was equally instrumental in shaping the Khalsa identity.[1]

The second chapter deals with the testimony of the *Bachittar Natak* and the creation of the Khalsa in Sainapat's *Sri Gur Sobha*. These contemporary texts project two opposing concepts of dharam. Accepted as the 10th Guru's own work, the *Bachittar Natak* became the authoritative narrative of the Guru's life in the eighteenth century. Later generations of Khalsa Sikhs would attempt to reconcile the courtly discourse on martial ethics, drawn from a larger pan-Indian cultural ethos rooted in notions of social hierarchy and noble birth, with the specifically Sikh rejection of caste privilege and the cherished corporate authority of the Panth.[2]

In Chapter 3, Dhavan states that Banda Singh's rebellion had a lasting impact on the Sikh community. He effectively utilized the network of the Khalsa Panth to gather support. The experience of an armed resistance and raiding and a growing emphasis on *dharamyudh* as a war against the Mughal state can be traced clearly to the years of Banda Singh's rebellion. Although many non-Sikh groups rejected his claim for Sikh sovereignty, his brief success demonstrated that organizing Jats and other peasant groups to oppose the elite powers in the Punjab was possible. Banda Singh, in his *hukamnama* recommended some non-Khalsa features such as a vegetarian diet and the salutation '*fateh-darshan*'.

The *Nasihatnama* (1718–19) is the first Rahitnama to emphasize the need for a Khalsa warrior to be armed at all times, and it is in such admonitions to the novice Khalsa Sikh that this text echoes sections of the *Dasam Granth*, which is not primarily concerned about establishing sectarian boundaries and looks, instead, to the larger shared devotional cultures of Punjab. Special attention is given to descriptions of valour, heroic models, and the sounds and feel of the battlefield.

By the mid-eighteenth century, Rahitnama writers like Chaupa Singh Chhibber were actively attempting to soften the boundaries that separated Khalsa Sikhs from non-Khalsa Sikhs and also from high-caste groups. In Chaupa Singh's Rahitnama, one can trace a trend toward accommodating the different practices of various castes and minimizing the differing practices of Khalsa and non-Khalsa Sikhs. Chaupa Singh advises Sikhs to follow the custom of caste and lineage for marriage. Chaupa Singh's narrative claims that the creation of the Khalsa was preceded by the worship of the warlike Devi.

Another feature of the Sikh texts written in the early part of the eighteenth century is to present dharamyudh as:

a religiously sanctioned war against Muslims in particular, signifying a growing rigidity with which Sikhs of this period differentiated between their own community and those of others. Most of the later authors claim to present the Guru's authentic message by attributing texts to either the Guru himself or to the close disciples of the Guru. Since the Sikhs were involved in an armed resistance against the Mughal and Afghan states through much of the eighteenth century, the reason for the shift in meaning becomes clear. If the context and dating of these sources is ignored, it is easy to read early sources as the Guru sanctioning a religious war against Muslims. But this reading masks the multivalent readings attributed to *dharam* and *dharamyudh* in earlier sources.[3]

Dhavan concludes that a hybrid Khalsa culture had emerged by the mid-eighteenth century, with appeal to a wide range of peasant communities in Punjab, which fostered ties with multiple Sikh groups that were not part of the Khalsa community. There were multiple sites, narratives, and interpretations of Sikh behaviour, and over time the boundaries between Khalsa and non-Khalsa Sikhs softened.[4]

Throughout her work, Dhavan talks of the Khalsa identity. Indeed, the formation of the Khalsa identity from the days of Guru Gobind Singh to the end of the eighteenth century lends unity to her study. It seems, however, that she does not make any difference between the formation of the Khalsa order and the formation of the Khalsa identity. The Panth, to be created in the *Bachittar Natak*, was to be distinct, and Sainapat equates that Panth with the arms-bearing Kesdhari Khalsa Singhs who are referred to in contemporary Sikh works as the third (*tisar*) Panth.

Dhavan talks of the great popularity of the *Bachittar Natak* during the eighteenth century. However, eighteenth-century Sikh literature does not seem to show a greater influence of the *Bachittar Natak* than that of the *Sri Gur Sobha*. A few verses of the *Bachittar Natak* are quoted in some of the eighteenth-century Sikh works, but, on the whole, the *Sri Gur Sobha*—which covers the creation of the Khalsa and the later confrontation of Guru Gobind Singh with the Mughal state—appears to have been more influential, depicting a clear image of the Kesdhari Singhs.

Much is made of the Rahitnama injunction against association with 'Turks' (equated with Muslims). A close attention to the use of the word 'Turk' suggests that it refers to Muslims associated with the affairs of the Mughal state. The connotation is primarily political rather than religious. In any case, the words *'dusht'* and *'mlechh'* are used in the *Bachittar Natak* and the *Sri Gur Sobha* for the same category of people.

Dhavan has argued that 'a hybrid Khalsa culture' emerged by the mid-eighteenth century in which the boundaries between Khalsa and non-Khalsa Sikhs were softened. The Khalsa Sikhs are actually the Kesdhari Singhs and the non-Khalsa Sikhs are those who have not taken *amrit*. The Khalsa, as Kesdhari Singhs, represented the dominant identity, so much so that the Khalsa came to be equated with the Sikh. In the time of Guru Gobind Singh, the Khalsa had two components: (*a*) the Kesdhari Singhs and (*b*) the Sikhs directly linked with the Guru. At the end of the eighteenth century, the non-Khalsa included even the former excommunicated groups.

It may be pointed out that the Sikh writers of the eighteenth century express little appreciation for Banda Singh. The ideal of sovereignty had come into currency before Banda Singh's appearance on the scene and this ideal survived the failure of his enterprise. The individuals who kept up the fight after the fall of Banda were not the followers of Banda but the Khalsa of Guru Gobind Singh.

Dhavan gives a lot of importance to Rahitnama literature in the period from 1716 to 1748. The *Nasihatnama* (1718–19) laid emphasis on nam, dan, and isnan as well as the need of the Khalsa warrior to be armed all the time. The Rahitnama associated with Chaupa Singh advocates marriage within the same caste and introduces the Goddess for creating the Khalsa. The community ensured its political survival through the creation of a more hybridized understanding of the Sikh dharam. It must be pointed out that the *Nasihatnama* talks of the Khalsa Raj to be inevitably established. In the Rahitnama associated with Chaupa Singh, Sahajdhari Sikhs (the non-Singh component of the Khalsa) are an integral part of the Khalsa Panth. With the passage of time, the Sahajdhari Sikhs of the days of Guru Gobind Singh disappeared, leaving the Kesdhari Singhs as the Khalsa.

Commendably, Dhavan makes considerable use of Sikh literature in her study, notably the *Bachittar Natak*, the *Sri Gur Sobha*, the *Nasihatnama*, the Rahitnama associated with Chaupa Singh,

and Koer Singh's *Gurbilas Patshahi 10*. However, the interpretation of the evidence of these literary works is sometimes open to
question. Dhavan's placement of all the Rahitnamas after the time
of Banda Singh affects her understanding of the early history of the
Khalsa most seriously and rather adversely.

Notes

1. Purnima Dhavan, *When Sparrows Became Hawks: The Making
of the Sikh Warrior Tradition, 1699–1799* (New York: Oxford University
Press, 2014 [2011]), pp. 7–16.

2. Dhavan, *When Sparrows Became Hawks*, pp. 23–6, 33–46.

3. Dhavan, *When Sparrows Became Hawks*, pp. 14–15.

4. Dhavan, *When Sparrows Became Hawks*, pp. 47–9, 56–9, 62–73.

Appendix 1B

Ani Rai's *Jangnama*

In the early 1940s, a retired army Jamadar of my village used to address people on the birth anniversary of Guru Gobind Singh and used to talk movingly about forced conversions in the time of Nauranga (the Mughal emperor Aurangzeb). Every day before eating his first meal, the emperor used to collect one and a quarter *maund* (a unit of weight equal to 38 kilograms) of sacred threads removed from the bodies of persons converted to Islam.[1] Equally important was his praise for Guru Gobind Singh's role in the situation: 'I know nothing of the present and I know nothing of the past, but this much I know that if Guru Gobind Singh had not been there, every male would have been circumcised'.

The statement about circumcision is attributed by some scholars to Bullhe Shah, a Sufi poet contemporary of Guru Gobind Singh. Bullhe Shah was certainly appreciative of Guru Tegh Bahadur, calling him a martyr (*ghazi*).[2] Guru Tegh Bahadur had given protection to all dharams of the world.[3]

The depiction of Guru Tegh Bahadur's martyrdom in the *Bachittar Natak* leaves no doubt that he was given the choice of Islam or death, and he chose death. Aurangzeb was surely held responsible for it. That there was resentment against Aurangzeb among the Sikhs is clearly indicated by the fact that a Sikh threw two bricks at the emperor in October 1676.[4] Guru Gobind Singh's mission in the *Bachittar Natak* is to destroy the wicked (dusht) and the hostile (*dokhi*).[5] Resentment is built into these terms, though rather subdued.

In the Rahitnama literature, the terms used for the enemy are generally 'Turk' and 'mlechh'. The former refers to Muslims, certainly the Muslims who were in the government and the administration, and those who actually supported the government. The term 'mlechh' was used for the 'outlandish barbarians' whose touch was polluting. The term was not coined for Muslims, but it included the Muslims. The Rahitnamas are quite explicit in expressing resentment against Muslims. Both forced conversion and resentment against Muslims were known in the India of Aurangzeb.

Piara Singh Padam says that Ani Rai's *Jangnama* relates to 'one of the last battles of Anandpur'.[6] This does not help us much in making sense of the *Jangnama* as a specific historical battle. Ani Rai's *Jangnama* can be appreciated in the general context of resentment over forced conversion. The *Jangnama* describes a battle between a Mughal noble and Guru Gobind Singh on the banks of the Sutlej towards the end of Guru Gobind Singh's stay in Anandpur. This battle cannot be identified with any of the known battles of the Khalsa, but it reads like a description of an actual battle. The names of some courtiers and of some eminent Sikhs of Guru Gobind Singh reinforce the impression of actuality. But the battle does not become really important as an actual event. It highlights the prowess of Guru Gobind Singh as a warrior and his success in the battle.

Ani Rai's *Jangnama* provides a larger setting for the battle and highlights the basic cause of the battle. Aurangzeb introduced his evil policy immediately on ascending the throne. He began to forcibly convert Hindus to Islam and destroy the temples dedicated to their gods. Complaints against these measures reached the divine court. God entrusted the task of punishing Aurangzeb for his evil deeds (*kutal karam*). Significantly, Guru Gobind Singh is called 'Hindupati Sultan' (Protector of the Hindus). Aurangzeb was apprised of the fact that Guru Gobind Singh had organized a Panth. It was suggested that he should not be allowed to live in the territories ruled over by Aurangzeb. The emperor's courtiers too were in favour of a serious action against the Guru. The emperor assigned to Azim Khan the duty of leading an expedition against Guru Gobind Singh. In the narrative of the battle, some of the Khalsa are praised for their valour, but nobody is comparable with Guru Gobind Singh, the true warrior of the Dark Age.[7]

Finally, it may be pointed out that forced conversion was a form of discrimination. There were some other forms of discrimination, such as: differential taxation, denial of employment in administration, denial of state patronage, curb on public demonstration of one's religious faith, and deprivation of space for religious worship. Discrimination in all forms was practiced against the Sikhs as well as the Hindus. Reaction to discrimination could take different forms: verbal criticism (like Guru Nanak's strong criticism of discrimination and oppression), a hostile act by an individual against those who seem to be responsible for discrimination, the deliberate sacrifice of an individual seen as martyrdom by his coreligionists, and a possible revolt against the authorities.

Credible evidence is available on all forms of discrimination and all forms of reaction to discrimination during the reign of Aurangzeb. In the case of the Khalsa, the form of reaction that lasted the longest, going much beyond the life of Guru Gobind Singh, was their revolt against the Mughal empire, which became the struggle for a sovereign Sikh state in the eighteenth century.

Notes

1. It is an interesting coincidence that Koer Singh talked of 1¼ maunds of sacred threads removed every day by Aurangzeb, *Gurbilas Patshahi 10*, p. 48.

2. J. S. Grewal, 'Bullhe Shah' in *Historical Studies in Punjabi Literature* (Patiala: Punjabi University, 2011), p. 184.

3. Sainapat, *Sri Gur Sobha*, edited by Shamsher Singh Ashok, pp. 10–11.

4. Khwajah Kamgar Husaini, *Ma'asir-i Alamgiri*, edited by Azra Alavi (Aligarh: Aligarh Muslim University, 1978), p. 94.

5. *Sri Dasam Granth Sahib: Text and Translation*, translated and edited by Jodh Singh and Dharam Singh (Patiala: Heritage Publications, 1999), vol. 1, p. 160.

6. Piara Singh Padam, 'Ani Rai' in *The Encyclopedia of Sikhism*, edited by Harbans Singh (Patiala: Punjabi University, 1992), vol. 1, p. 175.

7. Ani Rai, *Jang Nama Sri Guru Gobind Singh Ji*, edited by Shamsher Singh Ashok (Amritsar: Shiromani Gurdwara Prabandhak Committee, 1971 [1947]), pp. 17–32.

Appendix 1C

Koer Singh's *Gurbilas*

The Punjabi University published Koer Singh's *Gurbilas Patshahi 10* in 1968 with an introduction by Fauja Singh who pointed out that the original narrator of many an episode was professedly Bhai Mani Singh. Indeed, the work had been known as *Bhai Mani Singh da Gurbilas*. Fauja Singh quoted Baba Sumer Singh of Patna to the effect that Mani Singh prepared a *granth* called *Gurbilas*. At the end of the published *Gurbilas*, it is stated: 'Here ends the Gurbilas Sri Mani Singh'. The name of Bhai Mani Singh as the original narrator occurs at many other places in the work. According to Fauja Singh, Koer Singh's *Gurbilas* was written in 1751.[1] This is also the view of the editor, Shamsher Singh Ashok.[2]

In 1988, Surjit Hans questioned both the date and the authorship of the *Gurbilas*. His entire discussion was meant to establish that this *Gurbilas* was a work of the time of Maharaja Ranjit Singh. Its most important feature was heterodoxy. Moreover, Guru Gobind Singh was portrayed paradigmatically 'as a Hindu incarnation'. The doctrine of *Guru Panth* was kept in low key. The author of the *Gurbilas* did not show much sympathy for 'the people'. On the Mughal–Afghan conflict, certain statements appeared to be post-eventum prophecies. There are echoes of differences between the *Majha* and the *Malwa* Sikhs. The tone of the author of the *Gurbilas* towards the Muslims was conciliatory. All these points are supported by a long string of quotations from the text of the *Gurbilas*.[3] No external evidence is cited by Hans in support of the basic argument. In other words, the contents of the *Gurbilas* make better sense to him if the work is placed in the early nineteenth century. Logically, therefore, Koer Singh appears to borrow liberally from the *Gurbilas* of Sukha Singh written in 1797.

Madanjit Kaur refuted Surjit Hans on all the major points one by one. She argued that the statement made by Koer Singh on the date could be interpreted as 1754 or 1762. Fauja Singh and Ashok give 1751 as the year of the beginning the work. Bhai Vir Singh gives 1762 as the year of its completion. Madanjit Kaur talks of 1751–62 as the time of its composition. There was no indication that Koer Singh's work was later than that of Sukha Singh. On the point of heterodoxy, Madanjit Kaur says that in this respect, the text of Koer Singh was 'a typically medieval Indian text'. In other words, Koer Singh was not alone in expressing certain ideas which could be seen as heterodox. The charge of having no sympathy for 'the people' is explained by the suggestion that Koer Singh had 'strong Brahmanical sentiments' and merely repeated what was recorded in ancient texts. The Mughal–Afghan conflict was a phenomenon actually witnessed by the Khalsa in the 1750s. The idea of Sikh rule in the future was expressed much earlier than Koer Singh by Sainapat in his *Gur Sobha*. The differences between the Majhails and the Malwais could arise in the 1750s when it was clear that the basic attitude of the rising Sikh chiefs of the Malwa towards the Mughals and the Afghans was different from that of the Sikh leaders of the Majha. Madanjit Kaur concluded that Hans had failed to find credible support for his assertions about Koer Singh's *Gurbilas*.[4]

The debate has gone no further, but scholars in the field have tended to accept the view put forth by Surjit Hans. For Harjot Oberoi, Hans 'convincingly demonstrated' that this work should be placed in the early nineteenth century.[5] W. H. McLeod also placed it in the early nineteenth century on the authority of Surjit Hans.[6] Louis E. Fenech has consistently treated Koer Singh's *Gurbilas* as an early nineteenth-century text. He adds that Koer Singh was writing in 'a period in which Sikhs had assumed a position of substantial political power'.[7]

Anne Murphy takes notice of a 'significant debate' about the dating of Koer Singh's *Gurbilas Patshahi 10*. Surjit Hans had argued for a late eighteenth or early nineteenth century date for the text, drawing in part on Koer Singh's awareness of the British presence in the country, while Madanjit Kaur argues strenuously for taking the text as a product of the mid eighteenth century. Murphy talks of 'the mid-late eighteenth century account of the life of the 10th Guru' at one place, and at another that the *Gurbilas* 'hails from later in the eighteenth century'.[8]

Murphy goes on to say that in the *Gurbilas* of Koer Singh, 'there are also clearly state-oriented articulations of the meanings of sovereignty'. The Guru is explicitly called upon to counter the repressive state powers and to destroy the mlechh (foreigners). This vilification of the 'Turks' is directly related to state power, while its 'religious' meanings are ambiguous. The trappings of the Guru's authority are explicitly royal in form, and the vocabulary of state sovereignty runs through the text. This development reflects the ascendancy of sovereignty among the successors to Mughal authority, including the Sikh chiefs.[9]

On one point, Murphy does not agree with Hans. Koer Singh's 'conciliatory tone' towards the Muslims is only one side of the picture. Actually, Koer Singh's attitude towards Islam and Muslims is 'ambiguous and multi-dimensional'. Murphy refers to 'a deep hatred of Muslims' on the part of Koer Singh, noted by Gurtej Singh.[10] It may be added that Gurtej Singh does not enter into debate with Surjit Hans, but his understanding of Koer Singh's *Gurbilas* is very different. The image of Guru Gobind Singh as a liberator of the oppressed had a strong appeal for Koer Singh. One of the objects of the *pahul* ceremony was 'to establish a freely inter-dining casteless brotherhood, sharing common aspiration to political power'. The caste status was 'formally repudiated by abandoning the sacred thread on initiation'. The Khalsa belonged overwhelmingly to castes regarded as 'low'. Koer Singh gave importance to both Guru Granth and Guru Panth, but perhaps more to the latter. 'The declaration that the Guruship was henceforth merged in the Khalsa Panth is emphatically and repeatedly made.' The mission of Guru Gobind Singh was centered on 'the single point of resistance to Mughal domination'. Paramount for Koer Singh was to gather support for the militant Khalsa engaged in destroying the Mughal power. The imaginary story of the Goddess is used by Koer Singh as a sanction for the use of arms by the Khalsa, consisting of Shudras who were normally excluded from the use of weapons.[11] Thus, Koer Singh's *Gurbilas* when placed in the 1750s makes a lot of sense to Gurtej Singh.

The debate on the date of Koer Singh's *Gurbilas* has remained confined to internal evidence. Therefore, a piece of external evidence in this context acquires a special significance. In verse 14 of sakhi 24 of a new edition of Ratan Singh Bhangu's *Sri Gur Panth Prakash*, Bhangu says that an account of Bahadur Shah was given by 'Mani Singh Sant' and it was elaborated by Sukha Singh. The reference to Bhai Mani Singh is actually a reference to the *Gurbilas* attributed to Bhai Mani Singh. Clearly then, the account written first by Koer Singh was expanded by Sukha Singh.[12] This small piece of information confirms the impression that Koer Singh wrote earlier than Sukha Singh.

Notes

1. Koer Singh, *Gurbilas Patshahi 10*, 'Bhumika', edited by Shamsher Singh Ashok (Patiala: Punjabi University), pp. 1–2.

2. Koer Singh, *Gurbilas Patshahi 10*, p. 295 n 14–16.

3. Surjit Hans, *A Reconstruction of Sikh History from Sikh Literature* (Patiala: Madaan Publications, 2005 [1987]), pp. 247–50, 253–57 n 1–37.

4. Madanjit Kaur, 'Koer Singh, *Gurbilas Patshahi 10*: An Eighteenth Century [Work of] Sikh Literature', in *Recent Researches in Sikhism*, edited by Jasbir Singh Mann and Kharak Singh (Patiala: Punjabi University, 1992), pp. 160–9.

5. Harjot Oberoi, *The Construction of Religious Boundaries: Culture, Identity and Diversity in the Sikh Tradition* (New Delhi: Oxford University Press, 1994), p. 99 and 99–100n.

6. W. H. McLeod, *Sikhs of the Khalsa: A History of Khalsa Rahit* (New Delhi: Oxford University Press), 2003. p. 206; see also pp. 58, 72.

7. Louis E. Fenech, *Martyrdom in the Sikh Tradition: Playing the 'Game of Love'* (New Delhi: Oxford University Press, 2000) p. 11. See also Louis E. Fenech, *The Darbar of the Sikh Gurus: The Court of God in the World of Men* (New Delhi: Oxford University Press, 2008), p. 18. Louis E. Fenech, *The Sikh Zafar-Namah of Guru Gobind Singh: A Discursive Blade in the Heart of the Mughal Empire* (New York: Oxford University Press, 2013), p. 107.

8. Anne Murphy, 'An Idea of Religion: Identity, Difference, and Comparison in the *Gurbilas*', in *Punjab Reconsidered: History, Culture and Practice*, edited by Anshu Malhotra and Farina Mir (New Delhi: Oxford University Press, 2012), pp. 93, 98, 100.

9. Murphy, 'An Idea of Religion', pp. 100–1.

10. Murphy, 'An Idea of Religion', pp. 104–5.

11. Gurtej Singh, 'Compromising the Khalsa Tradition: Koer Singh's *Gurbilas*' in *The Khalsa: Sikh and Non-Sikh Perspectives*, edited by J. S. Grewal (New Delhi: Manohar, 2004), pp. 51–5.

12. Ratan Singh Bhangu, *Sri Gur Panth Prakash*, edited by Balwant Singh Dhillon (Amritsar: Singh Brothers, 2004), p. 69.

Appendix 1D

Guru Gobind Singh's Speech
on the Baisakhi of 1699

According to the Persian historian Ghulam Muhiyuddin, says
Max Arthur Macauliffe, the news writer of the period sent to the
Mughal emperor a copy of Guru Gobind Singh's address to the
Sikhs at Anandpur on the first of Baisakh Sambat 1756 (AD 1699).
It was as follows:

> Let all embrace one creed and obliterate differences of religion.
> Let the four Hindu castes who have different rules for their guid-
> ance abandon them all, adopt the one form of adoration, and
> become brothers. Let no one deem himself superior to another. Let
> none pay heed to the Ganges and other places of pilgrimage which
> are spoken of with reverence in the Shastras, or adore incarnations
> such as Ram, Krishan, Brahma, and Durga, but believe in Guru
> Nanak and the other Sikh Gurus. Let men of the four castes receive
> my baptism, eat out of one dish, and feel no disgust or contempt for
> one another.[1]

The report of the news writer himself was as follows:

> When the Guru had thus addressed the crowd, several Brahmans and
> Khatris stood up and said that they accepted the religion of Guru
> Nanak and of the other Gurus. Others, on the contrary, said that they
> would never accept any religion which was opposed to the teaching
> of the Veds and the Shastras, and that they would not renounce at
> the bidding of a boy the ancient faith which had descended to them
> from their ancestors. Thus, though several refused to accept the
> Guru's religion, about 20 thousand men stood up and promised to
> obey him, as they had the fullest faith in his divine mission.[2]

According to Bhagat Lakshman Singh, Ghulam Muhiyuddin
was 'a contemporary Muslim historian'. Lakshman Singh gives
a transliteration of the address of Guru Gobind Singh in Roman

script before he gives his own translation in English. It is only slightly different from Macauliffe's translation.[3]

Teja Singh and Ganda Singh state that Guru Gobind Singh spoke at length to the Sikhs about his mission on the Baisakhi day of 1699 and, according to Bute Shah (Ghulam Muhiyuddin) and Ahmad Shah of Batala, he was reported to have said among other things:

> I wish you all to embrace one creed and follow one path, obliterating all differences of religion. Let the four Hindu castes, who have different rules laid down for them in the Shastras, abandon them altogether and, adopting the way of co-operation, mix freely with one another. Let no one deem himself superior to another. Do not follow the old scriptures. Let none pay heed to the Ganges and other places of pilgrimage which are considered holy in the Hindu religion, or adore the Hindu deities, such as Rama, Krishna, Brahma and Durga, but all should believe in Guru Nanak and his successors. Let men of the four castes receive my baptism, eat out of the same vessel, and feel no disgust or contempt for one another.[4]

Teja Singh and Ganda Singh point out in a footnote that Ahmad Shah's text on the point was 'in supplement to Sohan Lal's *Umdat ut-Tawarikh*'.

Kapur Singh clarifies that the account given by Ahmad Shah of Batala (published as an appendix to Sohan Lal Suri's *Umdat ut-Tawarikh*) was almost identical to the one given by Ghulam Muhiyuddin. In other words, Ghulam Muhiyuddin simply copied the 'address' from Ahmad Shah's work. Kapur Singh gives his own translation, which is only slightly different from the one given by Teja Singh and Ganda Singh.[5]

Harbans Singh quotes Guru Gobind Singh and refers to 'a report' for another quotation:

> I wish you all to embrace one creed and follow one path, obliterating all differences of religion. Let the four Hindu castes which have different rules for their guidance abandon them altogether, adopt the one form of adoration and become brothers. Let no one deem himself superior to another. Let men of the four castes receive my baptism, eat out of one dish and feel no disgust or contempt for one another.[6]

Harbans Singh quotes from a report of the proceeding: 'Though several refused to accept the Guru's religion, about 20 thousand men stood up and promised to obey him, as they had the fullest faith in his divine mission.'[7]

Harnam Singh Shan has discussed 'Guru Gobind Singh's address' more recently. He talks of Ghulam Muhiyuddin, Ahmad Shah (in the appendix to Sohan Lal Suri's work), Muhammad Latif, Macauliffe, Bhagat Lakshman Singh, Teja Singh and Ganda Singh, Kapur Singh, and Harbans Singh among others to clarify the issue. He comes to the conclusion that the reported portion of the 'historic address' echoes some of the basic principles enunciated by Guru Gobind Singh on the Baisakhi day of 1699. It was based on the report of a news writer of the Mughal court and affirmed by three Muslim historians. Shan has reproduced the text in Persian, with its transliteration in Gurmukhi and an English translation.[8] Thus, Shan has reinforced the view that Guru Gobind Singh's address was recorded and reported by a news writer of the Mughal court.

However, the authority of the Guru's 'address' rests only on plausibility. The quotation becomes plausible only when it is taken out of its context. The speech which Ghulam Muhiyuddin ascribes to Guru Gobind Singh begins with a significant statement:

> You should remember that the Musalmans have maltreated us. They have killed our ancestors and, having been uprooted from our homes, we have taken refuge from their tyranny in these mountains. Now, in accordance with the mandatory wish of my father Guru Tegh Bahadur, I cherish the desire of avenging myself upon my father's murderers.[9]

This statement is significant because, in Ghulam Muhiyuddin's considered view, the one consuming passion of Guru Gobind Singh was revenge. 'So long as I live,' he is made to say earlier, 'I shall meditate revenge, to the point of risking my life in pursuit of this purpose.'[10] It was for this purpose that, according to Ghulam Muhiyuddin, Guru Gobind Singh had taken an irrevocable decision to muster armies and conquer territories, and it was for this very purpose that he created the Khalsa.[11]

Ghulam Muhiyuddin attributes this motive to Guru Gobind Singh on an obvious assumption about human psychology: a son would naturally think of vengeance upon his father's murderer. Ghulam Muhiyuddin's extremely faulty chronology could lend further support to his assumption. The creation of the Khalsa is placed by him soon after the execution of Guru Tegh Bahadur in 1675; all the battles of Guru Gobind Singh follow upon the creation of the Khalsa.

If Ghulam Muhiyuddin's whole account of Guru Gobind Singh is analysed, it becomes possible to see that he was basing himself on the tradition which had developed during the past 100 years rather than on any early record. This is evident from his treatment of the episode of the Goddess, the forecast about the end of the *masands* in the future, the wanderings of Guru Gobind Singh after the battle of Chamkaur, the composition of the *Dasam Granth* at Talwandi Sabo, and the cause and circumstances of Guru Gobind Singh's death. Ghulam Muhiyuddin does not betray any anxiety about early evidence, and we may be sure that the speech which he attributes to Guru Gobind Singh on the day of creating the Khalsa is purely an imaginative feat. Direct speech was a stylistic feature of historical works in Persian, and the *Tawarikh-i Punjab* is quite full of it. The passage on 'address' deserves no special credence.

If we analyse the chronicles of Buddh Singh, Bakht Mal, Khushwaqt Rai, Ahmad Shah of Batala, Ganesh Das, Sohan Lal Suri, and Aliuddin, we find that the character of their work is not essentially different from that of Ghulam Muhiyuddin's *Tawarikh*. One finds them depending occasionally on earlier chronicles for a small detail or another, but the creation of the Khalsa in their presentation is invariably related to the feeling of revenge and the episode of the Goddess.

Notes

1. Max Arthur Macauliffe, *The Sikh Religion: Its Gurus, Sacred Writings, and Authors*, vol. 5 (New Delhi: Low Price Publications, 1995 [1909]) pp. 93–4.

2. Macauliffe, *The Sikh Religion*, vol. 5, p. 94.

3. Bhagat Lakshman Singh, *A Short Sketch of the Life and Work of Guru Gobind Singh* (Patiala: Punjab Languages Department, 2002 [1909]), pp. 47–8.

4. Teja Singh and Ganda Singh, *A Short History of the Sikhs (1469–1765)* (Patiala: Punjab Languages Department, 2002 [1909]), pp. 67–8.

5. Teja Singh and Ganda Singh, *A Short History of the Sikhs (1465–1765)* (Patiala: Punjabi University, 1999 [1950]), pp. 67–8.

6. Harbans Singh, *Guru Gobind Singh* (Chandigarh: Guru Gobind Singh Foundation, 1966), pp. 76–7.

7. Singh and Singh, *A Short History of the Sikhs*, p. 68.

8. Harbans Singh, *Guru Gobind Singh* (Chandigarh: Guru Gobind Singh Foundation, 1966), pp. 76–7.

9. Harnam Singh Shan, 'Guru Gobind Singh's Address to the Baisakhi Congregation of 1699 on the Occasion of the Creation of the Khalsa', in *Guru Gobind Singh and Creation of the Khalsa*, edited by Madanjit Kaur (Amritsar: Guru Nanak Dev University, 2000), pp. 45–59.

10. Bute Shah, *Tarikh-i Punjab*, f. 400.

11. Bute Shah, *Tarikh-i Punjab*, f. 397.

2

The Mughal State and the Sikh Panth

The establishment of the Mughal empire under Akbar was in a way helpful to the Sikh movement in the sixteenth century. The Sikh Panth became a state within the state. Emperor Jahangir ordered stern action against Guru Arjan, eventually resulting in his martyrdom in 1606. A confrontation with the Mughal state in the early seventeenth century weakened the Sikh Panth due to sectarian cleavage. The martyrdom of Guru Tegh Bahadur in 1675, a glaring interference of the Mughal state in the affairs of the Sikh Panth, created a grave situation. The institution of the Khalsa left little room for reconciliation between the Mughal state and the Sikh Panth. The stage was set for a long political struggle between the 'House of Babur' and the 'House of Baba Nanak', extending beyond the life of Guru Gobind Singh. The vassal chiefs of the hills could play only a limited role in the larger context.

The Mughal Empire under Aurangzeb (1659–1707)

The Mughal empire covered nearly a whole subcontinent for about 150 years. The military power of the Mughals lasted long due largely to the system of assignments of land to maintain the *mansabdars* and their contingents. This system made the mansabdars completely dependent upon the will of the emperor. Akbar forged the main features of the provincial administration as well to give shape to a centralized apparatus through which an absolute monarchy could function.[1]

The Mughal emperor was assisted by a number of ministers. The *Khan-i-Saman* looked after the imperial household and managed the state factories (*karkhanas*). The diwan decided matters related to the collection or assessment of revenue, signed all orders of pay, and wrote letters called *hasb al-hukm* (by order) in his own name on behalf of the emperor. The *bakhshi* passed the salary bills of all civil and military officers and made payments to the field army. The *qazi* at the imperial court was the chief judge, and the law was expounded by the mufti. The highest judge in the empire was the emperor himself who held his court once a week. The *darogha* of Dakchauki received all reports to be presented to the emperor. Three classes of agents sent regular reports from all parts of the empire: *waq'ai-navis, swanih-nigar* (news writer), and *khufia-navis* (secret writer). The *muhtasib* was responsible for regulating the lives of the people in accordance with the Islamic law, and putting down the use of intoxicants and the practice of immorality.[2]

The Mughal empire was divided into provinces (*subas*). The chief administrator in a province was its governor (*nazim*), popularly known as *subadar*. He tried to play the role of the emperor in his province. Having a high *mansab*, ranging from 3,000 to 5,000, he had direct access to the emperor. His authority was limited to his province and he was not allowed to go on a large expedition on his own discretion. Furthermore, he had no formal authority over the diwan of the province who was responsible to the diwan at the centre. Similarly, the provincial bakhshi worked under the *mir* (chief) bakhshi at the centre. The qazi and the *sadr* in the province were responsible to their seniors in the central government. The *faujdars* and the news writers were also independent of the governor. The departments of the sadr and the *mutawalli* looked after the problems of the grantees under direct control of the centre.[3]

The province was divided into *sarkars*, each consisting of a number of parganas. Faujdars appointed to the sarkars and parganas represented the military or the police power of the imperial government. One of the main duties of a faujdar was to go to the aid of a *jagirdar* or an *'amil* of the *khalisa* to deal with local discontent among zamindars or peasants who refused to pay the revenue.[4]

The pargana, generally, was a unit under the zamindari of members of the same caste. But sometimes, there were two or three castes of zamindars in a pargana. The 'amil or the *'amalguzar* was the revenue collector of the pargana. The *amin* was the revenue assessor. A treasurer (*fotadar*) and an accountant (*karkun*) were a part of the revenue administration at the pargana level. Every pargana had a qazi to pass judgements on all cases among Muslims, on civil suits between Hindus and Muslims, or among Hindus. The law was expounded by the mufti. The *qanungo* was the permanent repository of information on revenue receipts, area statistics, local revenue rates, and practices and customs of the pargana. The *chaudhari* was an important functionary, chiefly concerned with the collection of revenue. He was generally a zamindar, and his position was often hereditary.[5]

The *muqaddam* and the *patwari* were the persons in authority in a village. The muqaddam was responsible mainly for the collection of revenue assessed on the village. He was answerable for any crime committed in or near the village. There could be a clash of interest between the muqaddam and the peasants. The patwari was the village accountant. His duty was to keep a record of the expenditure and income of the village. He could become powerful enough to oppress the small peasants.[6]

The territories from which revenues were collected for the imperial treasury were known as the khalisa. In the early part of his reign, Akbar tried to abolish the system of assignments (*jagirs*), but this turned out to be a temporary measure. In the 10th year of Aurangzeb's reign, the khalisa accounted for only 20 per cent of the total assessed revenue. It covered the most fertile and conveniently administered territories. Punjab was one of the provinces in which the most extensive areas were kept under the khalisa.[7]

The bulk of the revenue was alienated through jagirs. The jagirdars were entitled to collect the revenues assigned to them. They had to bear the risk of fluctuations in revenue collection.

In certain cases, when the loss was really excessive, they were given a compensation. Despite a rigorous system of inspection and checks to ensure that the assignees fulfilled their obligations, bribery was generally resorted to. A crisis in the *jagirdari* system developed towards the end of Aurangzeb's reign.[8]

The jagirdars were usually mansabdars, holding ranks (mansabs) given by the emperor. Their ranks were generally dual: *zat* and *sawar*. The former indicated personal pay and the latter determined the size of the contingent which a mansabdar was obliged to maintain. The pay scales for both were laid down. In the later years of Aurangzeb's reign, no claim was honoured for the time immediately following the grant of a mansab. The princes held mansabs much higher than the highest mansab bestowed upon any noble.[9]

Grants known generally as *madad-i ma'ash* (aid for subsistence) in the Mughal empire were different from jagirs. The grantee was given the right to collect revenue from a clearly demarcated piece of land but without performing any service for the state. Abu al-Fazl mentions four categories of persons who were given such grants: (a) men of learning, (b) religious devotees, (c) destitute persons having no sources of livelihood, and (d) persons of noble lineage who did not take to any employment. The bulk of the madad-i ma'ash grants went to the first two categories. The state had its own interest in maintaining them as a class. Jahangir refers to the grantees as the 'Army of Prayer'. The goodwill of Muslim scholars and divines was deemed to be important for the stability of the state.[10]

Akbar extended the scope of madad-i ma'ash grants to non-Muslims. In 1571, he gave 200 bighas of land by way of madad-i ma'ash to the *jogis* of Jakhbar in the upper Bari Doab of Punjab.[11] Jahangir was the first Mughal ruler to grant madad-i ma'ash to the Vaishnavas of Pindori in the upper Bari Doab.[12] Aurangzeb reversed Akbar's policy and ordered in 1672–3 the resumption of all grants held by Hindus. There is a reference to the order of resumption in the case of the jogis of Jakhbar. It is interesting to note that no one came forward to cultivate the resumed land. The provincial diwan of the *khalisa sharifah* (crown lands), Amanat Khan, gave a *pattah* for Rs 170 a year to the jogis who were willing to accept it.[13]

On the whole, the revenue assigned to madad-i ma'ash grantees was not large. In the reign of Akbar, it was 5.4 per cent of the total revenue in the province of Delhi, and only 1.8 per cent in Punjab. The area covered by grants formed only a small portion of the total cultivated area, and the grantees were not important in the agrarian society of the times.[14]

Within the imperial territories, there were persons authorized to collect revenues from the cultivators of a given area on behalf of the ruler. These 'intermediaries' between the emperor and the cultivators were known as zamindars. The 'zamindari villages' were clearly distinguished from the peasant-held villages, called '*ra'iyati*'. The intermediary zamindar was entitled to have 5 to 10 per cent of the revenue collected by him. His position was similar to that of a chaudhari in a pargana and the muqaddam in a village. However, he collected various kinds of cesses for himself too. His total income was not less than 15 to 20 per cent of the revenues in northern India. The zamindari was generally hereditary, and it could be divided into shares among the heirs. Moreover, it could be sold or given on lease. The zamindars' troops in the Mughal empire towards the end of the sixteenth century amounted to 384,558 cavalry, 4,277,857 infantry, 1,863 elephants, 4,260 guns, and 4,500 boats. Forts were the visible symbols of the armed power of the zamindars. A disloyal zamindar lost all his rights. If a zamindar did not perform his service well, he could be removed and replaced by someone else. The persons appointed by Aurangzeb as zamindars in cases of replacement were generally Muslims. The zamindars as a class were politically important.[15]

The power and authority of a vast centralized state was not easy to challenge.

Subordinate States

All the territories of the Mughal empire were not under imperial administration. Whole regions were left under the chiefs subordinate to the Mughal emperor due to geographical barriers—hills, rivers, forests, and deserts. From Kashmir to Kumaon, there were scores of states in the Himalayas. Some of these were founded in the fifteenth or sixteenth century, but others dated to the early centuries of the Christian era, or even earlier, such as Kashmir and Kangra.

Many of the states shared some general characteristics. As head of the state, the Raja exercised religious, feudal, and personal authority. He was the fountainhead of justice. He was venerated as head of the state religion, either in his own right or as vice-regent of a god. He was the supreme owner of the soil, and from him came the right of the cultivator to a share of the produce. His subjects owed him personal allegiance and service. The Raja could remit the rent as an act of favour to the holder, or assign it in jagir to a third party in lieu of pay, or as a subsistence allowance; the grazing fees due from the owner of each herd or flock were payable to the Raja.[16]

Immediately below the Raja in rank were the feudal barons. Some of these were Ranas and Thakurs whose ancestors had enjoyed partial or complete independence before the founding of the state, and had subsequently been reduced to the position of vassals. Others had received their rank and jagirs from the Raja. Some of the highest offices in the state were occupied by members of this class.[17]

The material resources of the hill states (see Map 2.1) were always limited, and probably only a few of them had revenue of more than four to six lakh rupees a year. Considering the restricted resources of the states, their wars were waged on a very limited scale. The hill states were able to maintain their political status for such a long period in great measure due to their isolated position, and the inaccessible character of the country.[18]

Early in Akbar's reign, the hill states became tributaries to the Mughals. A royal demesne was created by confiscation of territory from some of the states of the Kangra group. A large portion of the rich valley of Kangra was thus annexed, including the fort of Kangra which was placed under a Mughal qila'dar. Several expeditions were sent against the hills from Jammu to Kangra during Akbar's reign to keep them under the political control of the Mughal emperor.[19]

Every chief on his accession acknowledged the supremacy of the Mughal emperor by payment of the fee of investiture, after which he received a *kharitah* (patent of installation) with a *khil'at* (dress of honour) and other gifts from the imperial court. In letters and other documents, the chiefs were addressed as zamindars. The title of Raja was conferred as a personal distinction. As indicated by the letters and valuable presents received from the emperors, there seems to have been a friendly intercourse between the chiefs and the imperial court.

The autonomous chiefs had to pay a fixed annual offering (*peshkash*) which was regarded as the substance of submission. All the chiefs were left free to manage their internal affairs as they liked. They were free to levy cesses and duties on trade passing

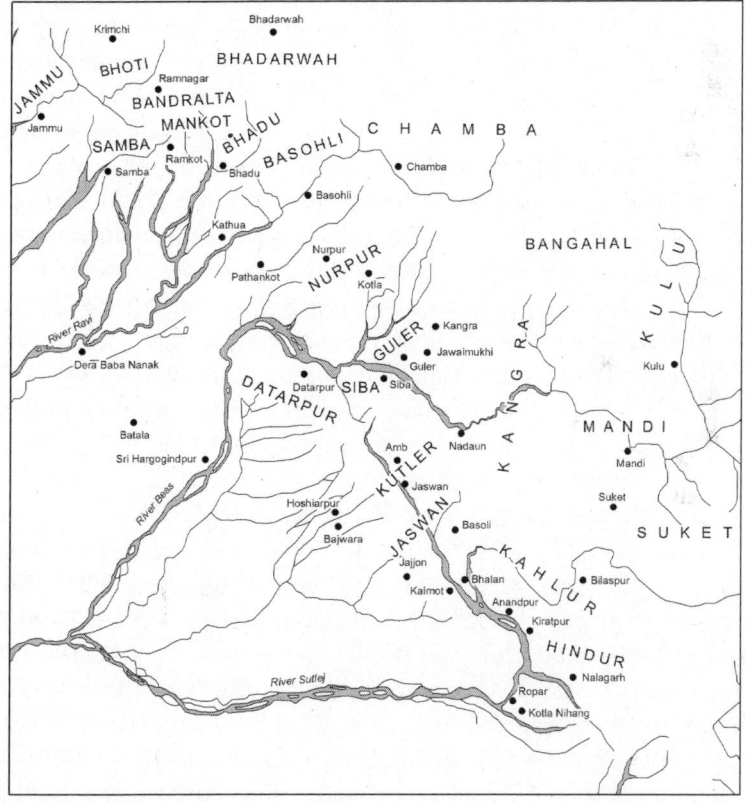

Map 2.1 The Punjab hill states (seventeenth century)
Source: Courtesy of the author.

through their territories at rates fixed by them. They did not have to follow the imperial methods of revenue administration.

The prerogatives of the chiefs were seldom questioned, and there was little interference in their internal affairs. Indeed, throughout the entire period of Mughal supremacy, the chiefs seem to have experienced liberal treatment. They were left generally to themselves in the government of their principalities, and allowed to exercise the functions and wield the power of independent rulers. They built forts and waged war against one another without any reference to the emperor, and sometimes even asked and received assistance in men and arms for this purpose from the Mughal faujdar or governor.[20]

Some of the chiefs entered the imperial service as mansabdars. Raja Jagat Singh of Nurpur was sent by Shah Jahan against the Uzbeks of Balkh and Badakhshan in 1645 with a force in which there were 14,000 Rajputs raised in his own territory and paid by the emperor.[21] His son, Raja Rajrup Singh, took a prominent part in the expeditions against Qandhar, first led by Aurangzeb and after him by Dara Shukoh. Aurangzeb raised the Raja's rank to 3,500 zat and sawars, and appointed him as the *thanedar* of a village on the frontier of Srinagar to guard the movement of Sulaiman Shukoh, who had taken refuge at Srinagar. Afterwards, he returned to the court and took part in the battle against Dara Shukoh at Ajmer.[22] He was succeeded by Raja Mandhata (1661–1700). The greater part of his reign was spent away from Nurpur in the service of the emperor. He was the last Raja of Nurpur to hold office under the emperor or to receive distinctions from him.[23]

The chiefs of Nurpur were the most notable among the rulers who gained considerably due to Mughal patronage and rose to positions of importance by entering the circle of mansabdars. The other chiefs to join the imperial service were the rulers of Chamba, Guler, and Jammu. The chiefs of Nahan were not mansabdars but they were occasionally associated with Mughal campaigns close to their state. It may be underscored that the submission of no single ruler could ensure Mughal control over the Punjab hills.[24]

The most important state for our present purpose was Kahlur because of the location of the headquarters of Guru Gobind Singh at Makhowal (Anandpur) within its territories. Hindur, an offshoot

of Kahlur, was also important for Guru Gobind Singh. The chiefs
of Hindur had cordial relations with Guru Hargobind and his successors at Kiratpur (in the territories of Hindur). There were two
other states with which Guru Gobind Singh came into contact in
his early career. One of these was located between the Sutlej and
the Jamuna, namely Sirmaur (later Nahan). The other state was
Srinagar (Garhwal), on the south of the Jamuna and, therefore, outside the Punjab hills.

In the north of the Sutlej, the boundary of Kahlur was close to
the state of Kangra with its capital at Vijaipur, founded by Raja
Vijai Ram Chand (1660–89). The first offshoot of Kangra was the
Jaswan state, founded by Purab Chand in the late twelfth century.
Another offshoot of Kangra was Guler. An offshoot from Guler
was Siba, founded by Sibarn Chand—the younger brother of the
ruling chief of Guler—who had made himself independent in the
mid-fifteenth century. He founded his capital, Siba, after his own
name. An offshoot from Siba was Datarpur, founded around 1550
by Datar Chand, a descendant of Sibarn Chand. The clan name of
the family was Dadwal from Dada, their original home. Situated in
the Jaswan hills, Kutlehr was the smallest of all the principalities
in the Kangra area.

Table 2.1 Contemporary hill chiefs

1. Kahlur (Bilaspur)	
Bhim Chand	1667–1712
Ajmer Chand	1692–1741
2. Hindur (Nalagarh)	
Dharam Chand	?–1701
Himmat Chand	1701–4
Bhup Chand	1704–?
3. Sirmaur (Nahan)	
Budh Prakash	1664–84
Mat Prakash	1684–1704
Hari Prakash	1704–12
4. Garhwal (Srinagar)	
Medni Shah	1662–84
Fateh Shah	1684–1717

(Cont'd)

Table 2.1   *(Cont'd)*

5. Kangra	
Vijay Ram Chand	1660–87
Udai Ram Chand	1687–90
Bhim Chand	1690–97
Alam Chand	1697–1700
Hamir Chand	1700–47
6. Jaswan	
Anirudh Chand	1588–89

He was succeeded by Samir Chand, Man Singh, Ajaib Singh,
Ram Singh, Ajit Singh and Jaghar Singh. Of these, Ram Singh was
certainly a contemporary of Guru Gobind Singh.

7. Guler	
Raj Singh	1675–95
Dalip Singh	1695–1730
8. Nurpur	
Mandhata	1661–1700
Dayadhata	1700–35
9. Mandi	
Shyam Sen	1664–79
Gaur Sen	1679–84
Sidh Sen	1684–1727
10. Kullu	
Bidhi Singh	1672–88
Man Singh	1688–1719
11. Jammu	
Gajai Dev	1675–1703
Dhrub Dev	1703–17

On the west of Kangra, between the Beas and the Ravi, was the
Nurpur state, already mentioned. This name was given to the state
by the Mughal emperor Jahangir in honour of his wife Nur Jahan.
On the east of Kahlur and north of the Sutlej was Suket, founded
by Bir Sen in the eighth century. The Mandi state to the north of
Suket was divided into two unequal parts by the Beas. Mandi and
Suket had always been rivals. In the north of Mandi was the state
of Kullu, one of the most ancient states of the Punjab hills. To the
northeast of Nurpur was the state of Chamba, founded before the

end of the sixth century and known after its capital on the right
bank of the Ravi in the Chamba valley proper.

The chiefs of the Jammu group of states do not seem to have
played any considerable role in the events of the reign of Aurangzeb.
But Jammu finds a mention in the *Bachittar Natak*. The presence
of the Mughal faujdar in the area to deal primarily with the affairs
of the hill chiefs made the chiefs of Jammu a little more active
generally in alliance with the Mughal authorities.

The roots of religion in the hills were deep and strong. The prestige and power of the Brahmans rested on the religious sentiments
of the people and the princes. The rulers generally displayed strong
religious sentiments. Innumerable temples and shrines dotted the
sparsely populated hills as tokens of the religious beliefs, feelings,
and sentiments of the people. Religion, above all, was the cement-
ing force for the society in the hills and hedged its princes with the
halo of divinity.[25]

Many important temples were dedicated to Mahadev and there
were numerous Shaiva shrines in the hills. The dominant religion was indeed Shaivism. Worship of the Goddess in her several
aspects and forms was very popular. She was worshipped mostly
in her terrible and fierce form. She was the family deity of the
proudest of hill Rajputs, the Katoches of Kangra. The recitation
of the *Durga* Saptashati was especially esteemed for ensuring
a safe return from a long journey. The tantric cult of the five
*makara*s (wine, flesh, fish, parched grain, and sexual intercourse)
was not unknown. A sizable proportion of the people appear to
have been worshippers of Devi. The sacrifice of animals (goats,
cocks, and buffaloes) at the Shaiva and Shakta shrines was not
uncommon. At a popular level, the worship of many minor gods
was common.

Vaishnavism was entering the hills. Indeed, contact with
the outside world was not unknown even before the hills were
brought into the vortex of the Mughal empire. The princes and the
people of the hills visited many parts of India, such as Hardwar,
Kurukshetra, Gaya, and Jagannath. The learned Brahmans of
Kashmir and Benares were always welcome to the Punjab hill
states. Sanskrit was still the language of the learned and vernacu-
lar was coming into vogue during the latter half of the seventeenth

century. The works of Bhushan, Keshodas, and Tulsidas were imported from the plains.

The chiefs of Guler and Nurpur associated themselves with Vaishnava *bairagis* in the early seventeenth century. Raja Suraj Sen of Mandi introduced Vaishnavism in his capital in 1648. The foundation of Nahan and its founder, Raja Karam Parkash, are both associated with a bairagi named Banwari Das. Temples dedicated to Vishnu and to Ram and Sita were erected in Kangra and Chamba by the chiefs of those principalities in the seventeenth century. It is worth noting, however, that the 'new' faith was introduced and patronized only by the chiefs.

The society in the Punjab hill states was very conservative. The whole social structure was deeply rooted in the past, sanctioned by the political power of the Rajputs and the religious authority of the Brahmans. It was marked by the 'tyranny of caste'. There was great respect for authority, privilege, and tradition.

The Sikh Panth

In the compositions of Guru Nanak (1469–1539), there is a thorough critique of the contemporary religious systems of India. He appreciates the idea of *bhagti* (loving devotion) but not the beliefs and practices of Vaishnava bhakti. He prefers the Sufis over the 'ulama, but does not appreciate all their practices. On the whole, there is no unqualified appreciation of any religious system, whether Hindu or Islamic, Brahmanical (Vaishnava, Shaiva, or Shakta), or of the ascetical sanyasis, jogis, bairagis, and Jain monks.[26]

Guru Nanak's critique of his milieu was extended to the contemporary social order, whether Hindu or Islamic, and the contemporary politics and government. The social order was marked by inequalities and the polity was marked by oppression, injustice, and discrimination based on religious differences. Guru Nanak's ideology, or a set of his interrelated ideas, carried the implication not only of a new religious dispensation with a strong sense of social commitment but also of an egalitarian social order.

Divinely inspired to spread the message of God, Guru Nanak assumed the position of a guide (Guru) for his followers (the Sikhs)

Table 2.2   The successors of Guru Nanak (1469–1539)

Guru Angad	1539–52
Guru Amar Das	1552–74
Guru Ram Das	1574–81
Guru Arjan	1581–1606
Guru Hargobind	1606–44
Guru Har Rai	1644–61
Guru Har Krishan	1661–64
Guru Tegh Bahadur	1664–75
Guru Gobind Singh	1675–1708

who were admitted to the new path (the Panth) irrespective of their caste, creed, or gender. They met at one place for congregational worship (*sangat*), singing the hymns composed by him, and for the community meal (*langar*). This sacred space was called *dharamsal* and the religious fraternity was called 'Sangat' or 'Sikh Sabha' by Guru Nanak himself. He installed one of his exceptionally devoted followers as the Guru in his place before his death. The successor was given the name of Angad (literally, a part of Guru Nanak's body, or as one with him). He was expected to conform to Guru Nanak's ideology and strengthen the institution of the Sikh Sabha, later called the Sikh Panth.

The Sikh Panth developed peacefully from 1539 to 1605 under the first four successors of Guru Nanak in the period covered largely by the reign of Akbar. All the four successors composed verses, like Guru Nanak, reinforcing and expanding his ideology. Their compositions were carefully preserved, like those of Guru Nanak, in Gurmukhi script which, in all probability, had been used by Guru Nanak for recording his own compositions. The compositions of all the five Gurus were systematically compiled by Guru Arjan in 1604 in the form of a *Granth* which he equated with God. It was meant to serve as the Sikh scripture. It is important to note that the Granth compiled by Guru Arjan contained not only Gurbani but also the selected compositions of Vaishnava *bhakta*s, sants, Sufi Shaikhs, Muslim bards, and Brahmans known as Bhatts. Their compositions also became sacred, like Gurbani, because of their inclusion in the Granth. The *bani* of Guru Tegh

Bahadur was incorporated in the Granth at proper places in the 1680s.[27]

Bhai Gurdas, who was closely related to Guru Amar Das and remained associated with his successors in the late sixteenth and early seventeenth centuries, felt gratified to find thousands of Sikhs in every city and lakhs in every country. Punjab was pre-eminent among these countries. But there were Sikhs in Kabul and Kashmir, and in the cities like Thanesar, Delhi, Fatehpur, Agra, Lucknow, Prayag, Jaunpur, Patna, Raj Mahal, Dhaka, Gwalior, Ujjain, and Burhanpur.[28] The author of the *Dabistan-i Mazahib*, who refers to himself as 'Mobad', states that the number of Sikhs had been increasing under the successors of Guru Nanak, and became very numerous in the time of Guru Arjan. He says, 'Not many cities remained in the inhabited region where the Sikhs were not settled in some number.'[29] The increase in the number of Sikhs and their concentration at a number of places in and outside Punjab had two major implications: appointment of the Guru's representatives away from his headquarters and the proliferation of dharamsals.

'Mobad' says that the *Nanak-Panthi*s or 'the Sikhs of the Guru' did not believe in images and idol-temples. The bani of Guru Nanak was in the language of the Jatts, or the rustics. They had 'no attachment to the Sanskrit language' which for Hindus was 'the language of angels'. They did not recite 'the mantras of the Hindus', and they did not believe in *avtar*s (incarnations). None of the austerities and customary forms of worship of the Hindus had any currency among the Sikhs. There were no restrictions on Sikhs in matters of commensality. There was a firm belief among the Sikhs that congregational prayer was more efficacious than that of an individual Sikh. Even the Guru 'consults the sangat or the assembly of Sikhs about his own wishes'. The Nanak-Panthis believed that all the Gurus were 'Nanak'. 'Mobad' talks of the *masand*s as the Guru's agents in the time of Guru Arjan and Guru Hargobind.[30]

Bhai Gurdas believed in divine sanction behind the path insti-tuted by Guru Nanak and followed by his successors. The sangat stands equated with the Guru in the *Var*s of Bhai Gurdas. The institutions of Guruship and the dharamsal became the hallmark of the distinctive Gurmukh Panth, both in the sense of a path and a community. The egalitarian character of the Sikh Panth distin-guished the Sikhs from all other communities. The Sikhs of the Guru were householders with a sense of social commitment. The criteria of distinction for Bhai Gurdas were both objective and sub-jective: the doctrine of the Name, the Sikh scripture, the institu-tions of Guruship, the dharamsal, and the character of the Sikh Panth.[31]

Turning to the successors of Guru Nanak, we find that Guru Angad pays homage to Guru Nanak by enunciating: 'If a 100 moons were to rise, and a thousand suns, despite all their light there would be darkness without the Guru.' For Guru Angad, Guru Nanak laid the foundation of a new dispensation based on divine revelation.[32] Guru Amar Das leaves no doubt that the dis-pensation of Guru Nanak was meant to transcend all the known religious traditions for universal redemption.[33] In the bani of Guru Ram Das, God enters history through the Guru, his bani, and his Sikhs for the redemption of the whole world. The whole dispen-sation of the House of Nanak appears to be an expression of the divine order and divine grace.[34]

Guru Arjan talks of '*halemi raj*' (mild rule) in which there is no oppression: 'Now the order of the Merciful One has gone forth that no one shall molest another'. Halemi Raj is the whole dispensa-tion: the Guru and the Sikhs, the organization of the Sikh Panth, its institutions, its human and materials resources, the autono-mous towns under the Guru's control where there was no fear of tax-gatherers, and an exclusive validity of the new path for libera-tion. This rule is everlasting under divine protection: 'All around us is the *chauki* of the *shabad* of the Guru for our protection.... All around us is the protective line of Ram.'[35]

Jahangir says that Guru Arjan used to live in the garb of a spiri-tual master and had induced a large number of simple-minded Hindus, and even some ignorant Muslims, to adopt his ways and customs. From all sides and directions, ignorant people were inclined towards him and reposed full faith in him. For a long time, the thought kept coming to Jahangir of putting an end to this 'shop of falsehood' or to bring Guru Arjan into the fold of the people of Islam. When the rebel Prince Khusrau went to Punjab,

Guru Arjan saw him, conveyed to him some far-fetched things, and put a fingermark in saffron on his forehead, which was held to be auspicious. The matter was brought to Jahangir's notice and he ordered that Guru Arjan be brought to his presence at Lahore. He gave over his houses and children to Murtaza Khan, the mir bakhshi, confiscated his goods, and ordered him to be put to death.[36]

The author of the *Dabistan-i Mazahib* states that Jahangir punished Guru Arjan for 'having prayed for the welfare' of Prince Khusrau, the rebel son of Jahangir. Khusrau himself was arrested and imprisoned. Many years later, he died in prison.[37] When Guru Arjan found himself powerless to pay the heavy fine imposed on him, he gave up his life.

Bhai Gurdas takes notice of Guru Arjan's martyrdom in a poignant stanza and refers to Guru Hargobind as a great warrior (*vad jodha*) and a vanquisher of armies (*dal bhanjan*). He was the master of the temporal as well as the spiritual realm (*din duni da patsah*); he was the king of kings (*patsahan patsah*).[38] Guru Hargobind adopted 'the style of soldiers'. Contrary to his father's practice, he 'girded the sword, employed servants, and took to hunting'. Jahangir sent him to the fort of Gwalior as a political prisoner. The Sikhs used to kneel before the wall of the fort with their foreheads touching the ground (to do homage to the Guru). At last, says the author of *Dabistan*, Jahangir released him out of kindness.[39]

Guru Hargobind fought a battle with the officers of the empire sent against him by Shah Jahan. Leaving Ramdaspur after the battle, the Guru went to Kartarpur. There too, a battle took place in which two imperial commandants were slain. Though 'many powerful forces' were sent to attack Guru Hargobind before and after this battle, he came out safe. He decided not to stay in any place near Lahore and went to Kiratpur in the Punjab hills—the territory of Raja Tara Chand, the chief of Hindur (Nalagarh), who did not pursue the path of obedience to Shah Jahan. The author of the *Dabistan* adds that Guru Hargobind had 700 horses in his stables, 300 battle-tested horsemen, and 60 musketeers in his service.[40]

The Vars of Bhai Gurdas and the *Dabistan* leave no doubt about the spiritual and temporal concerns of Guru Hargobind and his

Table 2.3   Guru Ram Das and his descendants

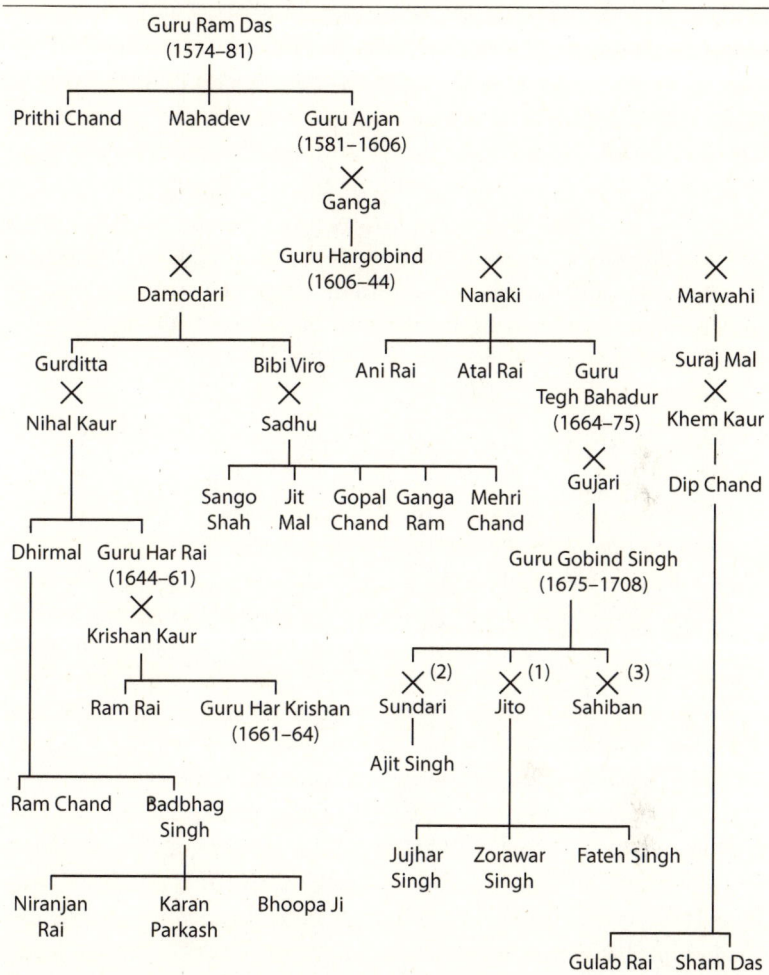

armed resistance against the Mughal authorities. The terms 'Akal Takht' and 'Miri-Piri' occur in the *Gurbilas Chhevin Patshahi*.[41] The eighteenth-century Sikh sources refer frequently to the *Akal Bunga*, carrying the implication that a structure was built over the original Akal Takht. At the time of rebuilding of the Akal Takht in the 1980s, a high platform could be seen at its base. This was the original Akal Takht.[42]

Guru Hargobind nominated his grandson, Har Rai, the younger brother of Dhir Mal, as his successor in 1644. His Guruship of about 17 years was rather uneventful. He moved temporarily to Thapal in the territory of Sirmaur (Nahan) not to embroil himself in an armed conflict between the Chief of Hindur and the Mughal commandants. He continued to maintain the retainers of Guru Hargobind, and met Dara Shukoh during his flight to Punjab. Sujan Rai Bhandari says that Dara Shukoh put up an appearance of preparations for a fight, but he was demoralized. He thought of proceeding to Multan and Qandahar. People intuitively realized that he would take to flight without daring to enter battle. As a result, they decided to separate from him.

> Thus Raja Rajrup departed with the excuse that he needed to go to his native territory (watan) to gather troops and conciliate the local chiefs (zamindars) of the Punjab hills. From expediency, he left his son as his agent at Lahore, but after some days, his son also departed one night. So too Guru Har Rai, the successor of Baba Nanak, who had come with a large force, left on the excuse of collecting more troops. Thus, most people separated themselves from Dara Shukoh.[43]

Aurangzeb called Guru Har Rai to his court. Guru Har Rai sent his elder son, Ram Rai, who tried to ingratiate himself with the emperor and changed the word *musalman* (a follower of Islam) to *be-iman* (one who has no faith) in a verse of Guru Nanak. Consequently, Guru Har Rai chose his younger son, Har Krishan, as his successor. Aurangzeb summoned him to Delhi too. Guru Har Krishan died there in 1664 after indicating that his 'grandfather' (baba) at the village Bakala was his successor. This referred to Tegh Bahadur, the youngest son of Guru Hargobind. Tegh Bahadur assumed Guruship at Bakala as the eighth successor of Guru Nanak. Within a year, he founded a new centre at a place called Makhowal, only a few miles from Kiratpur, in the territory of the Chief of Kahlur (Bilaspur).

Before the end of 1665, Guru Tegh Bahadur left Makhowal to establish contact with the Sikh congregations (sangats) in the Mughal provinces of the Gangetic plain. He was taken to Delhi under imperial orders. On the intercession of Kanwar Ram

Singh, son of Mirza Raja Jai Singh of Jaipur, he was released from detention in December. From Delhi, Guru Tegh Bahadur went to Agra, and from there to Prayag (Allahabad), Benares, Sahsaram, and Patna. He left his family at Patna to be looked after by the local sangat before he moved on to Monghir. There, he heard the news of the birth of his son at Patna. He was named Gobind Das. From Monghir, Guru Tegh Bahadur moved to Dhaka where Raja Ram Singh joined him early in 1668. He accompanied the Raja on his expedition to Assam and returned to Makhowal in April 1672.[44]

In 1673, Guru Tegh Bahadur moved out of Makhowal to impart his message to peasants in the province of Delhi. He moved from village to village in most of the districts now covered by the states of Punjab and Haryana. Guru Tegh Bahadur was making a public demonstration of his convictions at a time when Aurangzeb was bent upon discouraging such demonstrations. Whereas the emperor could use the power of the state in support of his policy, the Guru relied on moral courage inherited from a long line of predecessors.

After deep reflection on the situation, Guru Tegh Bahadur decided to court martyrdom. In July 1675, he moved out of Makhowal. He was arrested soon after he entered the Mughal pargana of Ropar and was kept in custody for nearly four months before he was taken to Delhi in November 1675. Three of his companions were put to death in his presence to impress upon him the consequence of refusal to accept Islam. But he refused to accept Islam and was beheaded on 11 November 1675 in the main market-square close to the Red Fort.

By this time, there was a serious cleavage in the Sikh Panth. After the death of Guru Arjan, his elder brother Prithi Chand did not recognize Guru Hargobind as the Guru and put forward his own claim to Guruship of the Sikh Panth. Prithi Chand's successor in 1645–6 was Harji. His followers called themselves 'bhagats', but the Sikhs of Guru Hargobind used for them the derogatory term '*Mina*'.[45]

Prithi Chand is called a Mina (a dissembling rogue) in the Vars of Bhai Gurdas. Virtually, a whole Var of 21 stanzas relates to him and his followers. In more than half of this Var, they are denounced in strong terms: they have blackened their faces by turning away from the true Guru; they are false and dishonoured; they eat carrion; they are bound for hell; association with them is a source of suffering; those who join them die without any hope for the life hereafter; they carry black marks on their foreheads; they are like false coins. In short, they claim to be the Guru, but they possess no merit.[46]

Bhai Gurdas supported the claim of Guru Hargobind with great vehemence. The critics of Guru Hargobind refer to his deviation from the practices of the former Gurus: he did not stay in one place; he was sent to the fort of Gwalior by the king; he roamed from place to place and knew no fear; he hunted animals; he did not recite Gurbani and did not listen to its recitation either; he gave precedence to outsiders over his disciples. But the true Sikhs were enamoured of Guru Hargobind; they knew that he was bearing an unbearable burden and that his new measures were no deviation. The Guru's outward appearance was a test of the disciple's faith. It was a hard test, but those who had the understanding remained firm in their faith. There was no Guru but Hargobind, the only legitimate successor of Guru Arjan, Guru Ram Das, Guru Amar Das, Guru Angad, and Guru Nanak. Guru Hargobind was the true king; the Minas were 'rebels', and rebels had no place in the realm of the king.[47]

When Guru Hargobind moved to Kiratpur, Ramdaspur was taken over by Miharban, the son of Prithi Chand. He wrote his own bani as 'Nanak' and claimed to be the seventh Guru. He composed a *Janamsakhi* (the life story) of Guru Nanak to buttress his own claims. His son, Harji, succeeded to his position at Ramdaspur in the 1640s as the eighth 'Nanak'.[48]

Dhir Mal, the elder brother of Guru Har Rai had moved to Kartarpur in the early 1640s, taking with him the original copy of the scripture prepared by Bhai Gurdas under the guidance of Guru Arjan. He was given revenue-free land at Kartarpur 'by way of *in'am*' (reward) by Shah Jahan.[49] On Guru Hargobind's death, Dhir Mal declared himself to be the seventh Guru.

Guru Har Rai nominated his younger son, Har Krishan, as the Guru. This was contested by Ram Rai who made a representation to Aurangzeb. Meanwhile, Tegh Bahadur was accepted as the

Guru by an influential body of Sikhs. Ram Rai refused to acknowledge Tegh Bahadur as the Guru, just as he had refused to acknowledge Guru Har Krishan. Eventually, under Aurangzeb's patronage,
Ram Rai received revenue-free land in the territory of the Raja of
Garhwal at a place that came to be called Dehra Dun.[50]

In 1675, thus, there were five groups of Sikhs: the central stream
who acknowledged Guru Tegh Bahadur as the only true Guru; the
followers of masands; the followers of Prithi Chand, Miharban,
and Harji; the followers of Dhir Mal and his successors; and the
followers of Ram Rai. Whereas the Sikhs of the central stream
were in confrontation with the Mughal emperors, the Minas, Dhir
Mallias, and Ram Raiyas were reconciled to the Mughal state and
accepted its patronage.[51]

The Sikh Panth developed as a state within the state till the
martyrdom of Guru Arjan in 1606. The martial activity of Guru
Hargobind led to a confrontation with the Mughal state, which in
turn encouraged cleavage in the Panth. Aurangzeb assumed the
position of an arbitrator for succession to Guruship. The execution of Guru Tegh Bahadur in 1675 was an act of extreme aggres-
sion. Thus, the young Guru Gobind was faced with the problem
of internal disunity and external interference. The institution of
the Khalsa was his well-considered response to a grave situation.

Notes

1. Irfan Habib, *The Agrarian System of Mughal India 1556–1707* (New
Delhi: Oxford University Press, 1999, 2nd. rev. edn.), pp. 364–5.

2. Jadunath Sarkar, *A Short History of Aurangzib (1618–1707)* (New
Delhi: Orient Longman, 1979), pp. 398–9, 405–7.

3. Muzaffar Alam, *The Crisis of Empire in Mughal North India:
Awadh and the Punjab 1707–1748* (New Delhi: Oxford University Press,
2013 [1986]), pp. 58–9, 87, 115. See also Chetan Singh, *Region and Empire:
Panjab in the Seventeenth Century* (Delhi: Oxford University Press,
1991), pp. 31–6.

4. Irfan Habib, *The Agrarian System*, pp. 2, 339. See also Chetan Singh,
Region and Empire, pp. 34–44.

5. Habib, *The Agrarian System*, pp. 281–2, 318–20, 324, 331–8. J. S. Grewal,
'The *Qazi* in the *Pargana*', *Miscellaneous Articles* (Amritsar: Guru Nanak

(Dev) University, 1974), pp. 38–73. See also Chetan Singh, *Region and Empire*, pp. 37–8.

6. Habib, *The Agrarian System*, pp. 160–8.

7. Habib, *The Agrarian System*, pp. 313–16.

8. Habib, *The Agrarian System*, pp. 298–313.

9. Habib, *The Agrarian System*, pp. 299–300, 311, 325.

10. Habib, *The Agrarian System*, pp. 342–3, 352–3.

11. B. N. Goswamy and J. S. Grewal (trans. and eds), *The Mughals and the Jogis of Jakhbar: Some Madad-i Ma'ash and other Documents* (Simla: Indian Institute of Advanced Study, 1967).

12. B. N. Goswamy and J. S. Grewal (trans. and eds), *The Mughal and Sikh Rulers and the Vaishnavas of Pindori* (Simla: Indian Institute of Advanced Study, 2010[1969]).

13. Goswamy and Grewal, *The Jogis of Jakhbar*, pp. 125–39.

14. Habib, *The Agrarian System*, pp. 360–1.

15. Habib, *The Agrarian System*, pp. 169–222.

16. Habib, *The Agrarian System*, pp. 222–9. For the rates of *jizya*, see also Iswar Das Nagar, *Futuhat-i Alamgiri*, edited by Raghubir Singh and Qazi Karametullah, translated by M.R. Lokhandwala and Jadunath Sarkar (Vado dare: 1995), p. 79.

17. J. Hutchison and J. P. Vogel, *History of the Punjab Hill States*, 2 vols (Simla: Department of Languages and Culture, Himachal Pradesh, 1982, reprint), pp. 65–7.

18. Hutchison and Vogel, *Punjab Hill States*, p. 70. In the war between Kangra and Kahlur (Bilaspur), Forster estimated the Bilaspur army at 'about 800 horsemen and 8,000 foot soldiers, armed with matchlocks, swords, spears and clubs'.

19. For a monographic study of the subordinate chiefs, see A. R. Khan, *Chieftains in the Mughal Empire During the Reign of Akbar* (Simla: Indian Institute of Advanced Study, 1977).

20. Hutchison and Vogel, *Punjab Hill States*, p. 73.

21. Hutchison and Vogel, *Punjab Hill States*, pp. 74–5.

22. Aqil Khan Razi, *Waqiat-i-Alamgiri* (Aligarh: Aligarh Historical Institute, 1945), Introduction, p. 44, n. 1.

23. B. N. Goswamy and J. S. Grewal, 'Some Persian Documents from Nurpur', in J. S. Grewal, *Miscellaneous Articles* (Amritsar: Guru Nanak (Dev) University, 1974), pp. 19–37.

24. Chetan Singh, *Region and Empire*, pp. 137–41.

25. This and the following four paragraphs are based on B. N. Goswamy, 'The Social Background of Kangra Valley Painting', Ph.D. diss. (Panjab University, Chandigarh, 1961).

26. For this and the following two paragraphs, see J. S. Grewal, 'The Gurmukh Panth: Guru Nanak', in *History, Literature and Identity: Four Centuries of Sikh Tradition* (New Delhi: Oxford University Press, 2013 [2011]), pp. 7–36. Also, J. S. Grewal, 'Guru Nanak and His Panth', in *The Sikhs: Ideology, Institutions, and Identity* (New Delhi: Oxford University Press, 2009), pp. 3–21.

27. J. S. Grewal, *A Study of Guru Granth Sahib: Doctrines, Social Context, History, Structure and Status* (Amritsar: Singh Brothers, 2009).

28. Grewal, *History, Literature, and Identity*, p. 128.

29. *Dabistan-i Mazahib* in *Sikh History from Persian Sources*, edited by J. S. Grewal and Irfan Habib (New Delhi: Tulika/Indian History Congress, 2001), p. 66.

30. *Dabistan-i Mazahib* in *Sikh History from Persian Sources*, pp. 61, 63, 66–7, 72–6.

31. Grewal, *History, Literature, and Identity*, p. 130.

32. Grewal, *History, Literature, and Identity*, pp. 37–47.

33. Grewal, *History, Literature, and Identity*, pp. 48–68.

34. Grewal, *History, Literature, and Identity*, pp. 69–84.

35. Grewal, *History, Literature, and Identity*, pp. 89–115.

36. *Tuzk-i Jahangiri*, in *Sikh History from Persian Sources*, p. 57.

37. Khwajah Kamgar Husaini, *Ma'asir-i Alamgiri*, edited by Azra Alavi (Aligarh: Aligarh Muslim University, 1978), pp. 86–7, 344.

38. *Varan Bhai Gurdas*, edited by Giani Hazara Singh (Amritsar: Khalsa Samachar, 1962 [1911]), I. 48.

39. *Dabistan-i Mazahib*, in *Sikh History from Persian Sources*, pp. 67–8.

40. *Dabistan-i Mazahib*, in *Sikh History from Persian Sources*, pp. 68–9.

41. *Gurbilas Chhevin Patshahi* (Patiala: Bhasha Vibhag Punjab, 1970), p. 138. This *Gurbilas* is placed by some scholars in 1718 and by some others in the early nineteenth century. The authorship of this work is also controversial.

42. Gurmeet Rai and Kavita Singh, 'Brick by Sacred Brick: Architectural Projects of Guru Arjan and Guru Hargobind', in *New Insights into Sikh Art*, edited by Kavita Singh (Mumbai: Marg Publications, 2003), p. 42.

43. Sujan Rai Bhandari, *Khulasatu't Tawarikh*, in *Sikh History from Persian Sources*, p. 94.

44. Jadunath Sarkar, *History of Aurangzib* (Northern India, 1658–1681) (Calcutta: M.C. Sarkar & Sons, 1921, 2nd edn), vol. 3, pp. 187–90, pp. 311–12.

45. *Dabistan-i Mazahib*, in *Sikh History from Persian Sources*, pp. 67–8.

46. *Varan Bhai Gurdas*, Var 36, pauris 1–11.

47. *Varan Bhai Gurdas*, Var 34, *pauris* 21, 24–5; Var 36, *pauris* 24–34; Var 38, *pauri* 20.

48. The Janamsakhis compiled by Prithi Chand's son Miharban and the latter's sons, Harji and Chaturbhuj, have been published with introductory essays by several scholars as *Janam Sakhi Sri Guru Nanak Dev Ji*, edited by Kirpal Singh and Shamsher Singh Ashok (Amritsar: Khalsa College, 1962, 1963). The compositions of Miharban and his sons are given in the third appendix to the first volume and also in the appendix to the second volume. In one of his compositions, Miharban denounces those who are proud of their Guruship. In some other ways too, the compilers of the Janamsakhi try to reinforce their claim. For instance, Guru Nanak is made to prophesy that the seventh Guru shall reveal the true meaning of his bani (*Janam Sakhi Sri Guru Nanak Dev Ji*, vol. 1 pp. vii, x, 25, 39).

49. Ganda Singh (ed.), *Makhiz-i Tarikh-i Sikhan* (Amritsar: History Society, 1949), pp. 51–2.

50. Ajit Singh Baagha, *Banur Had Orders: A Critical Study of an Hitherto Unknown 'Hukamnamah' of Guru Gobind Singh* (Delhi: Ranjit Printers and Publishers, 1969), pp. 57–61, 64–9, 76.

51. J. S. Grewal, 'Cleavage in the Panth', in *Sikh Ideology, Polity and Social Order* (New Delhi: Manohar, 2007), pp. 78–85.

II

The Pre-Khalsa Decades

3

From Birth to Manhood (1666–85)

At the beginning of his reign, Aurangzeb issued a number of orders known as 'Islamic ordinances'. In his orders of 1665 and 1667, a discrimination was made between Muslims and Hindus for the collection of custom duty. A general order was issued on 9 April 1669 'to demolish all the schools and temples of the infidels and to put down their religious teaching and practices'.[1] In 1672–3, all grants of land revenue to non-Muslims were ordered to be resumed.[2] That this order was implemented in Punjab is indicated by a couple of documents related to the *jogi* establishment at Jakhbar.[3] *Jizya* was ordered to be reimposed on the Hindus in April 1679.[4] That jizya was imposed in Punjab by Aurangzeb's *farman* (order) is indicated by the jizya returns of two villages near Lahore.[5] Aurangzeb's policy was clearly aggressive.

Saqi Musta'ad Khan, author of the *Ma'asir-i 'Alamgiri*, writes admiringly of Aurangzeb. The Hanafi (Sunni) creed gained greater strength in 'the great country of Hindustan' in his reign than in the time of any earlier sovereign.

By one stroke of the pen, the Hindu clerks (writers) were dismissed from the public employment. Large numbers of the places of worship of the infidels and great temples of these wicked people have been thrown down and desolated. Men who can see only the outside of things are filled with wonder at the successful accomplishment of such a seemingly difficult task. And on the sites of the temples lofty mosques have been built. His Majesty personally taught the credo to

many of the infidels who came to him, guided by their good fortune,
with a view to being converted to Islam, and he bestowed on them
robes of honour and other favours.

Musta'ad Khan admired the *Fatawa-i 'Alamgiri*, prepared at the
cost of Rs 200,000 which 'made the world independent of all other
works of jurisprudence'.[6]

It is important to note that Sikh *dharamsal*s or gurdwaras were
treated like Hindu temples. According to Khafi Khan, Aurangzeb
'ordered the temples of the Sikhs to be destroyed' and the Guru's
agents for 'collecting the tithes and presents of the faithful to be
expelled from the cities'. The reference here is to the masands.[7]

Early Life of Gobind Das (1666–75)

The *Bachittar Natak* refers to the birth of Gobind Das at Patna.
'My father was travelling towards the east, bathing at various
sacred places. When he reached Tribeni (Prayag) he gave charities
and stayed there for a few days. I was conceived there, and took
birth at Patna'.[8] No date is mentioned.

The date for the birth is given in two works of the middle
decades of the eighteenth century. According to the narrative part
of the *Chaupa Singh Rahit-Nama*, Guru Gobind Singh was born in
1661.[9] But, according to Koer Singh, he was born in 1666.[10] Kesar
Singh Chhibber and Sarup Singh Kaushish place the birth of Guru
Gobind Singh in 1661.[11]

The *hukamnama*s of Guru Tegh Bahadur are undated. But,
obviously, he could not issue a hukamnama before assuming the
Guruship. Indeed, it has been argued that nearly all his known
hukamnamas were issued from 1664 onwards. In one of these, Guru
Tegh Bahadur asks the *sangat* of Benares to look after his horse, Sri
Dhar, in its illness and to send it to Patna when it had fully recovered. Evidently, he was moving from Benares towards Patna.[12] In
two other hukamnamas to the sangat of Patna, he writes about his
halt at Monghir (on the way to Dhaka). Then comes the hukamnama in which he expresses his appreciation for the way in which
the sangat of Patna celebrated the birth of (his son) 'Gobind Das'.
In yet another hukamnama, he expected to join Rajaji (Raja Ram

Singh, whom he met in 1668).[13] Thus, there is strong contemporary evidence in support of the year 1666. The generally accepted date for the birth of Guru Gobind Singh is 22 December 1666.

Koer Singh states that Gobind Das used to go to the river for sport, and used to reward the boatmen generously. People used to bring small weapons for Gobind Das. He used to worship the weapons by offering incense, bowing his head to them, and going around them. The weapons mentioned are guns, matchlocks, arrows and quivers, swords, shields, and daggers of various kinds. Gobind Das was fond of the pellet bow (*gulel*). An incident is mentioned in this connection. There was a well of sweet water to which women used to come with their pitchers for carrying the water home. One day, a Muslim woman came to the well. Gobind Das aimed at the pitcher, but the pellet hit the woman's forehead and it began to bleed. She complained to Mata ji (Mata Gujari) who prayed for the water of the well to become saltish. Immediately, it became saltish.[14]

Sukha Singh gives all the four episodes mentioned by Koer Singh and adds two more. Both the additional incidents relate to the blessing of male children, one son in one case and five sons in the other.[15] It seems that the oral tradition about the childhood of Gobind Das was growing at Patna with the passage of time.

Both Koer Singh and Sukha Singh state that the cradle of Gobind Das was there in the Harmandar Sahib at Patna and the Sikhs used to worship it, making offerings of incense and flowers.[16] Evidently, the relics of the Gurus and their families were cherished by the Sikhs.

Koer Singh and Sukha Singh talk about the journey of Gobind Das from Patna to Makhowal, halting at a number of sacred places. At Benares, the local pandits asked him why he, a '*Surajvanshi Kshatriya*' (solar race or dynasty), accepted offerings. Gobind Das convinced them that the offerings made to him were absolutely voluntary and there was no imposition or compulsion of any kind. At Lakhnaur, Pir Arif Din came to pay homage to Gobind.[17]

In the *Bachittar Natak*, there is a bare reference to the stay of Gobind Das at Makhowal: 'I was brought to Madar Des (Punjab), and all kinds of nurses looked after me with affectionate care. I was given instructions of various kinds. At the age of *dharam karam* (when the sacred thread is put on), my father went to his heavenly abode.'[18] This statement refers to the early education of Gobind Das and the martyrdom of his father. In the *Sri Gur Sobha*, there is simply a reference to the true Guru's stay at Makhowal for many years, marked by his sport (*lila*) and wondrous acts (*kautak*) till his departure for Paunta.[19]

In the *Chaupa Singh Rahit-Nama*, the head of the male and female nurses who looked after Gobind Das is Chaupa Singh, the *khidawa* (who looked after the daily round of Gobind's life). Another person used to carry a sword and a shield, and a bow and arrows of small size, specially made for Gobind's sport. He played many games with boys. He was taught Gurmukhi and Takari by Chaupa Singh, and Persian by Bhai Kirpa Ram, a Brahman Sikh.[20] Kesar Singh Chhibber mentions Chaupat Rai (Chaupa Singh) as the person who taught Gurmukhi to 'Gobind Rai'. Initially, however, Gobind had learnt to read and write the Gurmukhi script from Harjas Rai, a Brahman Sikh who was known as *munshi* because he was well versed in Persian. Gobind Das learnt Persian from the 'Sikh munshi' in a year at the age of seven.[21]

Sarup Das Bhalla and Sarup Singh Kaushish place the accession of Gobind Das to the *gaddi* (seat of authority) before the martyrdom of Guru Tegh Bahadur. Bhalla says that before going to Delhi with the Raja (Ram Singh), Guru Tegh Bahadur thought of installing Gobind Das on the *singhasan* (throne). The ceremony of installation was performed before his departure for Delhi. Guru Tegh Bahadur called the sangat and declared that he had entrusted Guruship to Gobind Das.[22] In the *Guru Kian Sakhian*, it is stated that when the Brahmans of Kashmir came to Chak Nanaki (Makhowal) in 1675 to seek protection against persecution by Aurangzeb, Guru Tegh Bahadur was convinced that there was no other way than that of giving his own head. He told Diwan Dargha Mal to prepare for the installation of Gobind Das as the Guru. After the ceremony of installation, he told the Sikhs to regard Gobind Das as the Guru in his place.[23] The deliberate character of martyrdom gets amply underscored.

Among the contemporary writers, Sainapat expresses great appreciation for the martyrdom of Guru Tegh Bahadur. By this great act, he proved to be the protective sheet of the whole creation;

he saved the honour of *karam-dharam* (rites and rituals) and saved all the faiths; he saved the sacred mark, the sacred thread, and the dharamsal; and his praises were sung in all the three worlds.[24]

Some of the Sikh writers of the eighteenth century talk of the response of Gobind Das to the martyrdom of Guru Tegh Bahadur. When the head of Guru Tegh Bahadur was brought to Makhowal, the Master (Guru Gobind Das) cleaned it with a handkerchief with tears in his eyes. Then, he washed the head with Ganges-water (Ganga-*jal*). At this moment, Gobind Das uttered what became the last four lines of the stanza on the martyrdom of Guru Tegh Bahadur in the *Bachittar Natak*. After the head was cremated, Gobind Das wanted to know how many Sikhs had died along with Guru Tegh Bahadur. He was told that two other Sikhs had remained with him till the end. He wanted to know why only two. He was told that the Sikhs had no visible symbol of their identity. Gobind Das said that he would give them such a mark of identity that a Sikh would not remain hidden in a crowd of thousands.[25]

According to Koer Singh, when Guru Tegh Bahadur saw clearly that he had to give his head, he wrote to test his son (Gobind Das): '(T)here is no strength and no way out.' Gobind Das wrote back: 'There is all the strength and everything is possible.' Guru Tegh Bahadur felt satisfied and was now ready to lay down his life.[26] Both these verses occur in a *dohra* (rhyming couplet) of Guru Tegh Bahadur in the *Granth Sahib*.

Kesar Singh Chhibber's account of the response of Gobind Das to the martyrdom of Guru Tegh Bahadur remains close to that of the *Chaupa Singh Rahit-Nama* in all its detail.[27] Sarup Das Bhalla follows Koer Singh in quoting the dohra of Guru Tegh Bahadur by way of correspondence between the father and the son. Like the author of the *Rahitnama*, he quotes the last few lines of the stanza on the martyrdom of Guru Tegh Bahadur in the *Bachittar Natak*.[28] In the *Guru Kian Sakhian*, the head of Guru Tegh Bahadur is taken to Makhowal by Bhai Jaita and three other Sikhs. Bhai Jaita was a *Ranghreta* (a former outcaste) and Guru Gobind Das pronounced, '*Ranghreta, Guru ka beta*,' exalting him to the status of 'the Guru's son'.[29]

It is interesting to note that in the *Guru Kian Sakhian*, Guru Gobind expresses his appreciation for the martyrdom of Guru

Tegh Bahadur by uttering the first three lines of the stanza on martyrdom in the *Bachittar Natak* (which was composed over two decades later). The sangat responded to the words of the young Guru with 'praise be to Guru Tegh Bahadur', using for him the epithet *'Hind ki chadar'* (the protective sheet of India).[30] The full statement on the martyrdom is:

> God protected his sacred mark and sacred thread. He (Guru Tegh Bahadur) performed a great act of sacrifice in the Kaliyuga. He did so much for the *sadh*s; he gave his head, showing no pain. He performed a great deed for the sake of *dharam*. He gave his head, but did not reveal the secret. In contrast with charlatans, the devotees of God are shy of showing sham power. Breaking the pitcher of his body over the head of the ruler of Delhi, he left for the divine abode: Tegh Bahadur did what none else could do. The world was sorrowful on his departure. There were cries of anguish on the earth, but shouts of triumphant joy in the world of gods.[31]

The First Decade of Guruship (1676–85)

Most of the contemporary and eighteenth-century Sikh writers place the installation of Gobind Das as the Guru in 1676. An issue raised by the family priest on this occasion was that of the sacred thread. They talk also of the young Guru's interest in hunting wild animals, beating of the kettledrums (*naubat*), and keeping elephants. All these were regarded as a prerogative of royalty and, thus, became a source of tension between Guru Gobind Das and the Raja of Kahlur. It was primarily because of this mounting tension that the Guru accepted the invitation of the Raja of Srimaur to reside in his state. In the *Bachittar Natak*, it is simply stated that '(w)hen Guruship devolved upon me, I spread *dharam* to the best of my capacity. Hunting in the forest in various ways, I killed bears, *nilgao*s, and stags. Then, I was obliged to leave the country and I thought of Paunta'.[32] In the *Sri Gur Sobha*, as we noticed earlier, there is merely the statement that the true Guru stayed at Makhowal for many years before he went to Paunta.[33]

In the *Chaupa Singh Rahit-Nama*, the masands and the Sikhs approached Mata Gujari after all the mortuary rites had been performed to request that the *raj-tilak* ceremony of the *sahibzada* (Gobind Das) be performed so that he assumed the functions of the Guru's office. Mata Gujari told Gobind Das to sit on the gaddi and hold *darbar*. He told Pandit Devi Das to determine the auspicious time. With the consent of all the masands and the Sikhs, he assumed the office of the Guru. He asked the Chhibber Brahmans to serve the Guru's darbar like their ancestors. Sahib Chand Chhibber was appointed as diwan of the darbar and Dharam Chand Chhibber was made the *khazanchi* (treasurer) to look after the *Toshakhana* (storehouse of precious articles) as well.[34]

Koer Singh says that the family priest insisted that Gobind Das should put on the sacred thread, the time-honoured custom among the Hindus as the symbol of their identity. Gobind Das said that an old custom was not more sacrosanct than the command of God. He had been commanded by God to take up the sword and destroy the 'Turks'. The body remained bright (*ujjal*) with the sword put on. The thread of cotton did not last long. That was why Guru Nanak had asked for the thread of *daya* (compassion), *santokh* (contentment), *jat* (sexual restraint), and *sat* (spiritual power). The Brahman priest then requested Mata Gujari to get prepared a thread of gold. This was done and the priest was happy.[35]

Kesar Singh Chhibber says that Gobind Das went into seclusion for meditation after all the mortuary rites for Guru Tegh Bahadur had been performed. His austerities were meant to destroy the 'Turks'. A heavenly voice told him to 'take up the double edged sword' (*khanda*): the game of the 'Turks' was over. He came out of seclusion and sat on the throne (*raj* singhasan). The masands and the Sikhs came in large numbers to have *darshan* of Guru Gobind Das on the first day of Baisakh in 1676.[36]

According to Sukha Singh, Gobind Das came to Damdama to be installed as the Guru and to sit on the true throne (*sacha takht*), wearing the sword and the bow, and a *kalgi* on his turban. The family priest came with a sacred thread for Gobind Das to put on. Gobind Das said that he had put on the sword given to him by God (Mahakal) as the 'sacred thread'. The priest said that he should do what the Gurus before him had said. Gobind Das referred to the verse of Guru Nanak on the sacred thread.

The priest said despairingly that it was no good to set aside an ancient custom. Mata Gujari implored Gobind Das not to discard the sacred thread now, but at the time of instituting the Khalsa Panth. This was an acceptable compromise. Gobind Das assumed Guruship in 1676 and sat on the *ad singhasan* (original throne) at Damdama in Makhowal.[37]

In the *Chaupa Singh Rahit-Nama*, Guru Gobind Das starts going out for hunting.[38] Koer Singh gives a good deal of importance to hunting as it became linked with politics.[39] Sarup Das Bhalla states that Guru Gobind Das was accompanied by Sikhs when he rode out for hunting in the Terai.[40] In the *Guru Kian Sakhian*, it is stated that a huge drum called 'Ranjit Nagara' was prepared in 1679 to be beaten in the morning and the evening. It was beaten also when the Guru began to go out for hunting. In 1681, hukamnamas were issued to the Sikh sangats expressing the Guru's preference for good horses and weapons as offerings.[41]

According to the *Guru Kian Sakhian*, Guru Gobind Das left Anandpur for Sirmaur on the invitation of Medni Prakash, the Raja of Nahan, in view of the circumstances which had developed at Anandpur.[42] Koer Singh and Sukha Singh go into some detail of the circumstances. It was basically the tension between Raja Bhim Chand and Guru Gobind Das that weighed with the latter for leaving his '*des*' (country). An important cause of tension was the beating of the Ranjit Nagara at the time of hunting expeditions that were necessary for training warriors. The masands submitted to Mata Gujari that Raja Bhim Chand was sure to take offence over the beating of the drum. Mata Gujari called the Sikh concerned to tell him that no drum should be beaten at the time of the Guru going out for hunting. No drum was beaten.[43]

Guru Gobind Das asked the man in charge why the kettle-drum was not beaten. He told the Guru all that Mata Gujari had said. 'Are we so afraid of the Raja,' he thundered, 'that we cannot beat the drum?' He went on to add that his mission could not be kept concealed for long. Eventually, the drum was struck and all the hill chiefs trembled. The Raja of Kahlur called his ministers to discuss the matter. They said that the drum was beaten by Guru Gobind Das. He was compared with Rama and Krishna. On the suggestion of his ministers, the Raja came to see the Guru.

He was well received and was so pleased and happy that he thought of becoming a Sikh. But his attitude changed when he saw a rare elephant of the Guru. He wanted to have the elephant, but the Guru was not willing to part with it.[44]

Sukha Singh's account of the situation remains close to that of Koer Singh, but with some variations. In Sukha Singh's account, the masands tell Mata Gujari clearly that naubat was a prerogative of the Rajas and if Guru Gobind Das adopted this practice, the Rajas were bound to take offence. Mata Gujari told the head *nagarchi* (*naubates*) not to beat any drum. In reaction, Guru Gobind Das said that Mata Gujari did not know anything of the concerns of the brave warriors. Anyway, the implementation of the command of God could not be delayed for a long time.[45]

As narrated by Koer Singh, Bhim Chand wanted to know how an elephant came into the Guru's possession. He was told that it was offered to the Guru by Sham Sen, a Raja of the South (*Dakhan des*).[46] Bhim Chand left the place and Guru Gobind Das turned his attention to hunting. Bhim Chand, meanwhile, was thinking of how to get the elephant from the Guru, whether by force or diplomacy. He decided to send his wazir to make a submission to Guru Gobind Das. In all humility, he stated that the daughter of the Raja of Srinagar (Garhwal) had come to Bilaspur with attendants; the elephant was to be shown to them. He requested the Guru to lend the elephant to him for two or three days. Guru Gobind Das knew that Bhim Chand had no intention of returning the elephant. The wazir was told that the Raja could have anything but the elephant. On hearing the message from the Guru, Bhim Chand said in anger that he would call all the Rajas to his support and oblige the Guru to give the elephant to him.[47]

Bhim Chand dispatched letters to the warriors of all places about his intention and sought their support in his venture. The chief of Kangra observed that the two rulers could not live in the same place, just as two lions could not live in the same forest and two swords could not be kept in one scabbard. The Guru should be forced to leave the hills. Preparations for war began openly. The masands apprised Mata Gujari of the growing danger. Meanwhile, a messenger came with an invitation from the Raja of Sirmaur for Guru Gobind Das to go to his state. The masands pressed upon

Mata Gujari the need of accepting this invitation. Mata Gujari spoke to Guru Gobind Das and he reminded her of the purpose for which he had been sent by God. She said that he was too young to wage wars. He should wait for some time more. The Guru agreed to leave Makhowal and go to Nahan. Koer Singh mentions elephants, horses, cannons, and matchlocks in the procession from Makhowal to Paunta.[48]

Sukha Singh's account of how Guru Gobind Das came to think of leaving Makhowal for Sirmaur is similar to Koer Singh's, but with some variations. For example, the elephant which Bhim Chand demanded had come from Assam, and not from the South. Guru Gobind Das was prepared to lend an elephant to Bhim Chand, but not the one elephant which he was asking for.[49]

In retrospect, we can see that the most important event from the early life of Gobind Das was the martyrdom of his father, Guru Tegh Bahadur, in 1675. It was not insignificant that the young Guru Gobind took to hunting as a part of his activities. Before long, he adopted the beating of naubat with his legendary 'Ranjit Nagara' (the drum of victory in battle). He began to keep elephants. Because of the political dimension of these royal prerogatives, the chief of Kahlur became increasingly insistent on a formal acknowledgement of his authority by the Guru. On the Guru's refusal to accept any such terms, the situation was becoming increasingly tense. Guru Gobind accepted the invitation of the chief of Sirmaur to reside in his territory. This invitation had its own political implications. Guru Gobind was being drawn into the politics of the hills.

Notes

1. Jadunath Sarkar, *A Short History of Aurangzib (1618–1707)* (New Delhi: Orient Longman, 1979), pp. 90–4, 98, 130, 133. Jadunath Sarkar, *History of Aurangzib* (Northern-India, 1658–1681) (Calcutta: M.C. Sarkar & Sons, 1921, 2nd edn), vol. 3, pp. 265–6, 280–5 (Appendix V).

2. Irfan Habib, *The Agrarian System of Mughal India 1556–1707* (New Delhi: Oxford University Press, 1999, 2nd. rev. edn), pp. 356–7.

3. B. N. Goswamy and J. S. Grewal, *The Mughals and the Jogis of Jakhbar* (Simla: Indian Institute of Advanced Study, 1967).

4. Sarkar, *History of Aurangzib*, pp. 131–2. Sarkar, *History of Aurangzib*, vol. 3, pp. 268–75.

5. Irfan Habib, *The Agrarian System*, pp. 138–9.

6. Saqi Musta'ad Khan, *Ma'asir-i Alamgiri*, edited by Jadunath Sarkar (Calcutta: Royal Asiatic Society of Bengal, 1947), pp. 314–15.

7. Sarkar, *History of Aurangzib*, vol. 3, p. 312n. A *hasb al-hukam* to Wazir Khan, the *faujdar* of Sirhind, states that in accordance with the imperial orders, and in concert with the *qazi*, he had 'a temple' of the followers of Guru Nanak (called *Nanak-parastan* in the *hasb al-hukum*) destroyed in the town of Buriya and built a mosque in its place. The followers of Guru Nanak destroyed the mosque and killed its newly installed custodian. *'Ahkam-i Alamgiri'*, in J. S. Grewal and Irfan Habib (eds), *Sikh History from Persian Sources: Translations of Major Texts* (New Delhi: Tulika/Indian History Congress, 2001), p. 97.

8. *Sri Dasam Granth Sahib: Text and Translation*, translated and edited by Jodh Singh and Dharam Singh (Patiala: Heritage Publications, 1999), vol. 1, pp. 164–5.

9. *The Chaupa Singh Rahit-nama*, translated and edited by W. H. McLeod (Dunedin, New Zealand: University of Otago Press, 1987).

10. Koer Singh, *Gurbilas Patshahi 10*, edited by Shamsher Singh Ashok (Patiala: Punjabi University, 1968), p. 30.

11. Kesar Singh Chhibber, *Bansavalinama Dasan Patshahian Ka*, edited by Ratan Singh Jaggi, vol. 2 of *Parkh* (edited by S.S. Kohli) (Chandigarh: Panjab University, 1972), p. 81. Bhai Svarup Singh Kaushish, *Guru Kian Sakhian*, edited by Piara Singh Padam (Amritsar: Singh Brothers,1999 [1986]), pp. 58–9, 73–6.

12. Sukha Singh, *Gurbilas Patsahi 10*, edited by Gursharan Kaur Jaggi (Patiala: Bhasha Vibhag, Punjab, 1989), pp. 23–76.

13. Sabinderjit Singh Sagar, *Hukamnamas of Guru Tegh Bahadur: A Historical Study* (Amritsar: Guru Nanak Dev University, 2002), documents 12, 21, 23, 24, 25, 26, 28. Raja Ram Singh, son of Mirza Raja Jai Singh of Jaipur, was appointed to recover the Mughal losses in Assam in December 1667 and he reached Rangmati in February 1669. Guru Tegh Bahadur joined Raja Ram Singh in 1668. Sarkar, *History of Aurangzib*, vol. 3, pp. 187–90, 211–12.

14. Koer Singh, *Gurbilas*, p. 32.

15. Sukha Singh, *Gurbilas*, pp. 35–9.

16. Koer Singh, *Gurbilas*, p. 33. Sukha Singh, *Gurbilas*, p. 41.

17. Koer Singh, *Gurbilas*, pp. 33, 36–7, 42–3. Sukha Singh, *Gurbilas*, pp. 51–3.

18. Singh and Singh, *Sri Dasam Granth Sahib*, pp. 164–7.

19. Sainapat, *Sri Gur Sobha*, edited by Shamsher Singh Ashok (Amritsar: Shiromani Gurdwara Prabandhak Committee, 1967), p. 15.

20. *The Chaupa Singh Rahit-Nama*, p. 79.

21. Chhibber, *Bansavalinama*, p. 99.

22. Sarup Das Bhalla, *Mahima Prakash*, edited by Gobind Singh Lamba and Khazan Singh (Patiala: Punjab Languages Department\1972), part II, pp. 737, 740.

23. Sarup Singh Kaushish, *Guru Kian Sakhian*, edited by Piara Singh Padam (Amritsar: Singh Brothers, 1999[1986]), pp. 78–9.

24. Sainapat, *Sri Gur Sobha*, pp. 10–11.

25. *The Chaupa Singh Rahit-Nama*, pp. 80–1.

26. Koer Singh, *Gurbilas*, p. 58.

27. Chhibber, *Bansavalinama*, pp. 95–7.

28. Bhalla, *Mahima Prakash*, pp. 742–3, 746–7.

29. Kaushish, *Guru Kian Sakhian*, pp. 85–6.

30. Kaushish, *Guru Kian Sakhian*, pp. 85–6.

31. Singh and Singh, *Sri Dasam Granth Sahib*, pp. 152–3. Cf. Jaggi and Jaggi, *Sri Dasam Granth Sahib*, vol. 1, pp. 144–5.

32. Singh and Singh, *Sri Dasam Granth Sahib*, pp. 166–7.

33. Sainapat, *Sri Gur Sobha*, p. 15.

34. *The Chaupa Singh Rahit-Nama*, p. 81.

35. Koer Singh, *Gurbilas*, pp. 63–7.

36. Chhibber, *Bansavalinama*, p. 101.

37. Sukha Singh, *Gurbilas*, pp. 68–74.

38. *The Chaupa Singh Rahit-Nama*, p. 81.

39. Koer Singh, *Gurbilas*, pp. 69–70.

40. Bhalla, *Mahima Prakash*, p. 850.

41. Kaushish, *Guru Kian Sakhian*, p. 91.

42. Kaushish, *Guru Kian Sakhian*, p. 93.

43. Koer Singh, *Gurbilas*, p. 69.

44. Koer Singh, *Gurbilas*, pp. 70–3.

45. Sukha Singh, *Gurbilas*, pp. 75–8.

46. In an undated hukamnama of Guru Gobind Singh addressed to the sangat of Dhaka, Chitagaon, and others, the Guru asks for a good war elephant (*jangi hathi*). *Hukamname Guru Sahiban, Mata Sahiban, Banda Singh ate Khalsa Ji De*, edited by Ganda Singh (Patiala: Punjabi University, 1967), document 35.

47. Koer Singh, *Gurbilas*, pp. 72–7.

48. Koer Singh, *Gurbilas*, pp. 77–80.

49. Sukha Singh, *Gurbilas*, pp. 79–90.

4

In Battles and Politics (1685–98)

Aurangzeb conquered Bijapur in September 1686 and Golkunda in September 1687. Shambhuji was captured in February 1689 to be put to death in March. Throughout 1690 and 1691, the chief concern of Aurangzeb was to take possession of the vast territory that earlier belonged to Bijapur and Golkunda. The war in the Western Deccan continued to be indecisive. The Maratha problem was no longer the same as in the time of Shivaji (or Shambhuji). During 1695–9, the Marathas came nearer home and drove the Mughals into a defensive position.[1]

The author of the *Ma'asir-i Alamgiri* mentions the governors of Lahore, starting with the appointment of Sipahdar Khan as the *subadar* of Lahore in 1686 in place of Mukarram Khan. The three other subadars were Kokaltash Khan, Mahabat Khan Ibrahim, and Abu Nasr Khan. The most important person to be sent to the north-west in the late 1690s was the crown prince Muhammad Mu'azzam. He had received the title of Shah Alam Bahadur in 1676. He captured the city of Hyderabad in October 1685 and his *mansab* was raised to 40,000. In 1687, before the fall of Golkunda, he was imprisoned due to his intrigue with the besieged Sultan of Golkunda. Released in 1694, he was sent to Agra as its subadar. In July 1696, he was ordered to take charge of Multan and in April-May of 1698, he took charge of Kabul.[2] In order to establish peace in the north-west, Prince Mu'azzam was keen to have cordial relations with Guru Gobind Singh (see Image 4.1). There were signs of unrest.

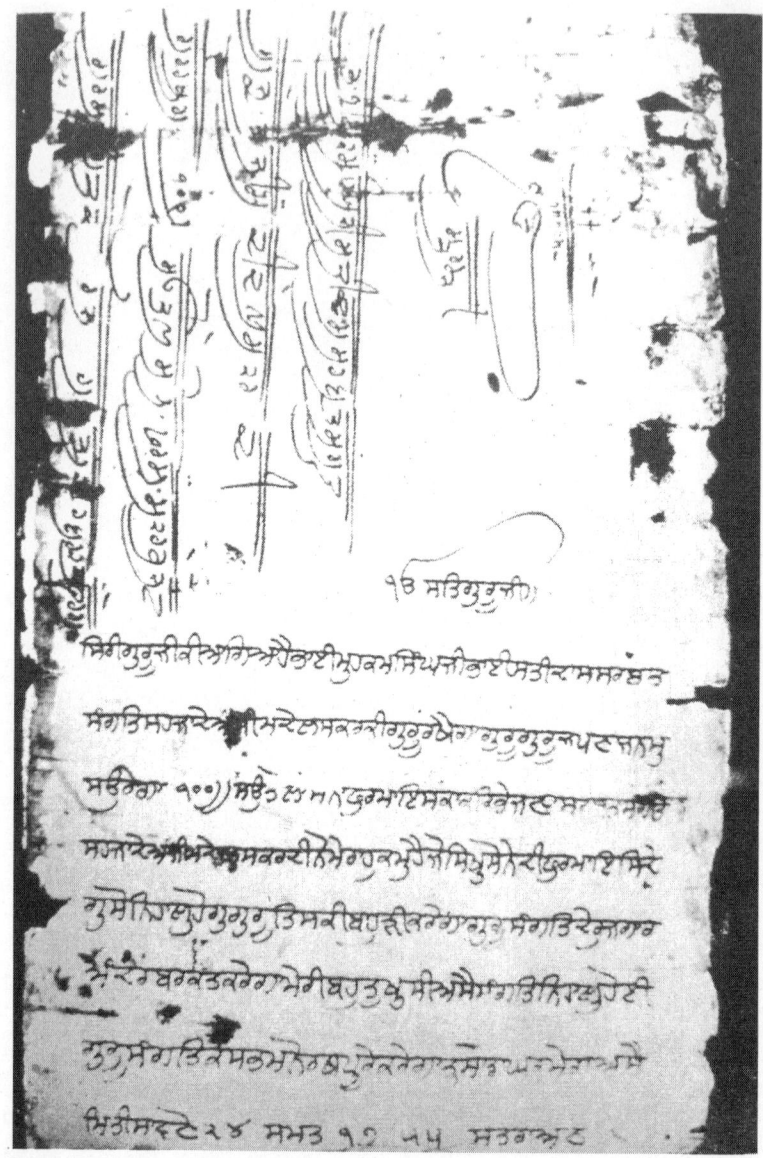

Image 4.1   Guru Gobind Singh's *hukamnama*, dated 24 July 1698 (document 45), addressed to the *sangat* of the army of Prince Azimuddin (son of Prince Mu'azzam). The *sangat* is asked to send 100 *tolas* of gold. Evidently, the presence of the Sikhs in the army of the prince was considerably important.
Source: Ganda Singh ed., *Hukamname*.

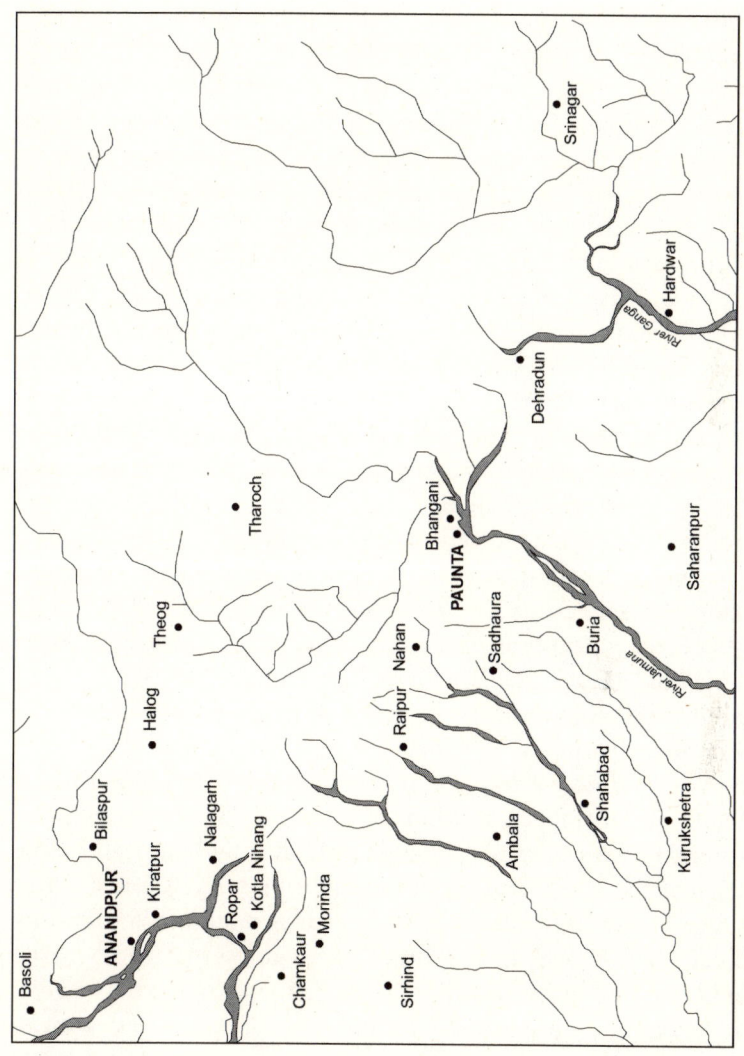

Map 4.1 The Anandpur–Paunta area
Source: Courtesy of the author.

The Battle of Bhangani

Koer Singh says that the relations of the Raja of Sirmaur with the other Rajas were not good and he hoped that the presence of Guru Gobind Das in his state would strengthen his position. He welcomed the Guru and said that his state was sanctified by the Guru's presence. When the Guru built a strong fort at Paunta (see Map 4.1), the Raja was pleased to see his border with the Raja of Srinagar strengthened. Guru Gobind Das assured him not to worry because his enemy would never be allowed to set foot on the territory of Sirmaur.[3] This was the first fort built by Guru Gobind Das.

There was a background of hostility between the rulers of Srinagar and Sirmaur. The former were independent, while the latter were vassals of the Mughal emperor. In the Mughal campaign against the rulers of Srinagar, the chiefs of Sirmaur used to support their suzerain. Generally, they were rewarded with the land wrested from the rulers of Srinagar. During the war of succession between Dara Shukoh and Aurangzeb, Sulaiman Shukoh was given refuge by Raja Prithvi Shah of Srinagar. However, Medini Shah, the son of Prithvi Shah, handed over Sulaiman Shukoh to the Mughals in December 1660. On succeeding Prithvi Shah, he accepted Aurangzeb's suzerainty. In 1684, Medini Shah was succeeded by his son Fateh Shah. Budh Prakash of Srimaur was succeeded by his son Medini Prakash, the chief who had sent an invitation to Guru Gobind Das. According to the *Guru Kian Sakhian*, Paunta was chosen in consultation with the Guru.[4]

In the *Bachittar Natak*, it is stated simply: 'On the bank of the Kalindari, I enjoyed all kinds of sport and killed a lot of lions, bears and *nilgao*s (antelopes). Raja Fateh Shah felt angry and came to fight without any reason.'[5] In the given situation, the activity of Guru Gobind Das could be regarded as a 'reason'. According to Koer Singh, hunting was a part of his daily routine. He used to ride out with other warriors, equipped with muskets, swords, and daggers. They hunted animals like lions, boars, rhinos, *nilgaos*, and rabbits. The Guru used to give long spears to the brave warriors to face intoxicated elephants. Sikhs from all parts of the country began to come to Paunta for the Guru's *darshan*.[6] Sukha Singh confirms that the Guru began to go out hunting in the thick forest where there were all kinds of wild animals: lions, elephants, wolves, boars, monkeys, stags, nilgaos, and deer. He used to take many warriors with him to encourage them to face lions with swords and shields. He himself had to kill a lion which none of the warriors could kill.[7] Hunting was not merely a sport but also a training for the warriors.

Koer Singh highlights Bhim Chand's role in persuading Fateh Shah to attack Guru Gobind Das. Bhim Chand's son was betrothed to the daughter of Fateh Shah. For the marriage ceremony, Bhim Chand had set out with a large party to go to Srinagar, the capital of Fateh Shah. He had to cross the Jamuna at a point near Paunta that was under the Guru's control. Bhim Chand sent his wazir to the Guru with the request to forgive him and to return to Anandpur. He praised the Guru as the *avtar* of Rama and Krishna, and requested for a safe passage. Guru Gobind Das told him that his master was not sincere and that he would have to face armed resistance if he tried to cross the Jamuna. The Guru added that he would return to Anandpur on his own with the beat of the drum.[8] Eventually, only the bridegroom was allowed to cross the Jamuna to reach Srinagar before the auspicious time fixed for marriage. Bhim Chand had to take a longer route and he reached late. He persuaded Fateh Shah to attack Paunta and dislodge the Guru. Among those who came to their support were the chiefs of Guler, Jaswan, Kangra, Kullu, Chamba, Jammu, Mandi, and Suket.[9]

Sarup Singh Kaushish adds another cause: the intervention of Guru Gobind Das in the affairs of his nephew, Ram Rai, at Dehra Dun in the state of Garhwal.[10] The Baisakhi festival of 1686 was celebrated by them together at Dehra Dun. In the rainy season of 1687 came the news of Ram Rai's death. Guru Gobind Das went to Dehra Dun to offer a formal condolence. He found that the prominent masands of Ram Rai were in favour of Mata Punjab Kaur to succeed her deceased husband, but a number of masands supported a masand named Charan Das Bahia and persisted in their demand. Guru Gobind Das punished the rebel masands and Mata Punjab Kaur was installed on the *gaddi*. The masands who were opposed to her made all kinds of allegations against Guru Gobind Das to invite Fateh Shah.[11]

On the first anniversary of Ram Rai's death, Guru Gobind Das
sent his Sikhs to look after all the arrangements. The opponents
of Mata Punjab Kaur tried to create trouble and saved their lives
by running away. Gurbakhsh Rai, their leader, went to Srinagar
and complained to Fateh Shah against Mata Punjab Kaur and the
Sikhs of Guru Gobind Das. He was emphatic that the Guru would
increase his influence in Dehra Dun through the willing coopera-
tion of Mata Punjab Kaur and by eliminating men like himself
who wanted the authority of Fateh Shah to be well established.
Raja Fateh Shah told his wazir that he did not wish to let the situation deteriorate further. 'The Guru has set his foot only in Dehra
Dun, but the day is not far when he would occupy a chunk of our
territory with the support of Raja Medini Prakash. Sant Gurbakhsh
Rai has told us everything. Further delay in this matter would not
be sound politics.'[12] Guru Gobind Das's intervention in the affairs
of Ram Rai was seen by Fateh Shah as an interference in the affairs
of his subjects and his state. This was the cause of the battle of
Bhangani.

Among the warriors who fought on the side of Fateh Shah,
according to the *Bachittar Natak*, were the hired Pathan commandants Hayat Khan, Najabat Khan and Bhikhan Khan, Raja
Gopal (Raj Singh) of Guler, Hari Chand (of Hindur), Madhukar
Shah Dadwal (of Siba), and the Raja of Jaswan. Among those
who fought on the side of Guru Gobind Das were Shah Sangram
(Sango Shah), Jit Mal, Mehri Chand, Ganga Ram, Lal Chand,
Daya Ram, Kripal, Nand Chand, 'Uncle' Kirpal, and Sahib Chand.
The first to be killed in the battle was Hayat Khan who was hit
on the head by Kripal with his staff. Sahib Chand killed a number of Khans and warriors. Hari Chand killed many warriors on
the Guru's side, including Jit Mal. Najabat Khan killed Sangram
Shah, but himself got killed. Guru Gobind Das took part in the
battle personally after the death of Shah Sangram. His first arrow
killed a Khan. His second arrow killed Bhikhan Khan's horse.
Hari Chand shot three arrows at the Guru, but only one of the
three pricked him slightly. Hari Chand was killed by the Guru's
arrow. The army of Fateh Shah left the field of battle. The Guru
was victorious through God's grace. He returned to Makhowal
and founded Anandpur.[13]

Sainapat's account of the battle of Bhangani in *Sri Gur Sobha* is based on the *Bachittar Natak* and remains very close to it. There are only some slight variations. Sainapat says explicitly that the source of Raja Fateh Shah's annoyance with Guru Gobind Singh was his activity in Paunta. Bhikhan Khan himself, and not his horse, got killed by the Guru. The title of 'Shah Sangram' was given to Sango Shah by Guru Gobind Das after his death on the battlefield. On the whole, Sainapat's account of the battle is shorter.[14]

According to Koer Singh, all the 500 Pathan mercenaries left Guru Gobind Das before the battle and joined the allied forces of the Rajas. The Guru's offer of one gold coin as the daily pay was rejected by them. Bhikhan Khan encouraged them to join the allies for a greater gain from the booty which they were sure to get after the Guru's defeat. All the 500 Udasis left the Guru for fear of his enemies, with the exception of Mahant Kripal who joined the battle. Koer Singh's account of the battle is similar to the account given in the *Bachittar Natak*. However, Mahru and Kahru are mentioned as two slaves of the Guru. Nand and Chand are mentioned as two brothers instead of 'Nand Chand' of the *Bachittar Natak*. Bibi Viro is mentioned as the Guru's sister, and not as the sister of his father, Guru Tegh Bahadur. There is also a reference to Kali and another to the creation of the Panth Khalsa in the future.[15]

The account of the battle in the *Guru Kian Sakhian* is brief and simple. Raja Fateh Shah marched from Srinagar with select warriors like Hari Chand and encamped near the Jamuna. Guru Gobind Das told the Sikhs that Fateh Shah had come to attack Paunta without any offence given to him. Diwan Nand Chand was told to intercept Fateh Shah on his way so that he did not reach Paunta. The following day, the Guru along with the Sikh army chose a spot between the Giri and the Jamuna to meet Fateh Shah in battle. His five cousins (sons of Bibi Viro), 'uncle' Kirpal Chand, Bhai Jaita, Purohit Daya Ram, Mahant Kripal, and others were with him. The army of Fateh Shah and his supporters was led by Hari Chand, Pahar Chand, Bir Chand, Najabat Khan, Bhikhan Khan, Hayat Khan, and some others. The warriors on both sides fought well. Two of the sons of Bibi Viro—Sango Shah and Jit Mal—became martyrs. To get killed on the side of Fateh

Shah were Najabat Khan and Bhikhan Khan, among others. The hill army took to its heels. Fateh Shah asked Mian Hari Chand, who was known to be the bravest warrior in the hills, to save his honour. Hari Chand quickly shot three arrows at Guru Gobind Das one after the other. Only one of these caused a small scratch. The Guru shot an arrow at Hari Chand and he fell down from his horse and died.[16] This was the end of the battle.

According to Koer Singh, the Sikhs were elated with the victory in the battle of Bhangani, feeling that they could conquer Srinagar, ransack Delhi, and establish their rule from Paunta to Anandpur. Guru Gobind Das smiled and asked them to be patient. Their power would increase, by God's grace, and they would conquer more and more territory. They would rule not only one but many countries. The grand objective was to destroy the 'Turks'. Thus, Koer Singh attached great political significance to the battle.[17]

According to Kaushish, Guru Gobind Das punished those who had not supported him in this '*dharamyudh*'. Raja Medini Prakash and Mata Punjab Kaur requested Guru Gobind Das not to leave Paunta. But he left Paunta exactly one month and 10 days after the battle.[18]

The Battle of Nadaun

According to the *Bachittar Natak*, Guru Gobind Das returned to Makhowal after the victory at Bhangani and founded Anandpur. He punished those who had not fought at Bhangani and rewarded those who had fought bravely in the battle. According to the *Guru Kian Sakhian*, Rani Champa of Kahlur and her son, Raja Bhim Chand, came for the Guru's darshan on the Baisakhi festival of 1689 and offered two villages, Agampura and Tarapur, in *bhet* to the Guru in his *darbar*. Guru Gobind Das declared that forts would be built on all sides of Anandpur. In due course, five forts were built, namely Anandgarh, Lohgarh, Taragarh (on the road of Naina Devi), Agamgarh, and Fatehgarh. Two more forts, Kesgarh and Holgarh, were added in 1699.[19]

Mian Khan (the Mughal *faujdar*) of Jammu sent Alif Khan to Nadaun. Bhim Chand marched towards Nadaun and requested

Guru Gobind Das to come for his support. Alif Khan had raised wooden defences on the top of a hill. Raj Singh of Guler and Ram Singh of Jaswan attacked Alif Khan. Several hill chiefs were on his side, notably Kirpal Chand from Kangra and Dayal Chand of Bijharwal. A fierce battle was fought. At a critical juncture, Guru Gobind Das shot one of the chiefs dead with his musket. Then, he shot four arrows in quick succession, three of them with his left hand. The battle stopped suddenly and Alif Khan and his supporters eventually crossed the river, abandoning the field of battle. Guru Gobind Das stayed at Nadaun for eight days and saw all its royal places. Bhim Chand and his supporters patched up peace with the Mughal faujdars and came to an amicable understanding with them. On his way back to Anandpur, Guru Gobind Das sacked Alsun (a village in the territory of Kahlur).[20]

In Koer Singh's brief account of the battle of Nadaun, a change in the attitude of Raja Bhim Chand towards Guru Gobind Das is explicitly mentioned. In view of his increasing popularity with all ranks of people from a prince to a pauper, Bhim Chand sent a sweet-tongued messenger to him to seek forgiveness for his past attitude and to seek permission to come personally to the Guru's presence. Bhim Chand then came to Anandpur with his wazir. He was impressed to see the Guru's darbar. He expressed admiration for the Guru as the avtar of Rama and Krishna and, in utter humility, implored the Guru to come to his aid in crisis. His past trespasses were forgiven and he returned home.[21]

According to the *Guru Kian Sakhian*, a year and a quarter after the return of Guru Gobind Das from Paunta, a messenger from Raja Bhim Chand came to Anandpur with a letter to the Guru, asking for help against the (Mughal) governor of Lahore who had invaded the hills. The Guru ordered Diwan Nand Chand to prepare for the Raja's support. Eminent warriors such as Diwan Nand Chand, Dharam Chand Chhibber, Bhai Mani Ram, and Bhai Alam Chand got ready. With the Sikh army, the Guru joined Bhim Chand and early in 1690 they reached Nadaun to fight against Alif Khan who was well known as a brave warrior. The Guru participated in the hard fight that followed, using his musket first and then his bow and arrows. Before sunset, the army of Alif Khan began to leave the field of battle in a disorderly fashion. Alif Khan rode his horse to escape alive. Among the dead were two of the Sikh warriors: Bhai Sohan Chand and Mul Chand. On the invitation of the chief of Nadaun, the Guru stayed in his palace for a week. On his way to Anandpur, he punished the Ranghars (Muslim Rajputs) of Alsun.[22]

Expeditions Sent by the Governor of Lahore

Aurangzeb appears to have taken serious notice of Guru Gobind Das in 1693. A news of November 20 from Sirhind is recorded in the *Akhbarat-i Darbar-i Mu'alla*.[23] The *waqai-navis* of Sirhind had reported about 'a person named Gobind who had assumed the name of Nanak'. The emperor commanded Bahramand Khan to issue orders to the faujdar of Sirhind to prevent crowds from collecting.[24]

Several years passed, says the author of the *Bachittar Natak*, before Dilawar Khan sent his son against Guru Gobind Singh. The Khanzada Dilawar Khan planned a night attack on Anandpur. When they crossed the stream near Anandpur, Alam Chand awakened the Guru. His warriors were awakened by the noise. They took up their arms and moved towards the enemy, sounding trumpets and beating drums. The noise created was so terrible that the enemy ran away without a fight. They left the field of battle shamelessly, using their horses to flee. On the way, they destroyed a village in impotent rage before they halted at Bhalan. The Guru and his warriors remained untouched.[25]

The Khanzada failed to explain his ignominious retreat. Husain Khan, a commandant under Dilawar Khan and legally his slave, was keen to undertake another expedition against Guru Gobind Das. (On his way to Anandpur) Husain Khan overpowered the Dadwal Raja and made many Rajputs captive. He plundered the whole area and distributed the booty among his soldiers. Husain Khan was supported by the Kahlurias and the Katoches. Raja Gopal (Raj Singh) of Guler accompanied Raja Ram Singh to offer tribute. Husain Khan demanded much more and Gopal left his camp without paying any tribute. His fort was besieged by Husain Khan and supplies of food were cut off. Gopal felt obliged to negotiate. Husain

Khan insisted that he should pay Rs 10,000. Gopal felt obliged to
fight. The battle is described in detail in the *Bachittar Natak*. The
bravery of some warriors on both sides is extolled. Among them
were Hari Singh and Himmat on the side of Husain Khan, and
the Jaswal Raja on the side of Gopal. Eventually, on Ram Singh's
suggestion, Gopal killed Himmat. Husain Khan and Kirpal Chand
Katoch also died fighting. Raj Singh and Ram Singh were victorious.
Guru Gobind Das had sent Sangat Rai (Sangtia) with seven horsemen
for their support; they all died fighting. Guru Gobind Das leaves
no doubt that Husain Khan's expedition was actually sent against
him. 'God protected us,' he says at the end, 'and the cloud of iron
burst elsewhere'.[26]

Sarup Singh Kaushish and Sukha Singh provide slightly varying versions. Kaushish says that Dilawar Khan was sore about his
son's failure. Husain Khan, the faujdar of Kangra, tried to console
him by saying that victory or defeat was inevitably the result of
any battle. He added that the result of a battle depended partly
on the tactics followed by a commander and offered himself to
lead a campaign. Husain Khan moved towards Anandpur, deal-
ing with the hill chiefs first. Many of them joined Husain Khan,
such as Raja Ajmer Chand, son of Raja Bhim Chand who had died
in 1692. Husain Khan laid waste the whole area and there was
no one to oppose him. He besieged Guler, the capital of Raja Gaj
Singh Gopal (Raj Singh). The Raja sent a messenger to Anandpur
to seek support from Guru Gobind Das. The Guru reached Guler
with Bhai Sangat Rai and seven other warriors. After discussing
the situation with Raja Gaj Singh, it was decided to negotiate with
Husain Khan to work out a peaceful solution. The Sikh warriors,
accompanied by Raja Gaj Singh, went to meet Husain Khan, but
the haughty faujdar did not care for anybody. In fact, he thought
of capturing the Raja. Getting an inkling of his intention, Raja Gaj
Singh and the Sikh warriors returned to Guler. The stage was set
for a battle.[27]

A few days later, a pitched battle was fought for several hours
in the plain close to Guler. Husain Khan was killed by an arrow
shot by Bhai Sangat Rai. Raja Kirpal Chand Katoch and Raja
Ajmer Chand of Kahlur came forward to take revenge. Bhai Sangat
Rai faced them boldly with the support of the army of Guler.

Eventually, an arrow shot by someone from the enemy side ended his life. The Sikh warriors fought bravely for the possession of his body. All seven of them died fighting. Both Kirpal Chand and Ajmer Chand were wounded and the armies left the field of battle. The victory of the Raja of Guler was due more to the Guru's grace than the support given by the Sikh warriors.[28]

Dilawar Khan now sent Jujhar Singh. He came to Bhalan where he was attacked by Gaj Singh Pamma. One side was supported by the Chandel (Raja of Kahlur) and the other by the Raja of Jaswan. They fought zealously. Two warriors, Chand and Narain, were killed. Left alone, Jujhar Singh was surrounded on all sides by his opponents. He killed many of them using different kinds of weapons before he fell to the ground and died.[29]

Sukha Singh says that Dilawar Khan was very sad over the death and defeat of Husain Khan. He consulted the *ahlkars* (officials) to decide what to do now. Jujhar Singh was sent with an army of 3,000 to collect the arrears of tribute for four years from the chiefs of the hills. Raja Ajmer Chand joined him with his army. A remarkable battle with the Raja of Jaswan was fought in 1696. Jujhar Singh's companion Narain Chand was killed in the battle. Jujhar Singh was furious over his death and rode alone to the spot where Narain Chand had fallen. Finding him alone, his opponents surrounded him on all sides and he died fighting. The army of Lahore left the field of battle.[30] Sukha Singh remains very close to the *Bachittar Natak* in his narration of the expedition of the Khanzada and the activity of Husain Khan.

Arrival of Prince Mu'azzam

According to the *Bachittar Natak*, after the failure of the campaigns of the Khanzada, Hussain Khan, and Jujhar Singh, it occurred to Aurangzeb to send his son to Punjab. The people were frightened and took shelter in the higher hills. An *Ahadi*, Mirza Beg, sent by Aurangzeb destroyed the homes of those who had turned away from Guru Gobind Das. They died a dog's death and were thrown into the pit of hell. Four Ahadis followed Mirza Beg and completed his task of destroying the homes of those who had left the Guru.

On the other hand, Guru Gobind Das and his Sikhs were safe under the protection of God.[31]

In the *Bachittar Natak*, there is a reference to the House of Baba Nanak and the House of Babur, suggesting a sort of relationship between the two.[32] Teja Singh and Ganda Singh state indeed that Bhai Nand Lal seems to have brought about some kind of an understanding between the government and the Guru who made the following statement:

> The House of the Baba and the House of Babur
> Both derive their authority from God Himself,
> Recognise the former as supreme in religion,
> And the latter supreme in secular affairs.[33]

However, Kapur Singh does not accept the view of Teja Singh and Ganda Singh. He gives his own translation of the verses to give them his own interpretation. Two forces claimed allegiance of men's souls on earth: (a) the truth and morality as religion, and (b) the state as an embodiment of utilitarian and secular politics. The primary allegiance of man was to truth and morality, and those who fail in this allegiance suffer under the subjugation of the state, 'un-nourished by the courage and hope which is born through unswerving adherence to the primary allegiance'. 'The Church must perpetually correct and influence the State without aiming to destroy or absorb it.'[34]

The author of the *Bachittar Natak* was concerned primarily with the moral dimension of the situation. Koer Singh was more concerned with the political dimension. Guru Gobind Singh was holding his court when a message was delivered that Aurangzeb had sent his son with a huge army against the Guru and that he was to decide whether to face the enemy or to move to a safe place. Many people left Anandpur out of fright. Some of the Sikhs went to Mata ji to underline the danger implicit in the situation. Guru Gobind Das, however, did not think of leaving Anandpur. He resorted to diplomacy. He explained to some intelligent Sikhs that they should meet the prince on his arrival in the territories of Sirhind and convince him that only the Guru and his Sikhs could help him against his brother Azam who was ambitious and competent enough to usurp the throne after Aurangzeb's death. This argument appealed to Prince Mu'azzam. He sent a letter to Guru Gobind Singh and went to Lahore, leaving the Guru undisturbed. Aurangzeb was annoyed with Mu'azzam and sent four Ahadis to punish the recalcitrant people. They punished those who had turned away from the Guru. Thus, Guru Gobind Singh protected his devout Sikhs.[35]

Sarup Singh Kaushish gives some detail of Mu'azzam's arrival. Dilawar Khan, the subadar of Lahore, having failed twice or thrice in the campaigns he had sent against Guru Gobind Singh, wrote to the Mughal court that the hill Rajas were in revolt and had paid no tribute for four years. The Guru at Anandpur was at their back and, consequently, they did not obey any order. Aurangzeb sent his son Mu'azzam with an army to help the Lahore governor. On the news of his arrival in Punjab, many Sikhs left Anandpur for the higher hills. The *Charitro Pakhyan Granth*, which was started in 1691, was completed at this time. A prayer for protection against the new threat was added to the *Charitro Pakhyan*:

> Protect us with your hand. Let the desire of my heart be fulfilled, with my mind centred on your feet. Protect me as your own.
>
> Destroy all our enemies, and save me with your hand. May my family live in comfort, and all my *sewak*s (attendants) and Sikhs O'Kartar.[36]

This prayer was efficacious. In any case, the Mughals went towards Lahore, leaving Anandpur alone. Aurangzeb was unhappy over this and, after the rainy season, sent back the Ahadi Mirza Beg. Still unsatisfied, Aurangzeb sent four more Ahadis. They confirmed what Mirza Beg had written earlier. An amicable understanding had been reached. Guru Gobind Das refers to this understanding in *Apni Katha*. He refers also to the way in which Mirza Beg treated the Sikhs who had deserted the Guru.[37]

Sukha Singh gives a whole chapter to Prince Mu'azzam and the Ahadis. After the defeat of the combined forces of the Mughals and the Rajas, some people went to the court of Aurangzeb to inform him that his army had been defeated. He was struck by surprise and wanted to know how this had happened. The messenger (*doot*) described the battle in detail. The emperor was much perturbed and wanted to hear from the ministers of the hill chiefs. They told him that Guru Gobind Das was a perfect person (*puran purkh*), even though the emperor saw him as a small fry. He was a succes-sor of Guru Nanak who was the redeemer of humankind, whether Hindu or Muslim. Babur had met Guru Nanak and got all that he wanted. The emperor should invite the Guru for a personal meet-ing or should go and meet him. Professional jesters impersonated the Khalsa at the court of Aurangzeb. They represented the Khalsa as fully armed. The Guru had built a number of forts in Anandpur which was the abode of the Khalsa. The Guru had prepared the Khalsa for *dharamyudh*.[38]

At the end of the chapter, Sukha Singh reiterates what Koer Singh had written, with only minor differences in detail. Guru Gobind Das was informed that Aurangzeb had sent his son with a huge army. The Guru would have to fight or seek refuge elsewhere. He remained unperturbed and there was no fear in the hearts of the Sikhs who were devoted to the Guru. But many others left him to seek refuge in the higher hills. They were destroyed by their own cleverness. Guru Gobind Das advised his trusted Sikhs to meet Prince Mu'azzam when he entered the territories of Sirhind and to put forth the proposition that he could depend upon the support of the Guru and his Sikhs in his competition with Azam for gaining the throne after the death of Aurangzeb. Sukha Singh mentions Bhai Nand Lal among the Sikhs of Delhi who persuaded Prince Mu'azzam to accept the proposition. The argument appealed to Mu'azzam and he came to an understanding with Guru Gobind Das, and went to Lahore. When Aurangzeb came to know of this, he sent an Ahadi, Mirza Beg, who punished those who had actually deserted the Guru. Mirza Beg was followed by four more Ahadis who completed the task. All the renegades were destroyed.[39]

In the summer of 1696, there was a sense of urgency, suggesting a warlike situation. The *hukamnama*s issued on 2 August 1696 to Bhai Taloka and Bhai Rama, and to Bhai Sukhia and the sangat of Rupeki, ask for a unit of horsemen, foot soldiers, and musketeers to come immediately to Anandpur.[40] Significantly, some other sources indicate that Mu'azzam was not hostile towards Guru Gobind Singh. In a later hukamnama, we find the Guru writing to 'Bhai Makhan Singh ji' and Bhai Sati Das of the sangat of the prince's *lashkar* (army), asking the sangat to send 100 *tola*s (a weight of about 30 grams) of gold.[41] This suggests that a considerable number of Sikhs of the Guru were now with the Mughal army.

In retrospect, we find Guru Gobind Das getting involved in several battles, which acquired an increasing importance in the political context of the Mughal empire. The battle of Bhangani, fought against the hill chiefs in 1688, ended in the Guru's victory and he returned to Makhowal. He founded Anandpur and started building fortresses for its defense. In 1690, he was approached by Bhim Chand for help against the Mughal faujdar at Nadaun. Though victorious, Bhim Chand patched up peace with the faujdar. Guru Gobind appeared to be the source of trouble. In 1693, Aurangzeb ordered that no crowds should be allowed to gather at Anandpur. Dilawar Khan, the faujdar of Jammu, sent three expeditions against Guru Gobind and the chiefs who had aligned with him, but all the three attempts failed. Aurangzeb sent Prince Mu'azzam in the summer of 1696 to set right the affairs in the Punjab hills. He left Guru Gobind Das alone for his own reasons. In fact, he developed cordial relations with the Guru.

In a painting of the Guru's court in this phase, Guru Gobind Das is seated on the gaddi with his three sons seated in front on the floor and the courtiers standing behind them in a row. Identified from other sources, the three sons are: Ajit Singh, born at Paunta in 1686; Jujhar Singh, born at Anandpur in 1690; and Zorawar Singh, born at Anandpur in 1697. The fourth son, Fateh Singh (born on 25 February 1699), was either not yet born or was too small to be seated. Ajit Singh was born to Mata Sundari, whom Guru Gobind Das had married in 1685 before leaving Makhowal for Paunta. The other three sons were born to Mata Jito, who had been married to Guru Gobind Das in 1677.[42]

Notes

1. Jadunath Sarkar, *A Short History of Aurangzib (1618–1707)* (New Delhi: Orient Longman, 1979), pp. 260–5.

2. Saqi Must'ad Khan, *Ma'asir-i Alamgiri*, edited by Jadunath Sarkar (Calcutta: Royal Asiatic Society of Bengal, 1947), pp. 93–4, 164, 173, 178, 217, 225–6, 233, 235, 240, 255.

3. Koer Singh, *Gurbilas Patshahi 10*, edited by Shamsher Singh Ashok (Patiala: Punjabi University, 1968), pp. 78–81.

4. Bhai Svarup Singh Kaushish, *Guru Kian Sakhian*, edited by Piara Singh Padam (Amritsar: Singh Brothers,1999 [1986]), pp. 93–4. Raja Fateh Shah also came and Guru Gobind Das succeeded in bringing about a conciliation among the two Rajas. The Raja of Sirmaur as well as Fateh Shah returned satisfied from Paunta. Sukha Singh goes on to talk about a messenger from Srinagar who had come to invite Guru Gobind Das to the marriage of Raja Fateh Shah's daughter to the son of Raja Bhim Chand. The Guru sent Nand Chand, Daya Ram, and a few warriors with presents for the occasion. Kaushish, *Guru Kian Sakhian*, pp. 94–5.

5. *Bachittar Natak*, in *Sri Dasam Granth Sahib*, edited by Ratan Singh Jaggi and Gursharan Kaur Jaggi (New Delhi: Gobind Sadan, 1999), vol. 1, p. 156.

6. Koer Singh, *Gurbilas*, p. 82.

7. Sukha Singh, *Gurbilas Patsahi 10*, edited by Gursharan Kaur Jaggi (Patiala: Bhasha Vibhag, Punjab, 1989), pp. 90–6. Guru Gobind Das issued hukamnamas to Sikh sangats to come to Paunta for the Diwali festival. The Sikh sangats of Delhi, the 'east', Assam, Majha, Doaba, Pothohar, Kabul, and other countries reached Paunta in large numbers. The Raja of Assam, Ratan Rai, came with costly presents. He was following the example of his father who had come to Chak Nanaki (Makhowal) when Ratan Rai was 11 years old. Among the costly presents then brought by the father was the elephant called 'Prasadi'. Similarly, offerings were brought by the sangats of other countries. Sukha Singh, *Gurbilas*, pp. 97–117.

8. Koer Singh, *Gurbilas*, pp. 83–5.

9. Koer Singh, *Gurbilas*, pp. 85–7.

10. Kaushish, *Guru Kian Sakhian*, p. 94. Ram Rai had left Delhi towards the end of 1681 to live in the state of Srinagar at a place which came to be known as Dehra Dun. Ajit Singh Baagha, *Banur Had Orders: A Critical Study of an Hitherto Unknown 'Hukamnamah' of Guru Gobind Singh* (Delhi: Ranjit Printers and Publishers, 1969), p. 61.

11. Kaushish, *Guru Kian Sakhian*, pp. 95–8.

12. Kaushish, *Guru Kian Sakhian*, pp. 98–100.

13. *Sri Dasam Granth Sahib: Text and Translation*, translated and edited by Jodh Singh and Dharam Singh (Patiala: Heritage Publications, 1999), vol. 1, pp. 166–72.

14. Sainapat, *Sri Gur Sobha*, edited by Shamsher Singh Ashok (Amritsar: Shiromani Gurdwara Prabandhak Committee, 1967), pp. 15–22.

15. Koer Singh, *Gurbilas*, pp. 88–98.

16. Kaushish, *Guru Kian Sakhian*, pp. 100–1.

17. Koer Singh, *Gurbilas*, pp. 98–9.

18. Kaushish, *Guru Kian Sakhian*, pp. 101–2.

19. Kaushish, *Guru Kian Sakhian*, p. 105.

20. Singh and Singh, *Sri Dasam Granth Sahib*, pp. 172–9.

21. Koer Singh, *Gurbilas*, pp. 100–02.

22. Kaushish, *Guru Kian Sakhian*, pp. 105–06.

23. Teja Singh and Ganda Singh, *A Short History of the Sikhs* (Patiala: Punjabi University, 1990 [1950]), p. 64, n. 2.

24. Chetan Singh, *Region and Empire: Panjab in the Seventeenth Century* (Delhi: Oxford University Press, 1991), p. 300, n. 120. *News Letter*, 20 November 1693. See also Sri Ram Sharma, *The Religious Policy of the Mughal Emperors* (Bombay: Asia Publishing House, 1962, 2nd edn), pp. 141, 146, n. 80, 81.

25. Singh and Singh, *Sri Dasam Granth Sahib*, pp. 179–81.

26. Singh and Singh, *Sri Dasam Granth Sahib*, pp. 180–95.

27. Kaushish, *Guru Kian Sakhian*, pp. 112–13.

28. Kaushish, *Guru Kian Sakhian*, p. 113.

29. Singh and Singh, *Sri Dasam Granth Sahib*, pp. 194–7.

30. Sukha Singh, *Gurbilas*, pp. 118–25.

31. Jaggi and Jaggi, *Sri Dasam Granth Sahib*, part I, pp. 185–9.

32. Jaggi and Jaggi, *Sri Dasam Granth Sahib*, part I, p. 186.

33. Singh and Singh, *A Short History of the Sikhs*, p. 64.

34. Kapur Singh, *Parasharprasna: The Baisakhi of Guru Gobind Singh (An Exposition of Sikhism)* (Jullundur: Hind Publishers, 1959), pp. 284–9.

35. Koer Singh, *Gurbilas Patshahi 10*, pp. 175–7.

36. Jaggi and Jaggi, *Sri Dasam Granth Sahib*, vol. 5, p. 670.

37. Kaushish, *Guru Kian Sakhian*, pp. 115–16.

38. Sukha Singh, *Gurbilas*, pp. 235–45.

39. Sukha Singh, *Gurbilas*, pp. 246–9.

40. *Hukamname Guru Sahiban, Mata Sahiban, Banda Singh ate Khalsa Ji De*, edited by Ganda Singh (Patiala: Punjabi University, 1967), documents 43, 44.

41. *Hukamname*, document 45.

42. Baagha, *Banur Had Orders*, p. 84.

III

Institution of the Khalsa

5

Literary Articulation (1685–98)

The Guru's Darbar

In his *Darbar of the Sikh Gurus*, Louis E. Fenech observes that early Sikh tradition displayed a number of Mughal symbols denoting power and royalty, such as kettledrums, tents, *siropa*s (robes of honour), decorative designs, portraits, and production of books. Indeed, the Islamicate courtly precedence provided in part the framework for 'a Sikh courtly world' coherent in its own terms. 'It was perhaps during the time of the 10th Guru that the Sikh community became adept at such revisions.' Guru Gobind Singh adopted many courtly symbols and features, and their accompanying Persian terminology.[1]

Rai Balwand and Satta refer to Guru Angad being seated on the throne (*takht*) of Guru Nanak. Some other terms used in connection with investiture are: true king (*sacha patshah*), canopy (*chhatar*), mark of investiture (*tikka*), and the court (*diwan*). Bhatt Nath refers to Goindwal as the city of God. In the descriptions of the Bhatts, Guru Ram Das is a saintly king (*raj-yogi*), surrounded by 'his bards and the holy congregation'. The '*manji* system' of Guru Amar Das became the '*masand* system' under Guru Ram Das. The latter had a courtly connotation. At the time of their departure from the Guru's court, the Guru conferred a turban upon each masand. In the *bani* of Guru Nanak, there is a metaphorical reference to robing in honour. The gifting of garments became an empirical reality under Guru Arjan.[2]

Guru Arjan founded three towns: Ramdaspur, Tarn Taran, and Kartarpur. Fenech does not say so explicitly, but these towns were autonomous in the context of the Mughal empire. Guru Arjan refers to 'gentle rule' (*halemi raj*) prevailing in Ramdaspur. Everyone lived in peace. Under the guidance of Guru Arjan, Bhai Gurdas and other scribes helped prepare the Sikh scripture now known as the *Kartarpuri Bir*.[3]

Guru Hargobind took to hunting and proved to be a great warrior. His armed bands were organized 'on the pattern' of the Mughal armies. He built *Akal Takht* (Throne of the Immortal) in the precincts of the 'Golden Temple' (Harmandar) and a fort called Lohgarh. He issued *hukamnama*s and founded the town named Sri Hargobindpur. There were *dhadi*s (minstrels) like Abdul and Natha at his court. Thus, according to Fenech, Guru Hargobind presents an image that is 'clearly royal and courtly in nature'. Guru Gobind Singh carried forward the legacy of Guru Hargobind.[4]

Guru Gobind Singh emerged as a great patron of literature. Anandpur–Makhowal became an attractive venue for poets due to a number of reasons. In some cases, the Guru himself invited poets to join his *darbar*. Some poets were uncomfortable at the Mughal court due to the religious attitude of Aurangzeb. There was no safer place than the Anandpur of Guru Gobind Singh for poets 'who were either oppressed or had fallen out of favour or were simply looking for a location to sell their wares'. Guru Gobind Singh could genuinely appreciate literary talent.[5]

Literary Activity Recorded in Eighteenth-Century Sikh Literature

Several Sikh writers of the eighteenth century refer to literary activity at the court of Guru Gobind Singh in the late seventeenth century. In the *Chaupa Singh Rahit-Nama*, it is stated that two *Granth*s were prepared by Guru Gobind Singh: *Samundar Sagar Granth* and *Avtar Lila Granth*.[6] Kesar Singh Chhibber adds that the former was thrown into the river by the order of Guru Gobind Singh in 1701. It was still unbound and some of its folios were salvaged by the Sikhs. Chhibber claims to have seen 91 lines of this Granth. The second Granth too was unbound and its folios got scattered during the battles. Chhibber claims to have seen seven of its folios in the possession of a Sikh in Lahore. Written in a peculiar style (associated with Anandpur), the scattered folios were collected by Bhai Mani Singh. Furthermore, he got the compositions of the *Dasvin Patshahi ka Granth* bound with the *Adi Granth*, separating Gurbani from the *bhagat-bani* (compositions of the bhagats). Chhibber goes on to state that in 1698 the Sikhs had asked Guru Gobind Singh if his Granth could be bound together with the *Adi Granth*. The Guru told them categorically that these two Granths were to be kept separate. The *Adi Granth* was to be the Guru and the other Granth, his sport (*khed*).[7]

Sarup Das Bhalla talks of three Granths prepared at Guru Gobind Singh's court: the *Chaubis Avtar*, the *404 Charitars*, and the *Bidya Sagar Granth*. According to him, Guru Gobind Singh decided to get a wide range of Sanskrit works translated into *bhakha*, the spoken language of the people. A number of poets and scribes were encouraged to participate in this project.[8]

According to the *Guru Kian Sakhian*, 52 poets presented themselves at Guru Gobind Singh's court at Paunta. Among them were Amrit Rai of Lahore, Tehkan of Gujrat, Ani Rai, and Alam. Guru Gobind Singh himself was a poet of a high order. A literary darbar began to be held every day at Paunta.[9]

Of all the court poets of Guru Gobind Singh, Bhai Nand Lal attracted the greatest attention of the pre-colonial Sikh writers. Kesar Singh Chhibber relates how Nand Lal received the title of 'Goya'.[10] Sarup Das Bhalla mentions the arrival of Bhai Nand Lal at Makhowal. He was in search of a perfect Guru and was delighted to find such a Guru in Guru Gobind Singh. He stayed at Makhowal for a considerable time. Bhalla mentions Bhai Nand Lal's learning in Persian, his service with Prince Mu'azzam (Bahadur Shah) as his Mir Munshi, his adoption of the Sikh faith, and the bestowal of the title of 'Mulla Goya' on him by Aurangzeb for his exposition of a theological point. Bhai Nand Lal presented his *Bandaginama*, a composition in Persian, to Guru Gobind Singh who changed its title to *Zindagi Nama*. It embodied the author's great appreciation for *Gursikhi* (the Sikh faith). Bhai Nand Lal's exceptional services in the *langar* were appreciated by the Guru. Bhai Nand

Lal's ghazal on Holi at the time of its celebration at Anandpur is quoted by Bhalla.[11]

According to the *Guru Kian Sakhian*, Bhai Nand Lal came to the Guru's darbar in 1682. He offered two books to the Guru, one called *Bandaginama* which was composed by Bhai Nand Lal himself and the other was Hirdai Ram Bhalla's *Hanuman Natak*. Guru Gobind Singh appreciated both these works. The former was a source of inspiration for starting a new life afresh. Therefore, he changed its title to *Zindagi Nama*. The *Hanuman Natak* was appreciated by the Guru for inspiring the reader with a martial spirit. Bhai Nand Lal wrote a *chhand* (ghazal) in Persian on this occasion. The Guru was so pleased with Bhai Nand Lal that he gave *charan-pahul* to him personally to make him a Sikh.[12]

The eighteenth-century Sikh writers refer to a number of works written by Guru Gobind Singh before the institution of the Khalsa. In the *Rahitnama* associated with Chaupa Singh, Guru Gobind Singh is stated to have composed the *Jap* and the *Akal Ustat* in 1677.[13] The *Charitro Pakhyan* was completed in 1696.[14] The author of the *Guru Kian Sakhian* says specifically that the *Krishan Avtar* was started at Makhowal in 1684 (with 1186 verses) and completed at Paunta in 1688.[15] The *Charitro Pakhyan* was started in 1691 and completed in 1696. The *Bachittar Natak* was composed in 1698.[16] The internal evidence of the *Dasam Granth* confirms that the *Krishan Avtar* was completed in 1688 at Paunta, the *Charitro Pakhyan* was completed at Anandpur in 1696, and the *Ram Avtar* was completed in 1698.[17]

The Sikh writers of the eighteenth century reveal interesting attitudes towards their sources. Sainapat does not acknowledge any source, though the early part of his work was based on the *Bachittar Natak*. Its echoes are loud and clear. Sewadas Udasi quotes two couplets from a *dohra* of Guru Tegh Bahadur, one carrying his message to Gobind and the other carrying the reply made by Gobind.[18] At another place, Sewadas says that three hours before his passing away, Guru Gobind Singh uttered the *Savvayya* opening with '*Pae gahe jab te tumre*':

> Ever since I have held your feet, I have not cast my eyes on anyone else. Ram and Rahim, the *Puranas* and the *Qur'an* say countless

things, but I recognize none. Smritis, *Shastra*s, and *Veda*s talk of
many secrets, but I know none of them. With your grace O', Wielder
of the Sword, not I but you have spoken everything.[19]

Koer Singh uses the dohra of Guru Tegh Bahadur in the same
situation and in the same way as Sewadas. He quotes the Savvayya
(*Sri Mukh Vak Patsahi 10*) opening with the line '*Sev kari inhi ki
bhavat*' (Cherishable is the service of these people).[20] The Brahman
who was being addressed began to weep and Guru Gobind Singh
recited the Savvayya starting with '*Jo kuchh lekh likhio bipna*'
(Whatever is written as our lot, O' Brahman).[21] Koer Singh quotes
verses from the *Akal Ustat* about divine protection.[22] After the
battle of Chamkaur, when Guru Gobind Singh is left alone, he
recites the verse starting with '*Mittar piare nun*' (To the beloved
friend).[23] It may be added that Koer Singh repeats a chhand of
Sainapat without indicating the source. It opens with '*Sis pai ta
jiga*' (With the aigrette over the head).[24]

In the Rahitnama associated with Chaupa Singh, there are
about a score of quotations from the compositions of the *Dasam
Granth*: *Jap, Akal Ustat, Bachittar Natak, Chandi Charittar Ukti
Bilas, Krishan Avtar, Nihkalank Avtar,* and *Charitro Pakhyan.*
There is the well-known Savvayya from the *Krishan Avtar* starting with '*Chhatri ko put hon, Bahman ko nahi*' (I am the son of a
Chhatri and not of a Brahman).[25] Even better known are the verses
on the martyrdom of Guru Tegh Bahadur in the *Bachittar Natak*.[26]
From the *Chandi Charittar Ukti Bilas* is the famous Savvayya
starting with '*Deh Shiva bar mohe eha*' (Give me the boon, O'
Shiva).[27] The compositions known as *Khalsa Mahima* are there
in connection with the institution of the Khalsa.[28] In connection
with the divinely commissioned purpose of Guru Gobind Singh's
life is quoted the verse beginning with '*Ham eh kaj jagat mei aye*'
(For this purpose have I come into the world).[29] There is a reference to the opening stanza of the *Jap* after invocation.[30] There
are about a dozen other references to matters related with Guru
Gobind Singh.[31]

Kesar Singh Chhibber in his *Bansavalinama* quotes the dohra of
Guru Tegh Bahadur which is supposed to be carrying his message
to Gobind and his reply.[32] There is the passage on the martyrdom

of Guru Tegh Bahadur from the *Bachittar Natak*.[33] There is a quotation from the *Bachittar Natak* on the purpose for which Guru
Gobind Singh was sent to earth by God as his son.[34] The passage
on the creation of demons and gods in the *Bachittar Natak* is
quoted by Chhibber in his *Bansavalinama*.[35] The verse in which
Guru Gobind Singh had asked for God's support for instituting the
Panth for fulfilling God's purpose is also quoted by Chhibber.[36] All
the verses called 'Khalsa Mahima' appear in Kesar Singh's work.[37]
Then there are verses starting with the lines: '*Chhatri ko pūt hon*'
(I am the son of a Chhatri), '*Jo ham ko Parmesar uchre*' (Whoever
called me God), and '*Dhan jio tehko man mein*' (Praise be to the
man who has in mind).[38] A verse from the *Nihkalank Avtar* and
a dohra in which God and his devotee are said to be one are also
quoted in the *Bansavalinama*.[39]

Sarup Das Bhalla reproduces much of the *Bachittar Natak* in
his *Mahima Prakash*[40] and quotes two other verses: one, on the
message sent by Guru Tegh Bahadur from Delhi to Gobind in
Makhowal and the latter's reply,[41] and the other on the martyrdom
of Guru Tegh Bahadur in the *Bachittar Natak*.[42] Sukha Singh's
Gurbilas has only a few quotations from the *Dasam Granth* or
the *Adi Granth*. But the *Guru Kian Sakhian* has about a score of
quotations from the *Dasam Granth*. We may give the opening lines
of only the new ones:

> *Hamri karo hath deh rachha* (Protect us with your hand).[43]
> *Babe ke Babar ke doū* (The House of the Baba and the House
> of Babar, both).[44]
> *Ham te bhag jo bemukh hoe* (Whoever turns away from us).[45]
> *Jis ke sar mastak hath dharia* (He on whose forehead my hand
> is placed).[46]
> *Jagat jot jape nis basar* (He who meditates on the Shining Light day
> and night).[47]
> *Kamal-i kamalat ka'im karim* (The height of perfection, eternal,
> merciful).[48]
> *Chu kar az hama hilat-i darguzasht* (When all other means fail).[49]

Ratan Singh Bhangu refers to sources in addition to what he
has to say independently on the basis of oral evidence, or only
briefly. He refers to the *Puratan Janamsakhi* and (Sukha Singh's)

Gurbilas.[50] He quotes a line from the *Bachittar Natak*: *Babe au Babar ke dou* (both the people of Baba Nanak and of Babar) and a couplet from the *Zafarnama*: *Manam kushtnam kohian but-prast, ke u but prastand o man butshikan* (I kill the idol worshipper of the hills for I am an idol breaker).[51] He quotes the *Khayal* that starts with *'Mittar piare nun'* (to the beloved friend).[52] Bhangu mentions the *Akal Ustat, Chandi Charittar,* and *Chandi di Var* for daily recitation.[53] At the time of initiation were recited the Savvayyae and *Chandi-bani* (compositions related to Goddess Chandi).[54] Bhangu mentions the *Guru Granth* and the practice of taking order (*vak*) from it.[55]

Verses from the works included in the *Dasam Granth* are cited also in connection with the daily round of worship by the Sikhs, the administration of *pahul,* and other such occasions. In the Rahitnama associated with Chaupa Singh, for example, a Savvayya from the *Chandi Charittar* is recited by Guru Gobind Singh in the process of administering pahul. This is the well-known Savvayya that starts with *'Deh Shiva bar mohe ihae'*.[56] In the *Guru Kian Sakhian,* Guru Gobind Singh recites three dohras from the *Shastar Nam Mala* while administering pahul to the *panj piara*s (the five beloved).[57] The liturgical compositions include the *Jap,* the *Savvayyae* (from the *Akal Ustat*), and the *Benati Chaupai* (from the *Charitro Pakhyan*).[58]

It is important to note that Sikh writers of the eighteenth century leave the impression that they looked upon Guru Gobind Singh as the author of the works included in the *Dasam Granth.* This would explain why efforts were made to collect such works and put them together as *Dasvin Patshahi da Granth.* The inclusion of Chandi literature in this Granth could lead to introduction of the *devi* episode in a number of Sikh works of the eighteenth century. Understandably, this would explain the veneration in which the Granth came to be held by many Sikhs.

Veneration for the Granth of Guru Gobind Singh led Kesar Singh Chhibber to propose that, like the *Adi Granth,* it could be regarded as 'Guru'. Chhibber's statement has to be read very carefully. He says that Guru Gobind Singh had vested Guruship in the *Adi Granth* and it was undoubtedly regarded as the Guru in his days. There was no Guru other than the *Granth Sahib.* However, the two Granths were real brothers. The Granth prepared by Guru Arjan was the elder and the Granth prepared by Guru Gobind Singh was the younger. It was dear to the Guru. Nevertheless, as mentioned earlier, when the Sikhs requested that the two Granths may be combined into one, Guru Gobind Singh pronounced that the *Adi Granth* alone was *(Guru) Granth Sahib*. But Chibber suggests that since his own Granth was dear to him, both the Granths could be regarded as Guru.[59]

The Poets of Guru Gobind Singh's Court

Piara Singh Padam in his *Sri Guru Gobind Singh Ji de Darbari Ratan* highlights that Guru Gobind Singh gave as much regard to the pen as to the sword. He quotes Kesar Singh Chhibber on the point that Guru Gobind Singh issued hukamnamas to Sikh *sangat*s to send learned persons to the Guru's court at the Guru's expense. As a result, the Guru's darbar at Anandpur became so crowded with men of letters in a short time that the poets were never tired of singing its praises. In the 1680s, the *Hitopadesh*, the *Pandav Gita*, and 50 *Upanishad*s were translated into bhakha. Translation of the *Mahabharat* into bhakha was completed in the 1690s. Indeed, the literary activity at the court of Guru Gobind Singh continued for 20 years, at a moderate pace from 1678 to 1688 and rapidly from 1689 to 1698.[60]

Poets came to the court of Guru Gobind Singh not only from Punjab but also from Delhi where they had enjoyed patronage of the Mughal court. Padam mentions three major attractions of the Guru's court: (a) the character of literature promoted by Guru Gobind Singh, (b) the nature of patronage extended by the Guru, and (c) his personality. The purpose of Guru Gobind Singh was to create a kind of literary efflorescence that could serve as the basis of a revolution. Himself a learned person, Guru Gobind Singh had genuine respect and appreciation for learning and literary talent. He was exceptionally generous in his patronage of poets.[61]

For an authentic picture of the patronage extended by Guru Gobind Singh to poets, Padam refers to the evidence provided by some of the court poets themselves. Alam Kavi refers to the true king, Guru Gobind, as a person who was as generous as the legendary Raja Bhoj. For Mangal Kavi, 'Guru Sahib Gobind Rai' was the bestower of bliss (*anand*). Whoever wanted to have bliss should come to 'the city of bliss' (Anandpur). Kavi Kuvresh says that Guru Gobind was the source of life for the poets who lived in Anandpur on the banks of the Sutlej. Hans Ram states that he received 60,000 *taka*s for translating a '*parab*' (section) of the *Mahabharat* into bhakha. Kuvresh refers to 'crores' given by Guru Gobind for translating another 'parab'. Mangal Rai talks of billions and trillions of wealth received from Guru Gobind. Not only cash, Guru Gobind used to give horses, weapons, pearls, and golden robes to poets. Ani Rai talks of a hukamnama given to him by the Guru. Padam cites other such examples to reiterate that Anandpur became a great source of attraction for poets from far and near.[62]

Padam argues that the court of Guru Gobind was different from the kingly courts in the country. The Mughal court under Aurangzeb was no more a great source of patronage for the men of letters. The Rajput courts extended patronage to poets to promote the personal or political interests of rulers who were no more sovereign. The literature produced at kingly courts had little relevance for the society in general. On the other hand, the literature produced at the court of Anandpur was meant to create a new awakening among the people in favour of change. It was not meant for the pursuit of sensual pleasures but for creating social awareness. The whole outlook of the poets at the court of the Guru was changed and given social orientation. The welfare of the people was brought to the fore. At the court of Guru Gobind, *shastra* and *shaastra*, the sword and the pen, went together.[63]

Padam points out that the number 52 for the poets at the court of Guru Gobind Singh was merely conventional.[64] Indeed, in his *Darbari Ratan* he has identified over a 100 names. Included among them are the names which occur in the Sikh literary works of the eighteenth century: Alam, Amrit Rai, Brahm Bhatt, Nannua Bairagi, Nihchal Fakir, and Tehkan Das. The list includes also the names of some well-known writers, such as Bhai Nand Lal, Bhai Chaupa Singh, Sainapat, Prahilad Rai, Ani Rai, and Gurdas Singh. However, the larger number of poets are little known even to scholars.

Brind had been associated with the Mughal court before he came to Anandpur. He refers to Guru Gobind as his 'master' (*Nath*) in his *Brind Satsai*. In another composition, the *Bhaw Panchashika*, there is the entry that Brind was a '*huzuri kavi*' (court poet) of Guru Gobind Singh who produced a number of compositions. Padam has listed six of his extant works.[65] The poet Chand, a gold-smith, rendered two sections of the *Mahabharata* into bhakha. He composed *Shabad Slok* in praise of the Sikh Gurus. The *Triya Charitr* of Chand is a large composition, with 50 tales of wile women. 'There is no limit to their *chalittars*' (deceitful conduct) says Chand. Those who wished to write about them were advised to serve Chandi day and night.[66]

In his translation of a section of the *Mahabharata* into bhakha in 1695, Hans Ram Bajpai praises the darbar of Guru Gobind and refers to the 'army' of poets at the Guru's court. He praises the Guru's personality and his sword. At the feet of Guru Gobind Singh, all the four *barans* (varnas) attain liberation. All the four barans and the four ashrams live happily in 'the city of bliss' (Anandpur).[67] Another poet, Husain Ali, wrote in praise of the Guru in the idiom of Islamic mysticism: 'Your light is everywhere; wherever I turn, I see your face. I have nothing to do with the temple or the mosque; my only desire is to see your face.' He tells others: 'If you have not seen the face of God, have a sight of Gobind; he is no different.' Husain does not leave his door; he has the shackles of slavery around his neck.[68]

Kavi Kuvresh came to the court of Guru Gobind from the Ganga–Jamuna Doab and translated the 'Dron Parab' into bhakha in 1695. He wrote in praise of the 10 Gurus, especially Guru Gobind.[69] Mangal Kavi translated the 'Shalya Parab' into bhakha in 1696 at Anandpur in the '*raj*' of Guru Gobind Singh. At the end of his translation, he writes that the 'Sodhi Sultan' had come into the world to exalt the sants, to redeem the world, and to destroy the enemies. Mangal Rai composed a letter in verse to request Mata Jito for financial help so that he could make arrangements for his daughter's marriage. Mangal Rai looked upon Anandpur as the city of bliss and expressed his admiration for the Ranjit Nagara.[70]

Pandit Sukhdev, who had come to the court of Guru Gobind at Paunta in 1687, wrote the *Adhyatam Prakash* in 1698. Padam has listed six other works of Sukhdev.[71] Tansukh of Lahore was the poet who translated *Hitopadesh* into bhakha in 1684. He gave his work the title *Rajniti Granth*. For him, Guru Gobind Singh was 'Gur Parmesar' (God-like Guru). He was the *paras* (philosopher's stone) which transformed iron into gold by its touch. He who joined his Panth attained liberation and all his wishes were fulfilled.[72]

Padam takes notice of two dhadis at the court of Guru Gobind Singh: Mir Chhabila and Mir Mushki. Padam comments that dhadis were important in an atmosphere of wars and battles.[73] Even in the time of Guru Nanak, dhadis used to sing of wars and battles. He refers to himself as a dhadi who was out of work and whom God assigned the service of singing His praises day and night. The metaphor of the dhadi occurs in the compositions of Guru Nanak's successors. Guru Amar Das, for instance, talks of the dhadi who loves God and performs His service; he reflects upon the Guru's *shabad*. In the time of Guru Hargobind, dhadis appeared at his court. In the time of Guru Gobind Singh, Dhadi Nath Mal composed a *var* in Persian on the incidents of the Guru's life at Nanded. In this var, Nath Mal talks of the dhadi's performance as an essential part of the daily life of the Khalsa.[74]

Bhai Kahn Singh Nabha's *Guru Mahima Ratnavali* has a list of 90 poets who wrote in praise of Guru Gobind Singh and his predecessors or, to put it differently, in praise of Guru Nanak and his successors. A number of those poets, such as Ani Rai, Amrit Rai, Alam, Sainapat, Kuvresh, Chand, Hir, Hans Ram, Tansukh, Nannua, and Mangal, figure in Padam's *Darbari Ratan*. Relevant extracts from their works are given in the *Guru Mahima Ratnavali*.[75]

Observations on Courtly Literature

Louis E. Fenech makes a number of comments on the *Dasam Granth* produced at the court of Guru Gobind Singh. Many of its compositions have 'courtly understandings'. Many contentious points about authorship of the entire text or of a particular composition are not altogether important. In any case, there is no sufficient evidence to make conclusive statements about the individual authorship or the history of the compilation of the

Dasam Granth. As courtly poetry, one of the fundamental dimensions of the compositions of the *Dasam Granth* and the works
of the court poets was their 'performative nature'. Most of these
works were prepared in order to fulfill the needs of 'Sikhs, authors,
patrons, and listeners alike'. The vast majority of the compositions
of the *Dasam Granth* were 'not meant to be understood in the
same way as the *Adi Granth*'.[76]

The best-known courtly poetry was that of Bhai Nand Lal Goya.
His works were formally designated as bani by the Sikh authorities
who prepared the *Sikh Rahit Maryada* in the mid-twentieth century. Bhai Nand Lal himself is regarded as 'a Sikh of exceptional
character'. Fenech argues that Nand Lal was 'first and foremost' a
court poet. In other words, he did not have to become a Sikh for
writing the kind of poetry he wrote. Fenech poses the question,
'Why did Nand Lal not become a member of the Khalsa, especially
since so many Khalsa Rahitnamas lay claim to him as their puta-
tive author?' A plausible answer to this question is that 'he was
not a Sikh to start with, and perhaps had no intention of becoming one'. Fenech finds an explanation in the fact that Bhai Nand
Lal was a 'seventeenth-century Indo-Persian Khatri', a category of
people opposed as a class to the institution of the Khalsa.[77] This is
not a strong argument. Perhaps, the relevant question is whether
or not he was sincere in writing what he wrote about the Sikh
Gurus and the Sikh faith. His admiration for the Sikh Gurus and
his appreciation of the Sikh faith appear to be genuine. The use of
Persian was important in its own way as the medium of communication with the literate of all faiths.[78]

Gurinder Singh Mann has observed that 'the layers of secu-
rity around Anandpur, the presence of the standing army, the
weaponry, the elephants, the horses, the flags, the seal, the offi-
cial stationery, the issuing of the hukamnama, the copper plates,
and the emergence of Mata Jito's place of cremation on the map
of Sikh sacred geography – all these need to be incorporated in
our understanding of Guru Gobind Singh's life, the nature of
his leadership, and the contours of his vision for the future of
the Khalsa Panth'. Such artefacts also serve as the markers of the
context in which the poets and writers of the time created their
compositions and, as a result, should be taken into consideration

while interpreting the textual sources created at Anandpur. In his view, the *Dasam Granth* and *Sri Sarab Loh Granth* were the markers of 'the aura of royalty' that the Sikhs tried to create at Anandpur.[79]

Mann refers to 'a hoard of court poetry' produced by nameless poets of Anandpur. Much of it was embodied in the texts known as the *Dasam Granth* and *Sri Sarab Loh Granth*. Some structural changes had to be made to adjust the compositions to the needs of the new situation. At the end of the *Krishan Avatar* and *Ram Avatar*, there are statements which carry 'thundering assertions of the futility of worshipping Krishan and Ram'. These statements make the texts 'presentable at Anandpur'. The inclusion of Guru Gobind Singh's compositions in these texts needs special attention. Relatively little is known about the precise corpus of the Guru's writings, the circumstances of their entry into these texts, the history of the *Dasam Granth*, and its position within the Sikh community.[80]

For a proper appreciation of Guru Gobind Singh's position, it is important to identify his own compositions. This does not mean, however, that the rest of the courtly literature has no great significance or relevance in the life of Guru Gobind Singh. It is indispensable for understanding his life and mission. The socio-political import of the literature produced at the court of Guru Gobind Singh cannot be ignored.

Notes

1. Louis E. Fenech, *Darbar of the Sikh Gurus: The Court of God in the World of Man* (New Delhi: Oxford University Press, 2008), pp. 4–10.

2. Fenech, *Darbar of the Sikh Gurus*, pp. 55–64.

3. Fenech, *Darbar of the Sikh Gurus*, pp. 64–7.

4. Fenech, *Darbar of the Sikh Gurus*, pp. 87–105.

5. Fenech, *Darbar of the Sikh Gurus*, pp. 132–6, 145–6.

6. *The Chaupa Singh Rahit-nama*, translated and edited by W. H. McLeod (Dunedin, New Zealand: University of Otago Press, 1987), p. 82.

7. Kesar Singh Chhibber, 'Bansavalinama Dasan Patshahian Ka', edited by Rattan Singh Jaggi, in *Parkh*, vol. 2, edited by S. S. Kohli (Chandigarh: Panjab University, 1972), pp. 135–6.

8. Sarup Das Bhalla, *Mahima Prakash*, edited by Gobind Singh Lamba and Khazan Singh (Patiala: Punjab Languages Department, 1972), part II, pp. 794–6.

9. Bhai Svarup Singh Kaushish, *Guru Kian Sakhian*, edited by Piara Singh Padam (Amritsar: Singh Brothers,1999 [1986]), p. 95.

10. Chhibber, *Bansavalinama*, pp. 144–5.

11. Bhalla, *Mahima Prakash*, pp. 766–78, 787–95.

12. Kaushish, *Guru Kian Sakhian*, pp. 62–3.

13. *The Chaupa Singh Rahit-Nama*, p. 82.

14. *The Chaupa Singh Rahit-Nama*, p. 82.

15. Kaushish, *Guru Kian Sakhian*, p. 93.

16. Kaushish, *Guru Kian Sakhian*, p. 128.

17. *Sri Dasam Granth Sahib*, edited by Ratan Singh Jaggi and Gursharan Kaur Jaggi (New Delhi: Gobind Sadan, 1999), vol. 2, p. 792; vol. 5, p. 674; vol. 1, p. 682.

18. Kharak Singh and Gurtej Singh (trans. and eds), *Episodes from Lives of the Gurus: Parchian Sewadas* (Chandigarh: Institute of Sikh Studies, 1995), pp. 131–2.

19. *Parchian Sewadas*, p. 162.

20. Koer Singh, *Gurbilas Patshahi 10*, edited by Shamsher Singh Ashok (Patiala: Punjabi University, 1968), p. 58.

21. Koer Singh, *Gurbilas*, p. 135.

22. Koer Singh, *Gurbilas*, p. 136.

23. Koer Singh, *Gurbilas*, p. 148.

24. Koer Singh, *Gurbilas*, p. 205.

25. *The Chaupa Singh Rahit-Nama*, p. 72.

26. *The Chaupa Singh Rahit-Nama*, p. 80.

27. *The Chaupa Singh Rahit-Nama*, p. 83.

28. *The Chaupa Singh Rahit-Nama*, pp. 90–2.

29. *The Chaupa Singh Rahit-Nama*, p. 117.

30. *The Chaupa Singh Rahit-Nama*, p. 129.

31. *The Chaupa Singh Rahit-Nama*, pp. 59, 73, 77, 85–6, 92, 112, 126, 129, 132.

32. Chhibber, *Bansavalinama*, pp. 90–1.

33. Chhibber, *Bansavalinama*, pp. 93, 95.

34. Chhibber, *Bansavalinama*, p. 108.

35. Chhibber, *Bansavalinama*, p. 109.

36. Chhibber, *Bansavalinama*, p. 114.

37. Chhibber, *Bansavalinama*, pp. 116–17.

38. Chhibber, *Bansavalinama*, p. 121.

39. Chhibber, *Bansavalinama*, p. 161.

40. Bhalla, *Mahima Prakash*, pp. 832–70.

41. Bhalla, *Mahima Prakash*, pp. 742–3.

42. Bhalla, *Mahima Prakash*, p. 746.

43. Kaushish, *Guru Kian Sakhian*, p. 115.

44. Kaushish, *Guru Kian Sakhian*, p. 116.

45. Kaushish, *Guru Kian Sakhian*, p. 116.

46. Kaushish, *Guru Kian Sakhian*, p. 124.

47. Kaushish, *Guru Kian Sakhian*, p. 125.

48. Kaushish, *Guru Kian Sakhian*, p. 165.

49. Kaushish, *Guru Kian Sakhian*, p. 193.

50. Ratan Singh Bhangu, *Sri Gur Panth Prakash*, edited by Balwant Singh Dhillon (Amritsar: Singh Brothers, 2004), pp. 16, 41, 43, 69.

51. Bhangu, *Sri Gur Panth Prakash*, p. 132.

52. Bhangu, *Sri Gur Panth Prakash*, p. 59.

53. Bhangu, *Sri Gur Panth Prakash*, p. 69.

54. Bhangu, *Sri Gur Panth Prakash*, p. 35.

55. Bhangu, *Sri Gur Panth Prakash*, pp. 147, 207, 361, 362, 420.

56. *The Chaupa Singh Rahit-Nama*, p. 83.

57. Kaushish, *Guru Kian Sakhian*, p. 123.

58. Ami P. Shah, 'Liturgical Compositions in the *Dasam Granth*', in *Journal of Punjab Studies* 15, nos. 1 and 2 (Spring–Fall 2008): 97.

59. Chhibber, *Bansavalinama*, p. 215.

60. Piara Singh Padam, *Sri Guru Gobind Singh Ji De Darbari Ratan* (Jalandhar: Hamdard Printing Press, 1994 [1974]), pp. 25–7, 59.

61. Padam, *Darbari Ratan*, p. 27.

62. Padam, *Darbari Ratan*, pp. 27–32.

63. Padam, *Darbari Ratan*, pp. 33–44.

64. Padam, *Darbari Ratan*, p. 45.

65. Padam, *Darbari Ratan*, pp. 166–70.

66. Padam, *Darbari Ratan*, pp. 148–56.

67. Padam, *Darbari Ratan*, pp. 134–8.

68. Padam, *Darbari Ratan*, pp. 205–6.

69. Padam, *Darbari Ratan*, pp. 138–43.

70. Padam, *Darbari Ratan*, pp. 129–34.

71. Padam, *Darbari Ratan*, pp. 161–6.

72. Padam, *Darbari Ratan*, pp. 96–101.

73. Padam, *Darbari Ratan*, pp. 210–12.

74. Nath Mal, *Amarnamah*, edited by Ganda Singh (Amritsar: Sikh History Society, 1953), pp. 27, 37–9. See also Michael Nijhawan, *Dhadi Darbar: Religion, Violence and the Performance of Sikh History* (New Delhi: Oxford University Press, 2006), pp. 47–54.

75. Bhai Kahn Singh, *Guru Mahima Ratnavali*, edited by Pritam Singh and Krishan Lal (Amritsar: Guru Nanak Dev University, 1984), pp. 103, 107–11, 151–3, 210–18, 220–1, 267–9, 276–7, 289, 356–9.

76. Fenech, *Darbar of the Sikh Gurus*, pp. 148–56.

77. Fenech, *Darbar of the Sikh Gurus*, pp. 228–38.

78. See Appendix 5.1 on Bhai Nand Lal.

79. Mann, 'Sources for the Study of Guru Gobind Singh's Life and Times', *Journal of Punjab Studies* 15, nos. 1 and 2 (Spring–Fall 2008): 246, 256.

80. Mann, 'Sources for the Study of Guru Gobind Singh's Life and Times', p. 258.

Appendix 5A

Bhai Nand Lal's Homage to the Sikh Gurus

The ghazals of Bhai Nand Lal often have a mystical dimension, like the lyrical poetry in Persian. The first *ba'it* of the first ghazal in *Bhai Nand Lal Granthavali* talks of *bandagi* as the cause of his descent to this earth[1]: 'In our small gathering there is no talk other than that of the beloved; enter the fold without a veil, there is no stranger.'[2] A handful of the dust of his *dargah* has the efficacy of alchemy; every beggar is made a king of the seven realms.[3] Whoever becomes desirous of the sight of the beloved sees nothing but his face everywhere.[4] Nand Lal talks of the perfect guide (*murshid-i kamil*) who teaches bandagi; his auspicious word leads us towards God.[5]

In the first quatrain, Nand Lal talks of the devotee of God who strives hard on the path of love; he plants his flag in all the nine skies of the universe. He who has recognized the right path to God, his arrival in this world and his departure from it were a matter for congratulation.[6] In the seventh quatrain, Bhai Nand Lal talks of the men of God who show the right path to those who have lost their way. If your eyes are keen to see God, the men of God would come to enable you to have the sight of God.[7] On the whole, the ghazals and *ruba'is* (quatrains) of Bhai Nand Lal reveal a spiritual or religious orientation which is not alien to the Sikh faith.

In the *Zindagi Nama*, Bhai Nand Lal makes some explicit or implicit references to the Sikh faith. Just as the pure *momins* (pious Muslims) gather for *namaz* (prayer), 'in our faith we meet in *sadh-sang* [association with pious people] to be dyed in the love of God'.[8] Throughout the *Zindagi Nama*, a great emphasis is laid on the 'remembrance of God (*yad-i haqq*) which is not an exclusive feature of the Sikh faith but certainly an essential feature. '*Murshid-i kamil*' could easily be taken as a reference to the

Gurus whose bani (*kalam*) has the fragrance of God.[9] In Hindvi, their name is *sadh-sangat*.[10] 'This is life. God's bandagi is life'.[11] 'To see them is to see God'.[12] 'I have seen God through them'.[13] Their appearance is wordly (*duniavi*), but their practice is marked by spirituality or religious faith (*din*). No one else in the world is comparable with them.[14] The men of God are not bound by the constraints of life and death.[15] With the guidance of the perfect guide (murshid-i kamil), you would know God.[16] Go to the perfect guide if you wish to see God face to face.[17] 'This book is full of the nectar of life; that is why it is called *Zindagi Nama*'.[18] Nand Lal prays at the end that his eyes may remain filled with the light of God's sight and everything other than God may be removed from his heart.[19] The *Zindagi Nama* is not about the Sikh faith, but it can be seen as representing the Sikh faith in terms of Sikhs as the men of God, the sadh-sang as congregational worship, and the Guru as murshid-i kamil.

The *Ganj Nama* is directly on the 10 Gurus. Guru Nanak, *Jagat Guru* (guide of the universe) of the Sikh tradition, is *murshid al-'alamin* (guide of the inhabitants of all the worlds) in the *Ganj Nama*.[20] Guru Angad too is murshid al-'alamin. Not only two but thousands of worlds were redeemed by him.[21] The third *patshahi*, Guru Amar Das, was the master of both the worlds and his greatness and grace were beyond computation.[22] Guru Ramdas, the king of kings, combined the qualities of a sultan and a faqir.[23] The fifth patshahi, Guru Arjan, was the vehicle of the revealed word.[24] Guru Hargobind was known for his *badshahi* (rulership) and *darveshi* (saintliness) rolled into one.[25] Guru Har Rai, too, was a *darvesh* and a sultan; he was the protector and cherisher of truth.[26] Guru Har Krishan was the redeemer of both the worlds; every particle of the light of the Sun was a manifestation of his grace.[27] Guru Tegh Bahadur was distinct from the distinguished for his total acceptance of God's will.[28] Guru Gobind Singh, the protector of human beings, was under God's protection. He was the king of kings and king of both the worlds.[29] He was '*badshah dervesh*' (kingly saint).[30] He was the friend of the helpless.[31] He was the guide (*murshid*) of the two worlds.[32]

In the *Jot Bigas* in Persian, Guru Nanak is compared with Narain who is *niranjan* (taintless) and *nirankar* (formless). He was created from the light of divine grace and the whole world received great gifts from him.[33] Thousands of kings are his slaves; thousands of suns and moons salute him with reverence.[34] He is Guru Angad, Guru Amar Das, Guru Ramdas, Guru Arjan, Guru Hargobind, Guru Har Rai, Guru Har Krishan, Guru Tegh Bahadur, and Guru Gobind Singh. They are one and the same light.[35] Guru Nanak has created *Satjug* in the midst of *Kaljug*; the young and the old now cherish the truth.[36] The face of justice has become bright; oppression and exploitation have been burnt.[37] All the slaves of his name cherish him as the Siddhs and the Naths, the Ghauses and the Pirs, the gods and the *munis* (sages), the kings and the beggars, all alike.[38] His *amritsar* is superior to the Ganges, and all the 68 places of pilgrimage are his servants.[39] Thousands of Maheshes and Ganeshes (great Gods) bow their heads at his feet. Thousands of Alis and Walis show him reverence.[40] Nand Lal prays at the end that his head may remain at the Guru's feet and his life may be a sacrifice to him.[41]

In the *Jot Bigas* in Punjabi, Guru Nanak exalts the sants and destroys the wicked; he is the perfect guide, adorned with numerous virtues. He is Guru Angad Dev, Guru Amar Das, Guru Ram Das, Guru Arjan, Guru Hargobind, Guru Har Rai, Guru Har Krishan, Guru Tegh Bahadur, and Guru Gobind Singh. They are all one, there is no difference whatsoever. All the gods and goddesses, all incarnations of God, all the worlds, all kinds of devotees and guides were subordinate to the Guru. Nand Lal, a slave of his slaves, has come to the true Guru for refuge. By the grace of sadh-sangat, he may receive the gift of the divine name.[42] Bhai Nand Lal's appreciation for the Khalsa is summed up at the end, in the *Khatimah*. The sky is the slave of the sangat and all gods and goddesses are the slaves of the Khalsa (of Guru Gobind Singh).[43]

Not many Sikhs could write about the Sikh faith, the Sikh Gurus, and the Sikhs so devoutly as Bhai Nand Lal. In the light of his compositions, it is easy to look upon him as a Sikh.

Notes

1. *Bhai Nand Lal Granthavali*, edited by Ganda Singh (Malaka (Malasia): Sant Sohan Singh, 1968), p. 1.

2. *Granthavali*, p. 8, ghazal 10, ba'it 1.

3. *Granthavali*, p. 27.

4. *Granthavali*, p. 69.

5. *Granthavali*, p. 45.

6. *Granthavali*, p. 52.

7. *Granthavali*, p. 54.

8. *Granthavali*, p. 61, vv. 19–20.

9. *Granthavali*, p. 75.

10. *Granthavali*, p. 80.

11. *Granthavali*, p. 81.

12. *Granthavali*, pp. 83, 84.

13. *Granthavali*, p. 84.

14. *Granthavali*, p. 85.

15. *Granthavali*, p. 97.

16. *Granthavali*, p. 119.

17. *Granthavali*, p. 121.

18. *Granthavali*, p. 130.

19. *Granthavali*, p. 131.

20. *Granthavali*, p. 135.

21. *Granthavali*, p. 141.

22. *Granthavali*, p. 143.

23. *Granthavali*, p. 143.

24. *Granthavali*, p. 145.

25. *Granthavali*, p. 146.

26. *Granthavali*, p. 147.

27. *Granthavali*, p. 149.

28. *Granthavali*, p. 150.

29. *Granthavali*, p. 152.

30. *Granthavali*, p. 155.

31. *Granthavali*, p. 156.

32. *Granthavali*, p. 158.

33. *Granthavali*, p. 161.

34. *Granthavali*, p. 164.

35. *Granthavali*, pp. 164–5.

36. *Granthavali*, p. 172. *Satjug* is the first of the four cosmic ages and is supposed to have been the best. *Kaljug* is the last of the four cosmic ages and is supposed to be the worst.

37. *Granthavali*, p. 174.
38. *Granthavali*, p. 179.
39. *Granthavali*, p. 182.
40. *Granthavali*, p. 184.
41. *Granthavali*, p. 186.
42. *Granthavali*, pp. 187–90.
43. *Granthavali*, p. 218.

6

Socio-Political Import of Courtly Literature

Kesar Singh Chhibber gives a brief account of how Bhai Mani Singh had the *Adi Granth* and the *Dasvin Patshahi da Granth* bound together. The compositions (*bani*) of the Bhagats were separated from those of the Gurus. It amounted to separating the limbs of the body of the *Guru Granth*. Bhai Mani Singh was cursed by a Sikh and eventually his body was cut up limb by limb. Already in 1698, Guru Gobind Singh had told the Sikhs very clearly that the two Granths were not to be bound together.[1] This account highlights the sanctity of the *Adi Granth* and its status as the Guru. Later in his *Bansavalinama*, Chhibber reinforces the point that Guru Gobind Singh had vested Guruship in the *Adi Granth*.[2]

On the whole, disagreements about the status to be accorded to the *Dasam Granth* centred on whether its compositions conformed to the normative Sikh theology. Controversies about some of the compositions led to a debate about the authorship of the *Dasam Granth*. Basic questions about its history and compilation are still unanswered. However, 'multiple manuscript versions of the *Dasam Granth* were in circulation by the mid to late eighteenth century, and many Sikhs appear to have taken the text as the authentic work of Guru Gobind Singh, granting it a place of honour in Gurdwaras alongside the *Guru Granth Sahib*'.[3] The *Dasam Granth* was certainly held in great esteem by a large number of Sikhs.

The literary efflorescence resulting from the literary activity at the court of Guru Gobind Singh, embodied partly in the *Dasam Granth*, is an intrinsic part of the life of Guru Gobind Singh. Equally important is the issue of its relationship with his political purposes. Three issues are important in this context: (*a*) Guru Gobind Singh's conception of God, (*b*) his outlook on the systems of religious beliefs and practices of the past and the present, and (*c*) the basic significance of the compositions of the *Dasam Granth* for what may be called Guru Gobind Singh's mission.

True Beliefs and Practices

The most important composition of the *Dasam Granth* for the Sikhs is the '*Jap Sahib*'. It concerns God. One view is that the Jap is an elaboration of what is popularly called the *mul mantar*, which emphasizes the unity of God and refers to the fundamental attributes of God. In His absolute state, God is formless; He alone is there in the beginning and the end. He alone is the creator and the destroyer. He is transcendent and immanent at one and the same time. The power of God is emphasized as much as His compassion and grace.[4] In the opening *chhand* of the Jap, God has no physical feature, no caste (*baran*), or sub-caste (*jati*); he is eternal, self-effulgent, possessor of infinite power; He is the God of gods and the Ruler of rulers. In the last chhand of the Jap, Guru Gobind Singh salutes God as the object of universal obeisance and the destroyer of all; who is indestructible; who is the Destroyer of wickedness; and the Fosterer of goodness. God is Truth, Consciousness, and Bliss; He is the Vanquisher of enemies. God pervades all four directions; self-created and Beauteous; an Embodiment of compassion and the Destroyer of the suffering of death and rebirth, ever present and bestower of all gifts.[5] There are 199 chhands in the Jap. There is repetition, but the total number of epithets used for God in the Jap makes it comparable with the thousand names of Vishnu.

At the opening of the *Akal Ustat*, there are two lines to the effect that Guru Gobind Singh was under the protection of Akal Purkh, *Sarab Loh* (all steel), and *Sarab Kal* (all time). The main text is a collection of a dozen units originally written as independent compositions. Apart from the praises of God, the *Akal Ustat* embodies Guru Gobind Singh's outlook on the nature of God, unity in diversity, *prem bhagti* (loving devotion), God's omnipresence and omnipotence, the equality of human beings, and various sectarian dispensations.[6]

The opening *chaupai* (quatrain) of the *Akal Ustat* has the author's salutation to the primal Ekonkar who permeates land and water; He is the Prime Being, unmanifest and indestructible, whose light shines in all the 14 regions of the universe. In the 10th chaupai, God creates all and subsumes all unto Him; He is the destroyer of sickness, sorrow, and suffering; he who meditates on Him even for a moment is not caught by the noose of death. The *Akal Ustat* ends with an emphasis on the grace of God: 'The net of His grace is spread unseen all over the seven skies and the seven netherlands.' That the whole human kind has the same jati and the same light is emphasized in a *Kabitt* (numbered 85) in the *Akal Ustat*. There are several sectarian entities and religious identities in the world, such as *mundia* (the shaven heads), sanyasi, *jogi*, or Hindu, Turk, Rafizi, and Imam Safi (Imam Shafi'). But the entire humankind should be regarded as one. The same Lord, the only One, is the creator and sustainer of all. It is the duty of all to serve Him. His light shines in all. In the Kabitt that follows, 'the temple and the mosque are the same'; all human beings are essentially one; and Allah and Brahma are the same. In Kabitt 87, all human beings are God's creation and they are absorbed in Him, like sparks in the fire, particles of dust in a heap, and the waves in water.[7] The idea of unity in diversity is depicted with great gusto.

However, unity in diversity is not the only important feature of the *Akal Ustat*. Differences are pointed out and assessed. Rituals are rejected as empty or devoid of any gain: 'Some worship stones or wear lingam around their neck; some see God in the South or bow their heads to the West; and some worship idols or the dead. The whole world is entangled in futile ritual and none finds the secret of God.'[8] The way out is *bhagti*. God created millions of Indras, Brahmas and Vishnus, Rams and Krishans, and the Messengers of God. None was accepted (in the divine court) without loving devotion (bhagti) to God.[9] Many committed the *Veda* to memory and many others announced themselves to be *shaikh*s; some called themselves *bairagi* and some others sanyasi; and some wandered in the garb of Udasis. Regard all their acts as futile (*phokat*) and all such *dharam*s as fruitless; without the support of the Name, all actions are based on illusion.[10] Those who discard all empty rituals and meditate deeply on the Compassionate One cross the ocean of fear and never take rebirth.[11] Without meditation on Bhagwan, the lords of the earth are of no count.[12] He who remembers God as the Primal Being redeems his entire family.[13] God protects the poor, exalts the *sant*s, and casts down their enemies; He never fails to bestow His gifts out of compassion.[14] No one among the Jain monks, *Siddh*s, jogis, jatis, demons and Gods, and the sants of all the different dispensations have the sight of God without His grace.[15] What is positively projected here is bhagti, or more precisely, the bhagti expounded by Guru Nanak and his successors.

The primary concern with religion is the mark of the *shabad*s and the *Savvayya*e. The shabads, nine in all, criticize the belief in incarnation, the practice of idol-worship, and the performance of rituals. There is emphasis laid on the performance of good deeds. The number of Savvayyae is 33. The first relates to the Khalsa. The conception of God in the religious scriptures (the *Veda*, the *Purana*s, and the *Qur'an*) is not adequate; God is above and beyond their conception. God is everywhere and knows the innermost thoughts of human beings. God does not incarnate. He always comes to the aid of His devotees. Asceticism and idol-worship stand rejected. The Name of God and meditation on Him are the main pillars of true faith. All other religious dispensations are devoid of merit (phokat) and do not lead to liberation.[16]

In the first shabad, *sanyas* (renunciation) is redefined in terms of the poet's own ideas of true faith and its values. The second shabad treats *jog* in a similar way. The third shabad advises human beings to attach themselves to the feet of the Supreme Being (Parm Purkh). In the fourth shabad, the honour of the devotee is safe in the hands of God. In the fifth, Kartar is the sole creator of everything. In the seventh shabad, *Kal* (time/death) is equated with Kartar (the creator). That liberation is possible only if one takes refuge in God is the main idea of the eighth shabad. In the ninth shabad, the one God who makes and unmakes is to be the only object of worship. In the 10th shabad, the poet talks of the indispensability of the Name for liberation.[17]

The 10th Savvayya underlines the efficacy of the Name for liberation to the exclusion of the *Veda* and the Semitic scriptures, and Smritis and Shastras. To regard Kartar as the only doer and to discard phokat dharam is the poet's advice in Savvayya 12; among the fruitless faiths are Vaishnava bhagti as well as Shaivism and Islam. The importance of prem is underlined in Savvayya 18. The poet talks of phokat *karam* (deeds) too in Savvayya 32.[18]

Agents of Change

Belief in a deity other than the Akal Purkh seems to be unthinkable in the light of Guru Gobind Singh's views and attitudes in the religious compositions considered in the foregoing paragraphs. However, the *Var Durga ki*, also called *Var Sri Bhagauti Ji Ki*, and popularly known as *Chandi di Var*, written in Punjabi, is generally attributed to Guru Gobind Singh. It may be relevant in this connection to note that *Var Durga Ki* could not serve any religious need or purpose. The opening *pauri* (stanza) of the *Var* is invocatory. All the nine predecessors of Guru Gobind Singh are mentioned, but only after Bhagauti, who is the Goddess for some scholars, while for others the sword is the symbol of the power of Akal Purkh.

In the second pauri of the *Var*, the poet talks of creation. The Divine Power created *khanda* first and then the universe. Brahma, Vishnu, and Mahesh were created to start the sport of the natural world, with the earth and the sky, the rivers and the mountains. Demons and Gods were created with their mutual hostility. Durga was created to destroy the demons. Ram was given the power to kill Ravan with his arrow and Krishan was given the power to dash Kans to the ground. Great sages and Gods practised austerities for ages, but failed to find the mystery (of the Supreme Being).[19]

Durga was created for destroying the demons to save the Gods. The first to be killed by Durga in an open battle was the demon-king Mahikhasur who had deprived Indra of his Indrapuri. Durga disappeared after killing Mahikhasur but reappeared when

Shumbh and Nishumbh rose to power to defeat the Gods. She killed Dhuma Lochan, a great warrior, who had been sent by Shumbh and Nishumbh against the Gods. Similarly, the demon-kings Chand and Mund were killed by Durga in a hard-fought battle. Rakatbij then took the field. He presented a peculiar problem for Durga. The drops of blood shed from his body produced new demons to fight. Durga created Chandi from her forehead. Both the Goddesses fought now to kill Rakatbij and to destroy the demons. Nishumbh then entered the field of battle to be killed by the Goddess. Finally, Shumbh was killed by Durga in a grim fight. Indra was seated on his throne. The praises of Durga were sung in all the 14 regions of the universe. The last two lines of the *Var* refer to its completion in stanzas (pauris) as the source of liberation for those who would sing it.[20]

Like the other two *Chandi Charitra*s, the *Var Durga Ki* was based on 'Durga Saptashati' of the *Markandeya Purana*. However, the poet selected the major events and presented the account of Durga in his own way in only 54 pauris and a dohra (couplet). The *Var Durga Ki* is a new kind of work in its description of the battles. It appeals to the martial spirit and not to any religious sentiments. In the titanic struggle between the forces of good and evil, Durga sides with the good as the divine instrument. The use of physical force is sanctified in a righteous war.

All the 24 incarnations of Vishnu are depicted in the *Chaubis Avtar*. By far the most important are Rama and Krishna. The *Ram Avtar*, in 864 chhands, was based largely on the *Ramayana* of Valmiki. The main purpose of the work was to present Rama as a great warrior who destroyed all enemies. At the opening of the *Ram Avtar*, it is stated that the gods were worried about the increasing power of the demons. Kal Purkh told Vishnu to descend to the earth as Raghunath, the ruler of Awadh. His grandson was Dasrath. Unwittingly, Dasrath killed Sarwan, the son of blind parents, and wanted to burn himself alive. But when Dasrath heard the *dev-bani* (divine utterance) that Vishnu was to take birth as Ram to destroy the wicked and redeem the whole world, he decided to go home.[21]

It may be pointed out that the battles against Ravan are not the only battles fought by Ram as an incarnation of Vishnu. He kills a number of demon kings before the battles in Lanka. Two other legendary figures killed are Parshuram and Bali. Towards the end, the forces of Ram have to fight against Lav and Kush. In fact, Lachhman, Bharat, and Ram die in three separate battles. Thus, the *Ram Avtar*, on the whole, has a considerable range of martial activity. To hear and to sing the *katha* of Ram was to remain immune from sin and sorrow; the reward was no less than that of the bhagti of Vishnu. The Savvayya and the dohra at the end of the *Ram Avtar* underline a strong commitment to exclusive worship of the sole Supreme Being.[22]

> Ever since have I become attached to your feet, I have not cast a glance at any other. I do not subscribe to any of the many things said in the name of Ram or Rahim, and in the *Puran* or the *Qur'an*. The *Smriti*s and *Shastra*s, and the Veda and the Semitic scriptures talk of many mysteries but I have not tried to know any one of them. By your grace, O' Wielder of the Sword, all that has been said is said by you, and not me.

In the dohra, the poet says: 'Leaving all other doors, I have come to your door. Protect the honour of having held my arm; Gobind is your slave.'[23]

The *Krishan Avtar* is the largest single composition in the *Dasam Granth*, with a total number of 2492 chhands of various poetic forms used; it covers the entire second part of *Sri Dasam-Granth Sahib* in 793 pages. In all, 1182 of the chhands were composed at Anandpur and the rest at Paunta in 1688. In the first six lines of this composition it is stated that Vishnu, terribly frightened by the widespread and heinous sins, complained to Brahma who was with Kal Purkh at that time, and Kal Purkh summoned Vishnu to tell him to take birth as Krishan in the Mathura region. As told by Kal Purkh, Vishnu took birth as Krishan for the sake of the sants.[24]

Chhands 5 to 8 of the *Krishan Avtar* are in praise of Sharda and Chandi. In the last dohra of the work, it is stated that the 10th *skanda* (chapter) of the *Bhagwat Purana* had been rendered into *bhakha* with the sole purpose of inspiring people for *dhara-myudh*. In the last Savvayya, the person who has God on his lips and the thought of battle in his heart is worthy of praise. The way to liberation is open for him. With patience, intelligence, and knowledge, he sweeps out timidity from his mind. In the Savvayya before the last, the poet refers to himself as the son of a Chhatri; he cannot take to austerities like the son of a Brahman. His earnest prayer now is that at the end of his life, he may die fighting on the field of battle. The primary purpose of the *Krishan Avtar*, thus, is not religious but ethical.

The features common to these three compositions of the *Dasam Granth* are, in a way, the most important. First of all, neither Durga, nor Ram, nor Krishan is the supreme deity: none of them is the creator; they are all created beings, created for a specific purpose or role. To destroy the forces of evil and to strengthen the forces of good is their common purpose. Secondly, they are good warriors and take up arms to fulfil their purpose. The use of physical force by them is not only legitimate but imperative because their enemies possess great power. Thirdly, their struggle, essentially, is for righteous power.

Guru Gobind Singh's Mission

It is possible now to see the close relation of the *Bachittar Natak* with the *Var Durga Ki*, the *Ram Avtar*, and the *Krishan Avtar*— redeemers of the first three cosmic ages. In Guru Gobind Singh's view of the cosmic drama, the creator of the universe intervened from time to time to reinforce good in its struggle against evil. The divinely appointed instruments of good were entitled to use physical force against the wicked. However, the divinely appointed instruments in the past had failed to establish exclusive worship of the Supreme Being. A new dharam instituted by Guru Nanak had superseded the earlier dispensations. It was now incumbent upon Guru Gobind Singh to defend the claims of this dharam with the use of physical force, if necessary.[25]

The *Bachittar Natak* has 14 chapters. The first is in praise of God, called 'Sri Kal Ji'. The poet bows to the Sword (Sri Kharag) as the power of God to destroy the wicked and to protect the sants. This sword is the slayer of the wicked. It brings peace for the pious and destroys the evil-doers. It is the source of creation and 'my protection'.[26] God has the power to create and annihilate Ramas and Krishnas, prophets and walis. All the Ramas who flourished met their death. All the Krishnas who were created would have to go. All the Gods and all the Buddhas would ultimately perish.[27] None except God is the cherisher of the poor, who makes (Meru) mountain of a blade of grass: 'O Lord, forgive my trespass for none is more liable to commit mistakes than myself.' Those who serve God, their homes are full of riches. In this dark age, none is more trustworthy than the mighty arms of death in the form of the sword.[28] Without the grace of God, none can please Him.

In the second chapter, on the poet's mythical genealogy, it is explicitly stated: They who perform good deeds are called 'gods' and they who do evil deeds are called 'demons'.[29] The poet traces his genealogy to the Sodhis who had descended from the Surajbansi (belonging to the solar dynasty) Raghu, through Dasrath and Ram. Lav and Kush, the sons of Ram, established their rule in Punjab, founding Lahore and Kasur. The descendants of Kush were driven out by their collaterals at Lahore. In due course, they mastered the *Veda* and came to be known as Bedis. The Sodhis of Lahore voluntarily entrusted their territories to them. The Bedis were to repay their debt to the Sodhis in the Kalyug.[30] At the end of Chapter 5, it is stated:

> In the family of those Bedis was born Nanak Rai who brought peace to all his Sikhs and aided them everywhere. He initiated a new *dharam* in the Kalyug and showed the right path to all the *sadh*s (of the world). He who adopts his path is never troubled by sin. They who adopt his path are relieved of all sorrow and suffering. They are never subject to suffering and hunger; they are never caught in the web of delusion and the cycle of death and rebirth.

His second successor, Guru Amar Das, repaid the old debt of the Bedis by passing on the Guruship to Sodhi Ram Das. The ignorant people regarded Guru Nanak and his successors as different, but the wise knew that they were one.[31] The poet gives eight lines to the martyrdom of Guru Tegh Bahadur, clarifying the conception of martyrdom and making it an integral part of the Sikh tradition:

> Master protected their sacred mark and the sacred thread. He (the Guru) performed a great act of sacrifice in the Kalyug. He did much for

·the *sadh*s: he gave his head, showing no pain. He performed a great deed for the sake of *dharam*. He gave his head, but did not reveal the secret. In contrast with the charlatans, the devotees of God were shy of showing sham power. Breaking the pitcher of his body over the head of the ruler of Delhi, he left for the divine abode: Tegh Bahadur did what none else could do. The world was sorrowful on his departure. There were cries of anguish on the earth, but shouts of triumphant joy in the world of gods.[32]

The sixth chapter of the *Bachittar Natak* is the most important for Guru Gobind Singh's conception of his mission. The *Bachittar Natak* was not composed immediately after the martyrdom of his father, Guru Tegh Bahadur, in 1675, but much later, around 1698. By this time, Guru Gobind Singh had thought long over the event and fought a number of battles. He had formed an idea of his position and his role in history. God created the demons first and they became so mad with their power that they forgot all about the worship of the Supreme Being. He created gods then, but they too became entangled in power and began to regard themselves as the Supreme Deities. Mahadev, Vishnu, and Brahma claimed themselves to be the object of worship to the exclusion of the Supreme Being. Similarly, the Siddhs and *sadh*s created their own paths and forgot about God. Included in this category are Datt, Gorakh, and the prophet Muhammad. Consequently, the worship of the Supreme Being was nowhere in evidence.[33]

Meditating on Mahakal and Kalka in the mountains known as the Sapt-sring, Gobind became one with the One Supreme Being. Akal Purkh said to Gobind: 'I have given you the status of my son; I have resolved to empower you to propagate the cause of a *panth* to establish dharam everywhere and to stop people from doing foolish things.'[34] Gobind said emphatically that he would not be able to create any panth without the support of God. Then, Gobind took birth as a human being in the world: 'Anyone who calls me the Supreme Lord shall fall into the pit of hell. Call me His slave and make no mistake in this matter. I am the veritable slave of the Supreme Being, come into the world to watch His sport.'[35] Guru Gobind Singh's mission was to spread dharam, to exalt the sants, and to destroy the wicked, root and branch. 'The Divine Guru has sent me for the sake of dharam: to spread dharam everywhere and to destroy the wicked enemies. For this very purpose, I have taken birth, O sadhs, understand it well. I am born to spread dharam, to raise the sants, and to root out the wicked.'[36] God and the men of God were one; there was no difference between them. They were like the water and its waves.[37] What God had told him, he would tell the people.

The seventh chapter has only 12 lines related to the birth of Gobind and his early life till the martyrdom of Guru Tegh Bahadur. The eighth chapter refers to the Guruship (raj-saj) of Gobind in four lines. In the rest of the chapter is described the battle of Bhangani near Paunta. Five chapters (9–13) relate to the battle of Nadaun, the expedition of the Khanzada, the battle in which Husain was killed, the battle in which Jujhar Singh was killed, and the arrival of Prince Mu'azzam and four Ahadis. At a few places in these chapters, there are references to the providential protection for Guru Gobind Singh. In the last chapter, there is a general statement that they who turn away from their Guru get no place to dwell in this or the next world.[38] In Chapter 14, the poet says that Sarab Kal exalts the sadhs and kills their enemies; He saves the Bhagats in all crises; and 'He saved me as His slave'. Sarab Kal provided the protection of iron for Guru Gobind and made him honourable by His grace.[39]

It is important to note that Sainapat identifies the panth referred to in the *Bachittar Natak* with the Khalsa.[40] Martyrdom was built into the Khalsa ideology. It was an integral part of the struggle for sovereign rule. The ideal was all the more important for having divine sanction.

Notes

1. Kesar Singh Chhibber, 'Bansavalinama Dasan Patshahian Ka', edited by Rattan Singh Jaggi, in *Parkh*, vol. 2, edited by S. S. Kohli (Chandigarh: Panjab University, 1972), pp. 135–6.

2. Chhibber, *Bansavalinama*, p. 215.

3. Robin Rinehart, 'The Dasam Granth', in *The Oxford Book of Sikh Studies*, edited by Pashaura Singh and Louis E. Fenech (Oxford: Oxford University Press, 2014), pp. 136–46.

4. *Sri Dasam-Granth Sahib*, edited by Ratan Singh Jaggi and Gursharan Kaur Jaggi (New Delhi: Gobind Sadan, 1999), pp. 19–25 (of the introduction) and pp. 2–29 (of the text).

5. *Sri Dasam Granth Sahib: Text and Translation*, translated and edited by Jodh Singh and Dharam Singh (Patiala: Heritage Publications, 1999), vol. 1, pp. 14–15.

6. Jaggi and Jaggi, *Sri Dasam-Granth Sahib*, pp. 25–29 (of the Introduction) and pp. 30–103. The whole work consists of 10 chaupais, 10 Kabitts, 10 Savvayyae, 20 *Tomar* chhands, 20 *Laghu Naraj* chhands, 20 Kabitts, 30 *Bhujang Paryat* chhands, 20 *Padhari* chhands, 20 *Totak* chhands, 20 *Naraj*, and 20 *Ruamal* chhands. The chhands from 201 to 230 appear to be irrelevant to the main theme of the *Akal Ustat*, with 10 dohras and 20 *Darigh Tribhangi* chhands. The last three units have 12 *Padhari* chhands, 10 Savvayyae, and 14 Kabitts.

7. Singh and Singh, *Sri Dasam Granth Sahib*, pp. 54–7.

8. Singh and Singh, *Sri Dasam Granth Sahib*, p. 42.

9. Singh and Singh, *Sri Dasam Granth Sahib*, p. 44.

10. Singh and Singh, *Sri Dasam Granth Sahib*, p. 46.

11. Singh and Singh, *Sri Dasam Granth Sahib*, p. 72.

12. Singh and Singh, *Sri Dasam Granth Sahib*, p. 40.

13. Singh and Singh, *Sri Dasam Granth Sahib*, p. 98.

14. Singh and Singh, *Sri Dasam Granth Sahib*, p. 94.

15. Singh and Singh, *Sri Dasam Granth Sahib*, p. 35.

16. Jaggi and Jaggi, Introduction, *Sri Dasam-Granth Sahib*, vol. 1, pp. 56–7.

17. Jaggi and Jaggi, *Sri Dasam-Granth Sahib*, pp. 384–7.

18. Jaggi and Jaggi, *Sri Dasam-Granth Sahib*, pp. 388–99.

19. Jaggi and Jaggi, *Sri Dasam-Granth Sahib*, p. 314.

20. Jaggi and Jaggi, Introduction, *Sri Dasam-Granth Sahib*, pp. 38–400.

21. Jaggi and Jaggi, *Sri Dasam-Granth Sahib*, pp. 506–11.

22. Jaggi and Jaggi, *Sri Dasam-Granth Sahib*, pp. 502–683.

23. Jaggi and Jaggi, *Sri Dasam-Granth Sahib*, p. 682.

24. Jaggi and Jaggi, *Sri Dasam-Granth Sahib*, part 2, p. 2.

25. J. S. Grewal, *From Guru Nanak to Maharaja Ranjit Singh* (Amritsar: Guru Nanak (Dev) University, 1972), pp. 45–50.

26. Singh and Singh, *Sri Dasam Granth Sahib*, p. 104.

27. Singh and Singh, *Sri Dasam Granth Sahib*, pp. 109–10.

28. Singh and Singh, *Sri Dasam Granth Sahib*, p. 118.

29. Singh and Singh, *Sri Dasam Granth Sahib*, p. 126.

30. Singh and Singh, *Sri Dasam Granth Sahib*, pp. 130–40.

31. Singh and Singh, *Sri Dasam Granth Sahib*, pp. 142–4.

32. Singh and Singh, *Sri Dasam Granth Sahib*, p. 159. J. S. Grewal, *Guru Tegh Bahadur and the Persian Chroniclers* (Amritsar: Guru Nanak Dev University, 1976), pp. 78–9. 10 Persian chronicles of the late eighteenth and the early nineteenth century have been analysed to examine what they have to say about Guru Tegh Bahadur, particularly his martyrdom. Eight of the chroniclers say that the Guru was asked to perform a miracle. This was supposed to be a test of a person's spiritual status and his nearness to God. Therefore, the one who could not perform a miracle was supposed to be a pretender who deserved to be executed.

33. Singh and Singh, *Sri Dasam Granth Sahib*, pp. 144–8.

34. Singh and Singh, *Sri Dasam Granth Sahib*, p. 148.

35. Singh and Singh, *Sri Dasam Granth Sahib*, p. 150.

36. Singh and Singh, *Sri Dasam Granth Sahib*, p. 160.

37. Singh and Singh, *Sri Dasam Granth Sahib*, p. 150–4.

38. Singh and Singh, *Sri Dasam Granth Sahib*, p. 186.

39. Singh and Singh, *Sri Dasam Granth Sahib*, p. 190.

40. When Sahibzada Ajit Singh died fighting on the field of battle, Guru Gobind Singh remarked: 'Today he has proved to be the Khalsa in the true Guru's court.' Sainapat, *Sri Gur Sobha*, p. 90.

7

The Baisakhi of 1699

Creation, institution, or manifestation of the Khalsa is generally associated with the removal of masands, initiation through *pahul* of the double-edged sword, and new injunctions for the Khalsa. The Khalsa *rahit* was amplified in the contemporary Rahitnamas. The distinct identity of the Khalsa was underlined. The purpose of its creation was the establishment of Sikh rule. Several Sikh writers of the eighteenth century introduced the Goddess in connection with the creation of the Khalsa. It is now treated as a myth.[1]

Removal of the Masands

The author of the *Dabistan-i Mazahib* says that during the time of the Afghan sultans, the nobles were designated *masnad-i a'la*. Through frequent use, the word was converted into 'masand'. Since the Sikhs regarded the Guru as *Sachcha Padshah* (True King), his representative was known as a masand. Before Guru Arjan, no *bhet*, that is tax, was taken from the Sikhs; whatever they presented as offerings was accepted. Every Sikh, according to his own resources, put together money and took it by way of an offering (*nazar*) to the masand. The masand did not keep it for himself. Whatever they brought to the masand as bhet for the Guru's establishment (*sarkar*) was taken to him. In the month of Baisakh, the masands assembled at the court of the Guru. Of their followers (*melis*), whoever so desired and possessed the means of travel went with the masand to the Guru. At the time of departure, the Guru conferred a turban on each of the masands. It may be added that 'Mobad' mentions the Jatt Masand Chanda was considered by his melis as their Guru. His melis did not go to Guru Hargobind's dharamsal or even see Guru Hargobind without his permission.[2] In other words, the masand was more important for his melis than the Guru.

Sainapat says that Guru Gobind Singh made the Khalsa mani-fest on the Baisakhi festival by discarding the masands. 'By remov-ing the masands, he purified the world.' The Sikh *sangat* was made the Khalsa. The Sikhs were told to send *kar-bhet* (offerings) to the Guru and to no one else. The followers of the masands became the Khalsa. Everyone heard the Guru saying, 'Leave the masands.' The removal of masands and the creation of the Khalsa appeared to be two sides of the same coin.[3]

According to the *Chaupa Singh Rahit-Nama*, Guru Gobind Singh became extremely annoyed with the masands towards the end of 1697. A masand named Cheto had concealed something, but all the masands reacted as a body (when Cheto was to be ques-tioned). Guru Gobind called them thrice, but they did not come. Guru Gobind ordered that all of them should be forcibly brought to his presence. Some of them ran away, but the others were caught and burnt alive. *Hukamnama*s were issued to the sangats, ask-ing them not to accept the authority of the masands and not to give any offerings to them. Diwan Sahib Chand submitted to Guru Gobind that three collaterals had already been excommunicated, as were now the masands. The Guru said that the followers of all the four should be thrown out (of the *Panth*). Chaupa Singh goes on to mention the items of the rahit to be followed by the *kesdhari* and *shastardhari* Singhs. Their uppermost duty was to fight and establish their own *raj* in place of the rule of the 'Turks'. To take away rulership from the 'Turks' and to give it to the Panth was a sort of revenge for the past atrocities of the 'Turks'.[4]

According to Kesar Singh Chhibber, Guru Gobind Singh dis-cussed the problem of the masands with Diwan Sahib Chand in 1698. They were exploiting the Sikhs and feared none. Sikh sangats were complaining against them. The Diwan did not sug-gest any strong action. Chhibber cites the case of Cheto who had misappropriated a huge amount of wealth. The masands sided with Cheto because they were afraid that their own misdeeds would be exposed later. They refused to come to the Guru's presence even when he called them. They had crossed the limit of insolence. Guru Gobind ordered that they should be forcibly brought to his court. They were beaten and killed; some of them were thrown into cauldrons of boiling oil. Hukamnamas were sent to the sangats, asking them not to have any association with the masands or their followers, nor with the followers of Dhir Mal, Ram Rai, and the Minas. The Khalsa Sikhs should give no *golak*, *dasvandh*, or *chaliha* to the masands; the Khalsa should come fully armed to the Guru with their offerings. They should follow the rahit.[5]

Koer Singh says that Guru Gobind Singh decided to set the house in order (*greh-sodh*). He went to the houses of the masands in disguise to see for himself how charitable they were. One masand gave him virtually nothing. Another gave him five small rotis. On the following day, Guru Gobind Singh called professional mimics and asked them to act as the masands. They presented a person riding a horse with a dancing girl. He goes to the house of a poor Sikh who prepares as good a meal as he could. But the 'masand' does not like it. He obliges the Sikh to bring alcohol and kebabs. Again and again, he tells the Sikh that 'the Guru' had come to his house and he should make the best offering he could. He extorts gold from the Sikh. The mimic said that the masands were a 100 times worse than what he had depicted. Guru Gobind wanted the masands to mend their ways, but they were not afraid of the young Guru. Ultimately, they had to be punished and removed from the mediacy between the Guru and the Sikhs.[6]

Sukha Singh says that after returning from Naina Devi, Guru Gobind decided to put the *darbar* and the sangat in order. The masands had become greedy. They appropriated much of the offerings, contributing little to the Guru's treasury. Whenever this question was raised, they maintained that they had to spend much of their collection on account of the *langar* (common kitchen). Their misdeeds were depicted by jesters (*bhands*) in the Guru's presence. An example is given of a degenerate and oppressive masand. Ultimately, they were severely punished and removed.[7]

According to Sarup Das Bhalla, Guru Gobind removed the masands due to their greed and baneful influence on the Sikhs who were misled by them. At the time of the Baisakhi festival, when the masands and the sangats used to come to Anandpur in large numbers, the Guru confronted the masands with the question why their offerings were so small, in spite of the fact that their sangats were very large. Bhai Cheto assured the Guru that the masands served him sincerely. The offerings from the Sikhs were not so large now as earlier. The Guru was too young, he said, to appreciate the situation. Many days passed. A Sikh came to Anandpur and wanted to know whether or not a rare bangle that he had sent with Cheto as an offering for the Guru had been received. Cheto was exposed. He had given that bangle to his wife. He was bathed in boiling water with which jaggery was mixed, and he died. All the masands were obliged to render their accounts. The guilty were punished and removed. The institution was abolished. 'My Sikh will recognize no masand,' declared Guru Gobind. The entire sangat became the Guru's Khalsa. Sarup Das Bhalla uses the metaphor of the *jagir* for the sangat under the authority of the masand. When the jagir was resumed, it became the *khalisa*, coming directly under the Guru's control.[8]

In the *Guru Kian Sakhian*, there is a *sakhi* on 'Bhai Pheru and reform of masands'. Like all other masands, Bhai Pheru was brought to the court of Guru Gobind. He was treated with consideration and honour. In fact, all those masands whose fault was not serious were leniently treated. But boiling oil was poured over the heads of the most serious defaulters, and they died. Henceforth, offerings were not to be given to the masands on behalf of the Guru. Hukamnamas were issued to the effect that dasvandh (one-tenth), chaliha (offerings for the last mortuary rite), and *mannat* (vow) should be sent direct to the Guru at Anandpur and not through the masands. The Sikhs of the Guru should avoid a masand more than an intoxicated elephant.[9]

In Bhangu's *Sri Gur Panth Prakash*, the masands are removed after the institution of the Khalsa. The masands appeared on the scene when Guru Gobind Singh began to bring the Khalsa to the fore in the affairs of the Panth in order to increase the number of the Khalsa for a programme of conquest on a wide scale. All good things were given to the Khalsa. They were given the privilege of performing *ardas* in Gurdwaras. The masands and *mewaras* (special messengers) were cut to the quick. They complained to Mata ji that the Guru was trying to make *padshahs* out of the Jatts. It amounted to asking the lambs to kill the lions and asking the sparrows to kill the hawks. This misadventure would lead to the destruction of others too when the rulers of the day sent their armies against the Khalsa. Mata ji accepted the truth of their representation. The masands called the *diwans* and *musaddis* and proposed to give Guruship to Sahibzada Jujhar Singh. Guru Gobind Singh was furious when he came to know of the machinations of the masands who had been foolish enough to set fire to the *Guru Granth* and raise a *dehura* over the spot. The misdeeds of the masands in general were depicted before the Guru by professional mimics. He ordered the Khalsa to offer the masands as a sacrifice to Chandi. They were all killed in various ways.[10]

The masands figure in the *Dasam Granth*:

If one goes to a masand (for guidance to liberation), he is told to bring all his wealth. The masand interposes himself between the devotee and God, but says nothing about the way to God.

If anyone wishes to perform service for a masand, he is asked to offer all his possessions to him. 'Think of me all the time and talk of none else.' The masand runs away during the night if he has to give something. He is never pleased without getting something.

The masands put oil in their eyes to draw tears to deceive people. They offered good food to a wealthy follower, but gave nothing to the poor; they did not show their face to the needy. The masands plunder the people and never sing God's praises.[11]

Thus, the masands were not performing the role for which they were originally appointed. They had become counterproductive in the organization of the Panth.

In Ganda Singh's collection, masands appear in a hukamnama of 12 March 1699, addressed to the sangat of Machhiwara: 'The sangat is my Khalsa'; 'have no faith in the masands'. The Khalsa are told to bring golak, dasvandh, and mannat personally to the Guru. By implication, none of these contributions meant for the Guru's treasury were to be given to the masands.[12] In the

hukamnama of 1 February 1700, the sangat of Patan Farid is told:
'you are my Khalsa' and 'you are not to have faith in any masand'.[13]
This is repeated in the hukamnama of 4 November 1700.[14] In the
hukamnama of this date to the sangat of Naushehra, it is added
that they should not participate in the mortuary or matrimonial
ceremonies of the followers of the masands.[15] Not to associate
with a masand or a masandia is stipulated in the hukamnama of
6 February 1702 to Bhai Mihar Chand, *peshkar* (chief clerk)of the
khufia-navis.[16] The masands are mentioned for the last time in
Ganda Singh's collection in a later hukamnama of 1702.[17]

In a hukamnama of Guru Gobind Singh, addressed to Bhai
Kalyan Rai and the sangat of Machhiwara in 1698, it is claimed
that 'the sangat is my Khalsa'; they should repose no faith in the
masands, and bring offerings (golak, dasvandh, and mannat) personally to the Guru.[18] In a hukamnama of 1698 to the sangat of
Banur, there is the additional instruction to come at the time of
Baisakhi and Holi, fully armed to take the Guru's pahul. Thus,
the hukamnama appears to confirm that the Baisakhi of 1699 was
the occasion for instituting the Khalsa.[19] Gurinder Singh Mann has
examined a similar hukamnama of 1698 and thinks that its contents suggest the existence of the new ceremony of initiation in
1698. This, in his view, reopens the question of the date of instituting the Khalsa.[20] The masands were ultimately removed, but
they seem to have remained a problem for Guru Gobind Singh for
several years.

Fresh Initiation: *Khande di (ki) Pahul*

Sainapat looks upon the institution of the Khalsa as the sole purpose of Guru Gobind Singh's life. He addressed a large gathering
of Sikhs at Anandpur on the first day of the month of Baisakh and
declared his intention of starting a panth. Those who volunteered
to join were given the *khande ki pahul* to be made powerful.[21]

According to the *Chaupa Singh Rahit-Nama*, Guru Gobind
Singh introduced '*kesan di pahul*' to impart a distinct identity
to the Sikh Panth in '1697'. This initiation made it obligatory to
keep the hair uncut. The pahul was prepared by stirring water

with *patasha*s in a large bowl by a dagger, while five *Savvayya*s were recited. Then, the pahul—called *amrit*—was administered to Chaupa Singh and he was asked to utter, '*Vaheguru ji ka Khalsa, Vaheguru ji ki fateh*' (To God belongs the Khalsa, to God belongs the victory). Amrit was administered to four other Sikhs on their request. Thus, five Sikhs became 'Kesdhari Singhs' and were authorized to initiate others.[22]

According to Kesar Singh Chhibber, Guru Gobind asked Chaupa Singh to bring a bowl full of fresh and clean water. He gave Chaupa Singh a dagger to stir the water in the bowl and to recite the *Japu* and the *Anand*. Patashas were added on the suggestion of Diwan Sahib Chand. This water was called 'pahul'. Guru Gobind administered pahul to Chaupa Singh, asking him to shout 'Vaheguru ji ka Khalsa, Vaheguru ji ki fateh'. Five or seven persons became 'Sikhs' by taking pahul on this occasion.[23]

Koer Singh is the first Sikh writer to refer to the call for heads. Addressing a huge gathering at Kesgarh on the Baisakhi day, Guru Gobind Singh asked, 'Is there any perfect Sikh who would offer his head to the Guru?' He gave the call three times before a Sikh stood up. He was taken into a tent where a male goat was slaughtered and its blood could be seen flowing out. The Guru gave another call and another Sikh stood up. He too was taken into a tent and a male goat was slaughtered. In this way, the Guru chose five volunteers. The people were critical of the Guru; he had destroyed the masands already and was now killing Sikhs like goats. But they all praised him when he brought out all the five Sikhs. Then, he poured some fresh, clean water into an iron vessel and began to recite *mantar*s over it. Kirpa Ram described the whole scene to Mata ji, who put some patashas in the water. When amrit was ready, ardas was performed, and it was administered to all the five volunteers. They were asked to utter 'Vaheguru'. The first was Daya Singh, a Sobti Khatri of Lahore; the second was Nihchal (Mohkam) Singh, a Chheepa of Dwarka; the third, Sahib Singh, was a Nai of Bidar; the fourth, Dharam Singh, was a Jat of Hastinapur; and the fifth was Himmat Singh, a Jhiwar of Jagannath.[24]

Kaushish remains very close to Koer Singh in his description of the call for heads and the selection of the five Sikhs. Each one of them was asked to slaughter a male goat inside a tent.

All the five were brought out. Their heads were washed and the five Ks (*kakar*s) were given to each one. The Guru also adopted their new form. Guru Gobind Singh told the congregation that when the Sikhs were tested in the time of Guru Nanak, only one Sikh, Lehna, had passed the test. Now, there were five, willing to die for the Guru. They were given the status of *panjpyare* and reference to them henceforth was to be made in the daily ardas. On this occasion, *charan-pahul* was replaced by khande ki pahul. Kaushish briefly describes the way in which pahul was prepared. The *bani*s recited were *Japuji*, *Jap*, Savvayyas, *Chaupai*, and *Anand*. Ardas was performed. Significance of the *khanda* was explained. Three *doha*s from the *Shastar Nam Mala* were recited. Amrit was administered to the panjpyare. The epithet 'Singh' was added to the names of the five. Guru Gobind Das himself became Guru Gobind Singh.[25]

According to Kaushish, the panjpyare prepared khande ki pahul and administered it to those five Sikhs who had volunteered to offer their heads. Guru Gobind Singh gave them the title of '*mukte*'. Their names are given as Deva Ram, Ram Chand, Tehal Das, Ishar Das, and Fateh Chand. The epithet 'Singh' was added to their names. Guru Gobind Singh recited four lines, starting with '*Jagat jot jape nis basar*' (He who meditates on the shining light day and night). 11 more persons were given amrit. Their names are given. Then the names of about a score of other persons are given. The whole day was spent in administering pahul to about 40 persons. On the day following, groups of five 'Singhs' administered pahul to the sangats who had come to Anandpur from other places. This activity continued for many days.[26]

After the martyrdom of Guru Tegh Bahadur, according to Ratan Singh Bhangu, Guru Gobind Singh thought of destroying the 'Turks'. He discovered that the Sikhs were not prepared to take up arms against the Mughals. He knew that this was due to the effect of charan-pahul. He decided to initiate the Sikhs all afresh through 'khande pahul', and to give them the epithet 'Singh' and the appearance of '*Chhatris*' (Kshatriyas). Every Khalsa horseman would become a sovereign ruler. With these ideas, Guru Gobind Singh selected five *bhujangi*s at a gathering at Kesgarh. They belonged to five *jati*s: Khatri, Jatt, Cheepa, Nai, and Jhiwar.

Their names are the same as in Koer Singh's *Gurbilas*. The first *pauri* (stanza) of *Var Bhagauti*, 32 Savvayyas, and *Chandi Bani* were recited for preparing the pahul to be administered to the five bhujangis.[27]

New Injunctions

Three obligations were a part of the new initiation: the Sikhs who took the pahul were to keep their hair uncut, add the epithet 'Singh' to their names, and bear arms. In other words, the person who takes khande ki pahul becomes a kesdhari, shastardhari Singh. Sainapat says that the Khalsa were created to destroy the demonic and evil-minded men. The Khalsa were to have no association with five categories of people: the followers of the masands, Dhir Mal and Ram Rai, the Minas, and those who cut their hair. They were to shun *hukka* and never observe *bhaddar* (*bhaddan*). The Khalsa of Vaheguru were never to smoke or cut the hair of the head or the beard. They were to sing God's praises in the *sat-sangat* (true association) and pray for the gift of nam.[28]

In the instructions for the Khalsa, the 'Turks' are mentioned in addition to the five categories of people to be shunned. A very essential part of the rahit was to keep uncut hair (*kes*), to bear arms, to carry a dagger (*kard*), to wear *kachh*, and to remain devoted to Gur-*shabad*. *Deg*, *teg*, and *fateh* (triumph) were ordained for the Khalsa. They were to rule in all the three worlds. The Sikhs of all the four *barans* (varnas) were to eat together at one place.[29]

Guru Gobind Singh told the panjpyaras that their previous *janam* (birth), *dharam*, *karam* (actions), *bharam* (illusions), and *saram* (labour) had been annulled. They were made Khalsa and were given the dress and the visible form of *Kal* (death); they should ensure the honour of their dress. They should never separate any of the five Ks (*keski* of blue colour [a piece of cloth worn on the head over which the turban is tied], *kangha* [comb], *kirpan* [sword], *kara* [bangle] of iron, and *kachhehra*) from their body. The four weighty elements of *kurahit* were to show disrespect for the hair in any way, to eat halal meat, to use tobacco, and to have association with a Muslim woman. The five categories of people with whom the

Khalsa should have no connection were the Minas, Dhir Mallias, Ram Raiyas, masands, and those who cut their hair. The Khalsa should worship Maha Kal (God) alone, and not a *matth*, a *marhi*, or a grave.[30]

Guru Gobind Singh instructed the Sikhs never to threaten anyone, nor feel afraid of anyone. They should have complete trust in Akal Purkh. He would protect them in all situations. They should work with their own hands and take out the 10th part of their earnings for the Guru. They should keep a golak in their homes. They should regard the poor man's tongue as the Guru's golak. A daily routine of worship at home and in the sangat was essential. Care for the kes is emphasized: washing the hair every fourth day, combing the kes twice a day, not to touch the kes with soiled hands, and to respect the kes like the Guru. Five other categories of people to be shunned were the killers of infant daughters, the smokers of hukka, those who lived on charity, those who performed misdeeds after taking pahul, and the enemies of the Guru. It was the duty of the Khalsa to protect the cow and the poor. They should regard the daughters of others as their own and other women as their mothers. They should teach Gurmukhi letters to their children, both male and female, and impart other forms of education available to them.[31]

Sukha Singh goes on to talk of the various dimensions of the Khalsa Panth. God created gods, demons, and human beings. Hindus and 'Turks' were opposed to each other. Whenever a critical situation developed in their affairs, God sent an avtar to redress the balance between the wicked and the saintly. In the Kali Age, the order of castes was upset and ignorance prevailed everywhere. Sukha Singh emphasizes that the *mlechh* 'Turks' became overwhelmingly powerful and Hindu dharma was on the verge of extinction. In order to redress their suffering, Maha Kal sent his servant. The Khalsa Panth was created to uproot the 'Turks'. To this end, Guru Gobind Singh had been sent to the world. Amrit was administered to the panjpyare to create the Adi Guru Khalsa. The sacred thread was replaced by the sword. The rahit of the Khalsa is enunciated here with emphasis on nam and *dan, seva* and *bhagti, astar* (long-range weapons) and *shastar* (hand-held weapons), and shabad and ardas. The Khalsa was made manifest as

distinctly superior (*sirtaj*) to Hindus and 'Turks'. All the four varnas were made one and they ate together at one place.[32]

According to Bhangu, Guru Gobind Singh himself took pahul
from the five to become '*apae Gur-chela*' (himself the guru and the
disciple). All distinctions of one's background were abolished: the
four varnas, the four *ashrama*s, the sacred thread, and the sacred
mark on the forehead. Guru Gobind Singh instructed the five not
to have any association with the masandis, the Ram Raiyas, those
who killed their infant daughters, and those who smoked hukka.
They should keep their kes uncut, wear kachhehra, and bear arms:
teg, *kara*, and *chakkar* (quoit). Bhangu goes on to say that the Sikhs
should contribute to the Guru's golak and offer *karha parsad* to the
Khalsa. They should tie the turban twice a day and bear arms all
the time. They should drink *sukha* and go out for hunting, and eat
jhatka mutton. They should never eat *kutha* meat (meat prepared
by slaughtering an animal the Muslim way). They should live in
accordance with the *Guru Granth* and have 'Akal' on their lips.
For daily recitation of *Gurbani*, the *Japu* and *Jap*, *Anand*, *Rehras*,
and *Chandi Bani* are specifically mentioned.[33]

Rahitnamas

There has been a debate in the recent decades about the dates of
the Rahitnamas, and their texts have been studied in detail.[34] Six
Rahitnamas are now placed in the time of Guru Gobind Singh.
It is important to note that the authors of the Rahitnamas do
not write with reference to the Baisakhi of 1699. They write on
the assumption that rahit is indispensable for the Khalsa. Much
of the matter in the Rahitnamas gets related to God, the Guru,
the Granth, and the Gurdwara, highlighting the importance of
religious life for the Khalsa. But there is enough about the Khalsa
to suggest that the scope of the norms laid down for the Khalsa
way of life was comprehensive. It covers the social and political
aspects of the Khalsa way.

We may illustrate this with reference to specific statements
made in the Rahitnamas. The Khalsa were forbidden to have any
connection with five categories of people: (a) the Minas, (b) the Dhir

Mallias, (c) the Ram Raiyas, (d) the masands, and (e) masandias. All of them were earlier linked with the Sikh Gurus but now stood excommunicated.[35] Among eight other categories to be shunned by the Khalsa are the Jogis.[36] The author of the *Tankhahnama* shows serious concern for the moral conduct of the Sikhs. The Khalsa are reminded of their hostility towards Muslims, generally referred to as 'Turk'. A Sikh who takes meat from a 'Turk' and eats it becomes liable to *tankhah*. He who places a Muslim ruler's *mohar* (seal, gold coin) over his head takes birth again and again. The Khalsa should fight against the mlechh. The 'Turk' would leave the field of battle in the face of Khalsa hosts.[37]

On the death of a close relative, even a *sahajdhari* Sikh should not shave his hair. He should arrange a *kirtan* in a dharamsal and take with him a large quantity of *prasad*. He should bathe before distributing the prasad. He should observe no mourning; he could do the *kirya-karam* as he liked. The ashes should be taken to Harsar. Kirtan and *katha* could be held for 11 to 17 days. At the same time, he should organize *bhog-path* of the *Granth Sahib* (the reading of Guru Granth Sahib as a funerary rite). He should give charity and offer food to Sikhs, and pray for the deceased.[38] A Sikh of the Guru should follow none of the Brahmanical rites and rituals.[39] For kirya-karam, a Sikh should read the *Anand*, perform ardas, and distribute *karha prasad*.[40] All the kirya-karam for the Sikhs had been performed by Akal Purkh, the True Guru.[41] For a critical situation, a Sikh should offer food to five Sikhs and ask them to pray for him. When this is done, everything is set right.[42] At the time of the *shraddh*s, a Sikh should get all kinds of food prepared and invite the Khalsa, recite the *Anand*, perform ardas, and feed the Khalsa. This was the proper way.[43]

The author of the *Tankhahnama* shows a serious concern for the moral conduct of the Sikhs. A Sikh should not appropriate the wealth of an *atithi* (guest), neither by force nor by fraud. A Sikh should not resort to backbiting to harm another person. A Sikh should not indulge in gambling.[44] To feed the poor was as meritorious as to contribute cash to the Guru's funds.[45] He alone is the Khalsa who protects the poor, who destroys the wicked, who recites the Name, who attacks the mlechh, who connects others to the Name, who transcends all earthly attachments, who rides the horse, who fights every day, and who takes up arms to destroy the wicked.[46]

One of the many injunctions for the Khalsa is obviously political: he who wishes to become a Sardar should serve the Khalsa.[47] The *Tankhahnama* falls into two informal parts. In verses 3 to 43, the author dwells on religious and social matters in relation to the Sikhs; in verses 44 to 62, he talks of political matters in relation to the Khalsa. The last verse of the *Tankhahnama* is memorable for the conviction with which the ideal of the Khalsa Raj is stated: 'The Khalsa shall rule and no one will remain obdurate. Humbled at last, they will seek refuge with the Khalsa.'[48] Guru Gobind Singh tells Bhai Nand Lal that he would make his own raj manifest. He would roll all the four varnas into one.[49]

The most remarkable feature of the *Sakhi Rahit Patshahi* 10 is an emphatic assertion of the Singh identity. Just as the sacred thread was a mark of Hindu identity, the kes, the turban, and the flowing beard served as the markers of Singh identity. A Singh did not remain concealed amidst thousands of Hindus and Musalmans.[50] The distinct appearance of the Singhs was a reflection of their distinct religious beliefs and practices.

The *Prem Sumarag* has the most comprehensive scope of rahit. Its 10 chapters relate to the religious life of the Khalsa; the ceremonies to be performed at birth, marriage, and death; food and occupations; governance and administration of justice in the Sikh state to be established; and the *sahaj* way to liberation. The *Prem Sumarag* covers thus the personal, religious, social, and political aspects of normative life for the Khalsa.[51]

In the beginning, the introduction of the Khalsa rahit created some problems within the Sikh social order. According to Sainapat, there was resistance among the Khatri and the Brahman Sikhs to join the order of the Kesdhari Singhs. There were local fights among the Sikhs in many towns and cities.[52] Sainapat narrates what happened in Delhi. The tension arose from the Khalsa rahit, especially over the rite of bhaddar. Sainapat mentions three cases in which the matter turned out to be serious. The *panchs* and the hakim of Delhi tried to intervene on behalf of the Khatri and Brahman Sikhs, but eventually the hakim became considerate towards the Khalsa and they came to dominate the Sikh sangat in Delhi and other places. Sainapat equates the sangat with the Guru.[53]

A report of 24 May 1710 says that Guru Gobind Singh dismissed the masands by one stroke of the pen and established the Khalsa. It was settled by him that the Sikhs of the Khalsa would not cut the hair of the head, moustache, and beard, and would be known as Sikhs of the Khalsa. Among the community of Khatris, a great disturbance occurred, and marriages and kinships (between the Khalsa Sikhs and others) were given up. First, at the village Chak, in pargana Patti, which is known as Chak Guru, it came to a fight. The Sikhs of the Khalsa came out victorious. The force sent from Lahore failed to control matters.[54]

The verses known as the 'Khalsa Mahima' are generally supposed to have been written with reference to the Khalsa. But the term used in the verses is 'these' people.

> I have won battles with the support of these people, and with their support have given charities. All crises are resolved with their grace, and with their grace our house is full again. Due to their grace, we have acquired learning, and due to their grace, all our enemies were destroyed. Due to their grace is adorned our establishment, otherwise there were millions of helpless people like me.
>
> Their service I cherish, and no other; all our charities are for them, and for none else. They will flourish in the world to overshadow others. All that we possess, our body and mind, our head and all our wealth are dedicated to these people.[55]

'These people' appears to include all the Sikhs dedicated to the Guru and his cause.

On the whole, the religious beliefs and practices of the Khalsa recommended in the Rahitnamas are different and distinct from those of the Hindus and the Muslims. The norms for social life of the Khalsa leave no doubt that they cover the most important aspects of social life, including the life-cycle rituals. The ideal of equality is enunciated and upheld without ambiguity, but certain empirical inequalities are accepted without much hesitation. The Brahmans are virtually ignored in the Rahitnamas. The Khalsa have a strong political commitment to establish their rule. The norms of ethical conduct are perhaps the most important. The distinct identity of the Khalsa is not merely a question of assertion: this identity is the result of the convergence of their religious, social, political, and ethical life.

In retrospect, it seems that Guru Gobind Singh changed the character of the Sikh Panth quite deliberately. The fresh injunctions he gave to the Sikhs on the Baisakhi of 1699 were added to the ideals of the Sikh faith cherished by his predecessors. '*Gur sangat kini khalsa*' (the Guru turned the Sikhs into the Khalsa) underlines that the old and the new were combined to forge a new kind of order.[56] The Rahitnamas projected this comprehensive objective and not merely the new injunctions. To consolidate and innovate at the same time appears to have been the intention. The old and the new norms in combination covered all important aspects of the Khalsa way of life.

Notes

1. See Karamjit K. Malhotra, 'Appendix: The Goddess in Eighteenth-Century Sikh Literature', in *The Eighteenth Century in Sikh History: Political Resurgence, Religious and Social Life, and Cultural Articulation* (New Delhi: Oxford University Press, 2016), pp. 290–300.

The Sikh writers of the eighteenth century seem to have assumed that a number of compositions included in the *Dasam Granth* were written by Guru Gobind Singh. This would explain in the first place why some Sikh scholars were keen to collect and compile these compositions. *Dasven Patshah ka Granth*, for them, was a compilation of the works of Guru Gobind Singh. This would further explain why some Sikhs were prepared to give it a status close to that of *Guru Granth Sahib*. Finally, the *Dasam Granth* contained compositions related to the Goddess, and the Sikh writers generally were inclined to accept the oral tradition that grew up about the connection of the Goddess with the Khalsa. The oral tradition varied from place to place. This variation is reflected in the works of the Sikh writers who invoke the Goddess. For most of these writers, the institution of the Khalsa was the only event for which the Goddess could be invoked. She has no role in the rahit of the Khalsa. The belief in the supremacy of Akal Purkh left little room for an effective role for any other deity. A myth was sought to be created to sanctify the Khalsa which, even otherwise, was of vital importance. The episode remains incongruous in the Sikh literary works of the eighteenth century, or later.

2. J. S. Grewal and Irfan Habib, eds, *Sikh History from Persian Sources: Translations of Major Texts* (New Delhi: Tulika/Indian History Congress, 2001), pp. 66–7, 73.

3. Sainapat, *Sri Gur Sobha*, edited by Shamsher Singh Ashok (Amritsar: Shiromani Gurdwara Prabandhak Committee, 1967), pp. 29–30, 33–4, 36, 40.

4. The *Chaupa Singh Rahit-Nama*, translated and edited by W. H. McLeod (Dunedin, New Zealand: University of Otago Press, 1987), pp. 84–5.

5. Kesar Singh Chhibber, 'Bansavalinama Dasan Patshahian Ka', edited by Rattan Singh Jaggi, in *Parkh*, vol. 2, edited by S. S. Kohli (Chandigarh: Panjab University, 1972), pp. 130–2.

6. Koer Singh, *Gurbilas Patshahi 10*, edited by Shamsher Singh Ashok (Patiala: Punjabi University, 1968), pp. 127–9.

7. Sukha Singh, *Gurbilas Patsahi 10*, edited by Gursharan Kaur Jaggi (Patiala: Bhasha Vibhag, Punjab, 1989), pp. 171–5.

8. Sarup Das Bhalla, *Mahima Prakash*, part 2, edited by Gobind Singh Lamba and Khazan Singh (Patiala: Punjab Languages Department, 1972), pp. 815–24.

9. Bhai Svarup Singh Kaushish, *Guru Kian Sakhian*, edited by Piara Singh Padam (Amritsar: Singh Brothers,1999 [1986]), pp. 118–20.

10. Ratan Singh Bhangu, *Sri Gur Panth Prakash*, edited by Balwant Singh Dhillon (Amritsar: Singh Brothers, 2004), pp. 42–3.

11. *Sri Dasam Granth Sahib*, edited by Ratan Singh Jaggi and Gursharan Kaur Jaggi (New Delhi: Gobind Sadan, 1999), vol. 3, pp. 396–9.

12. *Hukamname Guru Sahiban, Mata Sahiban, Banda Singh ate Khalsa Ji De*, edited by Ganda Singh (Patiala: Punjabi University, 1967), document 46.

13. *Hukamname*, document 50.

14. *Hukamname*, document 51.

15. *Hukamname*, document 52.

16. *Hukamname*, document 54.

17. *Hukamname*, document 59.

18. *Nishan Te Hukamname*, edited by Shamsher Singh Ashok (Amritsar: Shiromani Gurdwara Prabandhak Committee, 1967), document 74.

19. Ajit Singh Baagha, *Banur Had Orders: A Critical Study of an Hitherto Unknown 'Hukamnamah' of Guru Gobind Singh* (Delhi: Ranjit Printers and Publishers 1969), pp. 86–90.

20. Gurinder Singh Mann, 'Sources for the Study of Guru Gobind Singh's Life and Times', *Journal of Punjab Studies* (Special Issue on Guru Gobind Singh), vol. 15, nos. 1 and 2 (Spring–Fall 2008): 236–9, 261.

21. Sainapat, *Sri Gur Sobha*, pp. 11–13, 29–36.

22. *The Chaupa Singh Rahit-Nama*, pp. 82–3.

23. Chhibber, *Bansavalinama*, pp. 127–9.

24. Koer Singh, *Gurbilas Patsahi 10*, pp. 126–35.

25. Kaushish, *Guru Kian Sakhian*, pp. 118–20.

26. Kaushish, *Guru Kian Sakhian*, pp. 123–4.

27. Bhangu, *Sri Gur Panth Prakash*, pp. 36–7.

28. Sainapat, *Sri Gur Sobha*, pp. 30–5.

29. Koer Singh, *Gurbilas Patshahi 10*, pp. 134–8.

30. Kaushish, *Guru Kian Sakhian*, p. 124.

31. Kaushish, *Guru Kian Sakhian*, pp. 124–5.

32. Sukha Singh, *Gurbilas Patsahi Dasmi*, edited by Manvinder Singh (Amritsar: Guru Nanak Dev University, 2016), pp. 217–19.

33. Bhangu, *Sri Gur Panth Prakash*, pp. 30–8.

34. W. H. McLeod, *Sikhs of the Khalsa: A History of the Khalsa Rahit* (New Delhi: Oxford University Press, 2003), pp. 29–157. J. S. Grewal, *Four Centuries of Sikh Tradition: History, Literature, and Identity* (New Delhi: Oxford University Press, 2013 [2011]), pp. 206–24. Malhotra, *The Eighteenth Century in Sikh History*, pp. 5–13.

35. *The Chaupa Singh Rahit-Nama*, p. 58.

36. *The Chaupa Singh Rahit-Nama*, pp. 60–1.

37. *Bhai Nand Lal Granthavali*, edited by Ganda Singh (Malaka (Malasia): Sant Sohan Singh, 1968), verses 15, 29, 51, 58.

38. *The Chaupa Singh Rahit-Nama*, p. 63.

39. *The Chaupa Singh Rahit-Nama*, p. 133.

40. *The Chaupa Singh Rahit-Nama*, pp. 134–5.

41. *The Chaupa Singh Rahit-Nama*, p. 135.

42. *The Chaupa Singh Rahit-Nama*, p. 135.

43. *The Chaupa Singh Rahit-Nama*, pp. 135–6.

44. Nand Lal, *Granthavali*, verses 22, 27, 35; 18, 20, 32, 38–39.

45. *The Chaupa Singh Rahit-Nama*, pp. 58–60, 62–65, 72.

46. Nand Lal, *Granthavali*, verses 50–4.

47. *The Chaupa Singh Rahit-Nama*, pp. 68–9.

48. Nand Lal, *Granthavali*, pp. 195–9, verse 62.

49. Nand Lal, *Granthavali*, verses 56–62.

50. *The Chaupa Singh Rahit-Nama*, p. 134.

51. For detail, see J. S. Grewal, 'The Prem Sumarg: A Sant Khalsa Vision of the Sikh Panth', in *The Sikhs: Ideology, Institutions and Identity* (New Delhi: Oxford University Press, 2009), pp. 158–85.

52. Sainapat, *Sri Gur Sobha*, p. 56.

53. Sainapat, *Sri Gur Sobha*, pp. 42–55.

54. *Sikh History from Persian Sources*, p. 107 (A report from the court of Bahadur Shah, dated 24 May 1710).

55. Jaggi and Jaggi, *Sri Dasam-Granth Sahib*, vol. 3, pp. 400–1.

56. Gurdas (Singh), Var 41, in *Varan Bhai Gurdas*, edited by Giani Hazara Singh (Amritsar: Khalsa Samachar, 1962 [1911]).

Appendix 7A

Signification of the Term 'Khalsa'

The term 'Khalsa' appears in the hukamnamas of Guru Hargobind: 'the sangat of the east' is 'Khalsa of the Guru'.[1] In a hukamnama of Guru Tegh Bahadur to the sangat of Pattan Farid, the sangat is *'Guru ji ka Khalsa'*.[2] A hukamnama of Guru Gobind Singh, dated 25 April 1699, is addressed to *'sangat sahlang'* (a sangat initiated into the Sikh faith by a masand on behalf of the Guru) of the village 'Bhai Gurdas Bhagte Phaphre'. The word 'sahlang' in the *Dabistan-i Mazahib* refers to a person initiated into the Sikh faith by a masand on behalf of the Guru. Such a Sikh was called *meli* or masandia, distinct from the Sikh initiated by the Guru.[4] The term used for the latter was 'Khalsa', underlining the direct link between the Guru and the Sikh.

The masands and their followers did not disappear suddenly. The assertion that a particular sangat, or an individual, was the Guru's Khalsa continues to appear in the hukamnamas of Guru Gobind Singh after 1699. *'Sarbat sangat mera Khalsa hai'* (the entire sangat is my Khalsa) appears in a hukamnama of 1704[5] and a hukamnama of 4 March 1706.[6] The sangat of Dhaul is told in the hukamnama of 2 October 1707 that 'you are my Khalsa'.[7] And so is the sangat of Khara.[8]

A new situation arose with the abolition of personal Guruship. As if to meet the situation, the hukamnama of 3 February 1708, addressed by Guru Gobind Singh to the sangat of Benares, says that the entire sangat of Benares is 'Vaheguru ji da Khalsa' (see Image 7A.2).[9] In two hukamnamas of the time of Banda, the sangats of Bhai Rupa and Jaunpur are *'Akal Purkh jio da Khalsa'* (the Khalsa of the Immortal Being).[10] In the hukamnamas of Mata Sundari and Mata Sahib Devi, the Khalsa belong to Akal Purkh. The number of these hukamnamas is about a dozen, written from 1717 to 1732.[11] In a hukamnama issued from the Akal Takht (Amritsar), the issuing authority is referred to as 'Sat Sri Akal Purkh ji ka Khalsa'.[12]

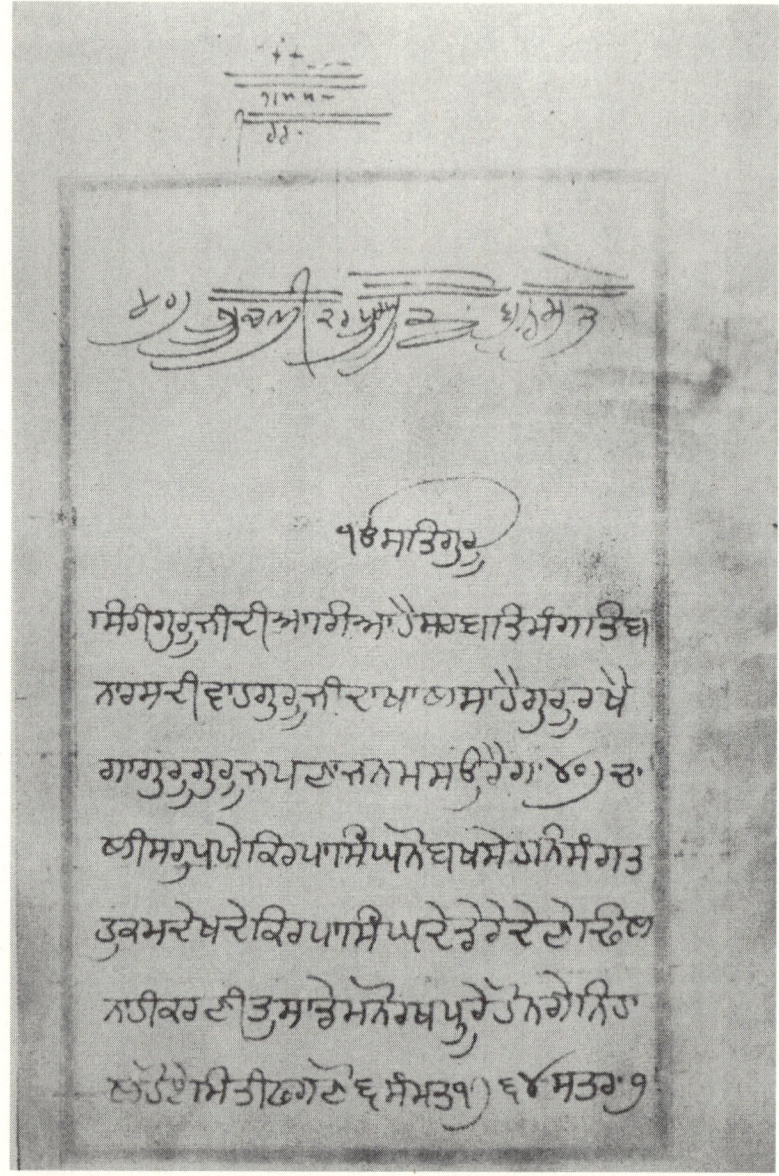

Image 7A.1 Guru Gobind Singh's *hukamnama*, dated 3 February 1708 (document 65), addressed to the *sangat* of Benaras. The *sangat* is addressed as 'Vaheguru ji ka Khalsa' and not as 'my Khalsa' or 'the Guru's Khalsa'.
Source: Ganda Singh ed., *Hukamname*.

By this time, 'Vaheguru ji ka Khalsa' was a familiar term used for both an individual and a group.

There was a further development. When Guru Gobind Singh introduced pahul of the double-edged sword, all the Khalsa did not accept it at once.[13] Those who took pahul became the arms-bearing Kesdhari Singhs. The followers of Guru Gobind Singh then could be seen as consisting of the Khalsa Sikhs and the Kesdhari Singhs. The Rahitnamas were addressed primarily, if not exclusively, to the latter. The term 'Khalsa' came to be used for them more and more frequently. Before the end of the eighteenth century, the 'Khalsa' stood equated with the 'Singh'. Thus, in the early eighteenth century, to be a Sikh of Guru Gobind Singh was to be a Khalsa, and in the late eighteenth century, to be a Khalsa of Akal Purkh was to be a Singh. The Khalsa as Singhs constituted the mainstream among the Sikhs.

Notes

1. *Hukamname*, document 3
2. *Hukamname*, document 8.
3. *Hukamname*, document 47.
4. *Sikh History from Persian Sources*, pp. 66–7.
5. *Hukamname*, document 60.
6. *Hukamname*, document 61.
7. *Hukamname*, document 63.
8. *Hukamname*, document 64.
9. *Hukamname*, document 65.
10. *Hukamname*, documents 66–7.
11. *Hukamname*, documents 68, 70–2, 74–5, 77–9, 81–3.
12. *Hukamname*, document 86.
13. The Rahitnama associated with Chaupa Singh alone talks of Sahajdharis with reference to those Sikhs who had not taken pahul. Kesar Singh Chhibber alone, among the other eighteenth-century Sikh writers, refers to Sahajdhari Sikhs.

Image 7A.2   A contemporary portrait of young Guru Gobind Singh
Courtesy: Dr Anurag Singh, Ludhiana.

Image 7A.3 *Nishan* (invocation) of Guru Gobind Singh on an illuminated folio of the *Adi Granth*.

Source: Collection of Takht Sri Harimandir Sahib, Patna.

Image 7A.4   Opening folio of the *Zafarnama* manuscript at Gurdwara Bhai Daya Singh, Aurangabad.

Source: Courtesy of Bhayee Sikandar Singh and Roopinder Singh, *Sikh Heritage: Ethos & Relics* (New Delhi: Rupa Publications, 2012), p. 58.

IV

Direct Confrontation with the State

8

Ouster from Anandpur (1699–1704)

In 1699 began the last stage of Aurangzeb's career in which sieges of successive forts were conducted by him in person. In each case, there was nearly the same tale: a hill fort captured by him after a vast expenditure of time, men, and money, its recovery by the Marathas from the weak Mughal garrison after a few months, and its siege by the Mughals again which began a year or two later. The siege of eight forts took five and a half years from 1699 to 1705.[1]

On 31 January 1700, Prince Mu'azzam was appointed the *subadar* of Lahore on the removal of Ibrahim Khan. Later sometime Zabardast Khan was made the subadar, but Mu'azzam was reappointed in September 1705. Mun'im Khan, *diwan* of the establishment of Mu'azzam, was made diwan of Punjab in 1704, and in 1705 he was made *naib* (deputy) *subadar* of Punjab and *faujdar* of Jammu.[2]

Muhammad Qasim Lahauri refers to the honoured orders issued from the imperial court to Wazir Khan, the faujdar of Sirhind, to warn Guru Gobind Singh to live like other religious persons, and his own ancestors, and shun the words used by his followers, giving him the title of the king (*padshah*). He should not imitate the ways and practices of sovereigns, like showing one's face in the *jharoka* (a large window) and receiving *sijda* (bowing in reverence to the emperor) from the people. If he did not heed the warning, then Wazir Khan should exert himself to the utmost to devastate the places under his control and expel him from his territories.[3]

A newsletter of 16 April 1699 refers to the report brought by the imperial messenger, Asad Khan, who had been sent to Wazir Khan and Dilawar Khan, the faujdar of Jammu, with instructions to admonish Guru Gobind Singh.[4] The faujdar of Sirhind, Mirza 'Askari, titled Wazir Khan, was of Iranian descent and his family had long been in the Mughal service. He held the rank of 2,000 *zat* under Aurangzeb.

Sikh writers of the eighteenth century take notice of the battles of Guru Gobind Singh after the institution of the Khalsa in 1699. Sainapat devotes four chapters to the battles resulting in Guru Gobind Singh's ouster from Anandpur in 1704. Sainapat talks of the first battle of Anandpur, the battle of Nirmoh, the battle of Basoli, the victory at Kalmot, and the second battle of Anandpur. The objective of the hill chiefs was to oust Guru Gobind Singh from the hills if he did not accept a clearly subordinate political position. With the support of their suzerain, Aurangzeb, they obliged Guru Gobind Singh to leave Anandpur. A local issue became an issue of the state in which the head of the state and Guru Gobind Singh were ranged on opposite sides.[5]

Koer Singh's *Gurbilas* has six chapters on the battles leading up to the evacuation of Anandpur. But two of these are misplaced: one on the expedition of Husain and the other on the arrival of Prince Mu'azzam. The first two (Chapters 10 and 11) relate actually to the first battle of Anandpur, and the last two (Chapters 14 and 15) relate to the second battle. There is nothing about the battles of Nirmoh, Basoli, or Kalmot.

In the *Guru Kian Sakhian*, eight *sakhi*s relate to the battles of Guru Gobind Singh after the institution of the Khalsa, leading up to the evacuation of Anandpur. The subject matter of one sakhi is new: the fight over the fort of Taragarh. Separate sakhis are given to Duni Chand, Bachittar Singh, Guru Gobind Singh's return to Anandpur, and his final departure from Anandpur. All the eight sakhis relate to three themes: the early battle of Anandpur, the battles of Nirmoh and Basoli, and the last battle over Anandpur.[6]

In Sukha Singh's *Gurbilas*, there are eight chapters (13–20) after the institution of the Khalsa up to Guru Gobind Singh's final departure from Anandpur.[7] However, Chapter 16, on the arrival of Prince Mu'azzam in Punjab, should have been placed before the institution of the Khalsa. Chapter 19, on the four wondrous acts (*charitar*), has nothing to say about battles. Chapter 13, which relates to a battle between the Khalsa and the Ranghars and Gujjars of Bajrur, has no political significance. In Chapter 17, there is no mention of any battle. Thus, only four chapters of Sukha Singh's *Gurbilas* are relevant for the battles of Guru Gobind Singh during the phase under consideration. Two of these four relate to the first battle of Anandpur, another relates to the battle of Nirmoh, and the last one to the second battle of Anandpur.

The First Battle of Anandpur

After the great event of 1699, some of the Khalsa left Anandpur and went to various places. They were keen to ensure the ascendancy of the Khalsa in Sikh sangats and the introduction of the Khalsa rahit. At many places, the situation of internal tension arose, such as the one in Delhi.

The Khalsa who remained at Anandpur were prepared for war. In any case, the Raja of Kahlur wrote to Guru Gobind Singh to leave 'our land'. He should either pay *dam* (by way of tribute) or fight. With his raj and reputation firmly established, Guru Gobind Singh told the Raja that he could not have the tribute for the asking; he had to get it 'at the point of the spear'.[8] The Raja of Kahlur wrote to the chief of Hindur that they should make a concerted attack from both sides. This was acceptable to the latter. Then they approached the other chiefs. The combined forces of the hill chiefs encamped near Anandpur. They besieged the town, allowing no one to enter or to go out. Guru Gobind Singh told the Singhs to be ready for an attack on the enemy. Ajit Singh, the eldest son of the Guru, led a sortie. The Raja of Kahlur began to think of an agreement for peace. On the advice of his minister, however, he decided to fight.[9]

Sainapat mentions the order in which the warriors used their weapons: musket, followed by the bow and arrows, followed by the sword. The Singhs fought with great bravery and effect, with two additional weapons: the spear and the *jamdhar*. Sahibzada Ajit Singh fought with exceptional courage and turned the tide in favour of the Khalsa. The hill chiefs admitted their failure.[10]

Koer Singh says that after the institution of the Khalsa, Guru Gobind Singh sent letters to Sikh sangats in all the four directions to come to Anandpur at the time of Diwali. A large number of countries and places are mentioned in this connection. Anandpur was crowded with the Khalsa. To get fodder and wood, they plundered the neighbouring villages. The hill chiefs led by the chief of Kahlur, made a representation to Aurangzeb, seeking justice from their overlord. They stressed the point that Guru Gobind Singh had come to Kahlur from outside (actually Sirmaur), founded Anandpur, and invoked the Goddess to create a new Panth called the Khalsa. He wanted the hill chiefs to become his followers and to support him in subverting the Mughal rule. The chiefs did not agree and he started plundering their territories. They needed protection. They would pay tribute regularly if Anandpur was taken away from the Guru and placed under their jurisdiction.[11]

Consequently, Aurangzeb sent an army of '10,00,000' against Guru Gobind Singh. When this army was encamped at Sirhind, the local Sikh sangat informed the Guru of this threat. He was well prepared to meet the combined forces of the Mughals and the hill chiefs when they attacked Anandpur. The Guru gained an initial victory. He reassured the Khalsa that they were under the protection of God who had bestowed upon them the armour that kept them safe in all situations. The Subadar of Lahore was told that Guru Gobind Singh was not a mere human being but a person with an element of divinity. He possessed four elephants offered to him by Raja Man Singh and Raja Sham Sen, and two others received from the South and the lands beyond Sind. The Guru defeated all the hill chiefs and invoked the Goddess for her blessing. He had built a number of forts, such as Taragarh, Bajaigarh (Fatehgarh), Agamgarh, Holgarh, and Kesgarh. The family of Guru Gobind Singh was residing in Agamgarh and it became a special target for the enemy. Sahibzada Ajit Singh played a vital role in its defence. Active among the opponents were Sher Khan, Hayat Khan, Khan Muhammad, Nahar Khan, Dilawar Khan, and Husain Khan. Sukh Dev and Kesari were the famous warriors among the Rajputs. Heavy artillery was used by both sides. Ultimately, the Singhs defeated the invaders. Some of them were killed and others left the trenches to run away.

Guru Gobind Singh rewarded the Singh warriors with robes of honour and gold.[12]

Koer Singh goes on to say that Zabardast Khan now took the initiative to recover the lost ground. A siege was laid to Lohgarh. On the Guru's side, Duni Chand, a masand, did not accept Guru Gobind Singh's advice to redeem himself by facing an intoxicated elephant sent by the enemy to break open the gate of Lohgarh. He was frightened and left Anandpur in the darkness of the night. He broke his leg by accident. Bachittar Singh, on the other hand, accepted the Guru's advice and struck the intoxicated elephant with his spear so forcefully that the elephant turned its back and trampled many on the enemy's side. Thousands of Turks were killed in this war. Among the dead was Raja Kesari Singh of Jaswan. Guru Gobind Singh won the battle with the support of the Khalsa.[13]

According to the author of the *Guru Kian Sakhian*, Raja Ajmer Chand, the son and successor of Raja Bhim Chand of Kahlur, occupied the fort of Taragarh, which was at some distance from Anandgarh. But Sahibzada Ajit Singh and Bhai Udai Singh, leading two different bands of the Khalsa, recovered the fort. Raja Ajmer Chand tried to occupy Fatehgarh and Agamgarh on two successive days, but he was repulsed. On the suggestion of Raja Kesari Chand of Jaswan, it was decided to attack Lohgarh using an intoxicated elephant to break open its gate. Guru Gobind Singh indicated that Duni Chand, a grandson of Bhai Salo, would face the elephant. Duni Chand thought that the Guru wanted him killed. He tried to persuade eminent Singhs such as Bhai Daya Singh and Bhai Bachittar Singh to suggest to the Guru some other way of facing the elephant, but no one listened to him. He left Anandpur during the night and went to Majitha. There, he died of a snake bite. Trying to run away from death, he fell into the jaws of death. Guru Gobind Singh asked Bhai Bachittar Singh now to face the elephant and he agreed. He went out of Lohgarh, riding a horse, shouted '*Sat Sri Akal*' (the immortal one alone is true), and fell upon the elephant like the lightening, striking his spear (*barchha*) on its forehead with such great force that it pierced the steel plate and penetrated the elephant's forehead. The elephant turned back in pain and trampled many men of the hill chiefs. Bhai Udai Singh, who was watching the scene from the gate, shouted 'Sat Sri Akal' and galloped to face Raja Kesari Chand Jaswal who was approaching them from behind the elephant. Given the chance to strike first, Kesari Chand struck his sword, but to no effect. Bhai Udai Singh, in turn, struck him so hard with his sword that Kesari Chand's head was cut off from his body. Udai Singh carried it on the tip of his spear back to the gate.[14]

Sukha Singh talks of the first battle of Anandpur in Chapters 14 and 15. A large number of Sikhs came to Anandpur at the time of Diwali. Before long, there was a shortage of wood and grass. This was brought to the notice of Guru Gobind Singh. He is said to have remarked that if no wood or grass was available on price, it could be taken by force. The subjects of the hill chiefs complained to their rulers about the way wood and grass were forcibly being taken from them. The hill chiefs made a representation to the emperor, seeking justice and making a strong case against Guru Gobind Singh. He had received blessings from the Goddess and become very strong. In fact, he possessed supernatural powers (*karamat*). He had created a new Panth called the Khalsa to replace both Hindus and Muslims. All the four varnas were made one. He claimed to have given *raj* and *jog* (temporal and spiritual matters) to the Khalsa and prepared them to fight against the emperor. The Mughals and other Muslim rulers would pay tribute to them. They would exercise lordship over the earth. He had the support of the God (*Kharagket*) and the Goddess (*Kalka*). 'The carpet of the *mlechh* was now to be rolled up.' The hill chiefs implored the emperor to give Anandgarh to them.[15]

Sukha Singh says that Aurangzeb sent a huge army against Guru Gobind Singh. When this army arrived in Sirhind, the local Sikh sangat heard about it. They informed Guru Gobind Singh secretly of the purpose for which this army had been sent. The Guru was forewarned. The Khalsa fought well in a battle near Anandpur. They firmly believed that they were under God's protection. Sukha Singh weaves the episodes of Duni Chand and Bachittar Singh into his narrative. Despite the large number of combatants and artillery on the Mughal side, the Guru was ultimately victorious. The Rajas went to Aurangzeb and told him sorrowfully of the Guru's victory.[16]

Battles around Anandpur

According to Sainapat, the Raja of Kahlur thought of a devious way of attaining his objective. In order to appeal to the Guru's sense of honour, a cow tied to a manger was left behind, asking Guru Gobind Singh to leave Anandpur as the 'cow's fodder' (*gau-bhat*). The Guru left the place and went to Nirmoh.[17]

At Nirmoh, the Khalsa had to subjugate the villages around it. Sahib Chand emerged conspicuous in this action. He was killed. The Khalsa fought hard to take possession of his body. It was cremated in Nirmoh. He was perfectly fortunate in 'becoming the true Khalsa by laying down his life'. When the Khalsa captured a large number of villages, the Raja of Kahlur sent a messenger to Aurangzeb to complain that Guru Gobind Singh had occupied his villages by force. Aurangzeb deputed one of his men to go to Sirhind with a large army and to act in concert with its administrator. The sangats of many villages went to the *darbar* of Guru Gobind Singh. He armed them to fight. The faujdar of Sirhind led the combined forces against Guru Gobind Singh at Nirmoh. It was besieged. Artillery was used with deadly effect. The fight went on for 21 hours before the imperial troops made a retreat. Guru Gobind Singh decided to cross the river Sutlej. Attacked on the banks of the river, the Khalsa had to fight for more than four hours. Eventually, the enemy was repulsed by the Khalsa. Guru Gobind Singh went to Basoli where he was warmly received by its Raja.[18]

According to Kaushish, the Rajas had a consultation at Bilaspur after their defeat in the first battle of Anandpur. The loss of Kesari Singh, who was regarded as the bravest and the wisest of them all, was felt by everyone. There was also a general feeling that something should be done to retrieve the prestige they had lost on the field of battle. An appropriate letter was addressed to Guru Gobind Singh and entrusted to Parmanand, the wazir, to be handed over to the Guru. It was attached to a sacred thread put on a cow that was tied to something immovable in front of the gate of Anandgarh. The letter addressed to the Guru was to the effect that the chiefs would never make the mistake of attacking Anandpur. They swore on the mother-cow (*gau-mata*) and the sacred thread, and wanted Guru Gobind Singh to save their honour and prestige by leaving

the fort of Anandgarh. He could return to it after some time. This
was a face-saving device. Guru Gobind Singh did not trust the hill
chiefs, but in consultation with Bhai Daya Singh and Bhai Udai
Singh, he decided to leave Anandgarh on the following day as a
politic measure.[19]

Ajmer Chand sent Parmanand with a letter to Sirhind, asking for help against Guru Gobind Singh. Rustam Khan arrived
with 'Turk' soldiers. However, he was killed by an arrow of Guru
Gobind Singh. His brother, Nasir Ali Khan, was killed by an arrow
of Bhai Udai Singh. Many others died in the battle. On the following day, Ajmer Chand led an attack with great vigour. Raja Salahi
Chand of Basoli invited Guru Gobind Singh to cross the Sutlej into
his territory. Ajmer Chand attacked the Khalsa on the banks of
the Sutlej. Bhai Udai Singh and other warriors kept him in check.
Guru Gobind Singh crossed the river and reached Basoli, the capital of Raja Salahi Chand. Ajmer Chand returned to Bilaspur after a
loss of men and materials.[20]

Sukha Singh's account of the battle of Nirmoh has all the familiar elements with some additional matter coming from some oral
tradition. First of all, there is the stratagem of the cow conjointly
presented. It is followed by Guru Gobind Singh's choice of Nirmoh
as an alternative to Anandpur. The specific feature of the battle of
Nirmoh is the death of Sahib 'Singh' and the fight over his body.
Guru Gobind Singh goes to Basoli on the personal request of its
Raja. The Ranghars and Gujjars of Kalmot are punished for plundering Sikh pilgrims to Anandpur. Among the new elements are:
the question by a Singh on why Guru Gobind Singh decided to
leave Anandpur; the mention of two tombs and a *shahidganj* in
connection with the battle of Nirmoh; and that the place where
Guru Gobind Singh stayed in Basoli was named Gobindgarh.[21]

According to Sainapat, the Raja of Kahlur came to Basoli with his
army. The battle fought near Basoli was witnessed by Guru Gobind
Singh. It ended in the flight of the troops of Kahlur: like an arrow
shot from the bow. Many days later, Guru Gobind Singh went on
a hunting expedition. The people of Kalmot came out to encircle
some of the Khalsa on the road. In a fight that followed, men from
both sides were killed. When Guru Gobind Singh was informed of
it, he came to Kalmot and laid siege to it. The Kalmotians were

overpowered after a hard fight. The Raja of Kahlur now came to meet Guru Gobind Singh as a token of his submission. The Guru returned to Basoli. Soon, he was back in Anandpur.[22]

Out for hunting one day, says Kaushish, Bhai Udai Singh saw a tiger cub coming out of the forest near Basoli and wounded it with a bullet. It ran towards Kalmot, with the Khalsa in pursuit. The Ranghars and Gujjars of Kalmot came out. A dispute about some minor point led to a fight between them and the Khalsa. They could not withstand the Khalsa and saved their lives by running away. Meanwhile, Raja Salahi Chand used his influence to work out a conciliation between Guru Gobind Singh and Raja Ajmer Chand. Guru Gobind Singh returned to Anandpur. Peace was restored.[23]

Kaushish alone of the Sikh writers of the eighteenth century mentions a battle at Anandpur before what is called the second or the last battle of Anandpur. According to him, the Raja of Basoli died two years after the battle of Nirmoh (placed in 1700). Ajmer Chand began to create problems for the Khalsa who used to collect grass as the fodder for their horses from places in the territory of Kahlur. In 1703, Ajmer Chand and the Raja of Hindur, with some others, invaded Anandpur. In a pitched battle that lasted for more than six hours, many fighters were killed on both sides. On the following day, no one dared to attack.[24]

Last Siege and Evacuation of Anandpur

The only contemporary account of the last battle of Anandpur is that of Sainapat (see Map 8.1 for an early twentieth-century map of Anandpur Sahib). It is rather short, but clear. On Guru Gobind Singh's return from Basoli to Anandpur, the Khalsa began to come for his *darshan* in increasing numbers. All the neighbouring villages were 'conquered' by the Khalsa. Their general practice was to ride into the villages to collect voluntary offerings (*bhet*). Those who did not bring any offering were plundered. This went on for over two years. The Rajas began to think that their authority was being thwarted. In all four directions was the raj of the true Guru. The Rajas collected their armies and moved towards Anandpur. They asked Guru Gobind Singh to leave Anandgarh. Both sides began to prepare for armed action.[25]

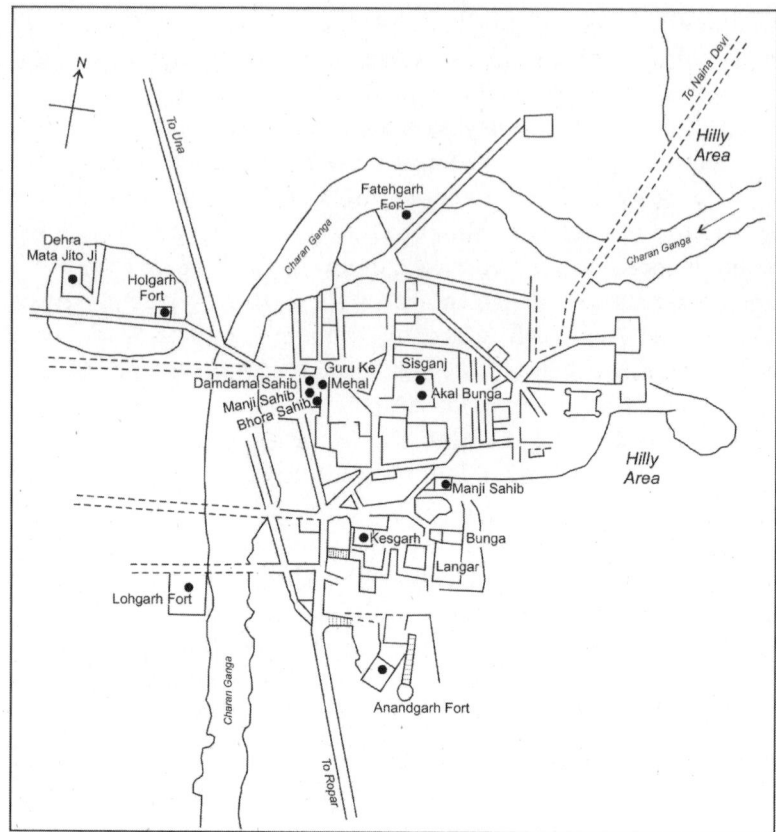

Map 8.1   Anandpur Sahib (early twentieth century)
Source: Courtesy of the author.

The Khalsa used artillery and went out to attack the combined forces of the Rajas. Some of them actually got killed. Many of their brave warriors died on the field of battle. Feeling helpless, the Rajas decided to approach the 'Turk'. They explained to him the situation in detail and begged for support. They wanted Anandpur to be taken away from the Guru and given to them. This was the basic issue.[26]

The resources of the Mughal faujdars and the hill Rajas were mobilized against Guru Gobind Singh, but they failed to dislodge him. The battle fought with muskets, arrows, and swords was grim. The Rajas eventually thought of laying siege to Anandpur.

No one was allowed to go in or come out. There was an acute shortage of food and water. The night attacks of the Khalsa for supplies became increasingly hazardous. It became impossible for many people to survive. Some of even the Khalsa Singhs began to say that it was advisable to leave Anandpur. Guru Gobind Singh asked them to take responsibility for the consequences in a written statement (*tauhad*). All the people at Anandpur were now ready to vacate the town. The treasury was distributed among the Khalsa who were fully armed with five weapons. All other materials and goods were burnt. They were ready to leave 'the city of bliss'.[27]

Koer Singh talks of the last battle of Anandpur and the evacuation in Chapters 14–15 of his *Gurbilas*. He refers to the plundering of villages of the Rajas by the Singhs and the predicament of the rulers. They approached Aurangzeb with their tale of woe to seek his support in ousting the Guru from the hills. However, even the combined forces of the Mughals and the hill chiefs failed to take the forts of Anandpur by storm. The Mughal commanders decided to lay siege to Anandpur. In due course, the suffering due to hunger and thirst increased due to the growing shortage of food and water. The Khalsa who came for the Guru's darshan found the place under siege and went back. The bodies of the besieged were shrinking to become frames of bones. Some people persuaded Mata ji to advise the Guru to work out the terms of peace with his enemies. Guru Gobind Singh said that the Rajas could not be trusted. A Qazi arrived with a message of peace. Pressed for peace, Guru Gobind Singh demonstrated the insincerity of the enemy. He agreed to leave the forts and sent out a party with loads of trash. The party was attacked and plundered. Guru Gobind Singh exposed thus the real intentions of the enemy.[28]

Eventually, a letter came from Aurangzeb, reassuring Guru Gobind Singh of his good intentions and suggesting a personal meeting. The people of the town came to Guru Gobind Singh and submitted that they were on the point of starving to death without food. Guru Gobind Singh told them to hold on for a few days more. Then they could have the choicest food. The Sikhs submitted that it was not a bad idea to leave Anandpur. The Guru said, 'You will be responsible for the consequences.' Preparations were then made for leaving Anandpur with bag and baggage. The treasure was disbursed among the Singhs who were armed with five weapons. The heavy gun was consigned to the river, so was all the cash, including *ashrafi*s (gold coins). All kinds of costly cloth were taken out and burnt. A Sikh from the South offered to him a studded pair of golden bangles worth Rs 25,000. This too was thrown into the Sutlej. The sants knew well that all this was the Guru's sport (*khed*).[29]

Kesar Singh Chhibber does not say anything about the battles of the Khalsa at Anandpur, but he does take notice of the last siege of Anandpur. When the Rajas made a representation to Aurangzeb, he sent Rustam Khan and Dilawar Khan with a large army. The combined armies laid siege to Anandpur. Guru Gobind Singh knew that the hill chiefs were motivated by greed. Therefore, he decided to get rid of *maya*. All kinds of costly goods and cash were either burnt or consigned to the river. The estimated worth of the former was Rs 435,250 and of the latter, Rs 1,732,735. The Sikhs were not aware of the designs of the Rajas, but Guru Gobind Singh knew them well. He exposed them by sending out boxes of trash. The Rajas took possession of those boxes. When they found the boxes full of trash, they tried to explain that some other people, and not they, were the real culprits. Later, the Rajas took an oath not to attack the evacuees. The Sikhs asked them, and also Rustam Khan and Dilawar Khan, to sign written statements. Guru Gobind Singh asked the Sikhs to wait for eight days, but the Sikhs insisted that they should be allowed to leave. Guru Gobind Singh had to leave Anandpur against his own judgement of the situation.[30]

Sarup Das Bhalla too underlines that Guru Gobind Singh did not trust the hill chiefs and their oath. When they mentioned the proposal of taking an oath on the cow, the Brahman, and the sacred thread, it was rejected by Guru Gobind Singh. They sent Pamma, the Brahman wazir, to Mata Nanaki for the same purpose. Mata Nanaki tried to convince the Guru that the Rajas meant what they had conveyed through Pamma. But Guru Gobind Singh said categorically that neither the cow nor the sacred thread carried any weight. Mata Nanaki asserted nonetheless that the hill chiefs would never betray him. Guru Gobind Singh said at last that she could do what she liked. People marched out of Anandpur with their baggage the following day. Guru Gobind Singh was at the rear.[31]

Sarup Singh Kaushish talks of the assurances given by Aurangzeb to Guru Gobind Singh in response to his letter. The imperial Qazi arrived at last from the South with a royal *parwana* (order) pasted in a copy of the holy Qur'an. Addressed to Guru Gobind Singh, it stated that Guru Gobind Singh should leave Makhowal and come to Qasbah Kangar where the emperor would meet him personally. Guru Gobind Singh discussed it with the prominent Singhs, such as Bhai Daya Singh. Eventually, it was decided to leave Anandpur.[32]

Sukha Singh's narrative of the last siege of Anandpur resembles that of Koer Singh in terms of the main content. He talks of the aggressive activity of the Khalsa in the villages around Anandpur; anxiety of the Rajas over this threat to their authority and power; consultation among them and their approach to Aurangzeb for help; the positive response of Aurangzeb; the attack on Anandpur by their combined forces; their failure to take it by storm and resort to a long and close siege; hardships faced by the besieged and their inclination to leave the town; assurances given by the Rajas through Mata ji, who uses her own influence with the Guru to persuade him to leave; Guru Gobind Singh's extreme reluctance to leave Anandpur; and his deep suspicion of the motives of the hill chiefs. Finally, the letter comes from Aurangzeb with his oath on the Qur'an, asking the Guru to leave Anandpur for a personal meeting to sort out the problems. Guru Gobind Singh was now prepared to leave, destroying all costly articles and goods and consigning all the cash to the river. The Gurdwara Sisganj was entrusted to Gurbakhsh Udasi for upkeep.[33]

Ratan Singh Bhangu does not refer to the battles fought before the institution of the Khalsa. Even after the institution of the Khalsa, he concentrates on the last battle. Guru Gobind Singh's Khalsa attacked a village like Kalmot which was known to be hostile. The hill chiefs attacked the Guru near Kalmot, but were repulsed. Another battle was fought at Anandpur in which the hill chiefs were defeated. They approached the emperor for help. They asserted that the Guru wanted to put an end to the Mughal power. He was called 'Sachaha Patshah'; in contrast, the Mughal emperor was a 'false ruler'. He had no dearth of wealth; many alchemists were with him (to transform base metals into gold). Aurangzeb was worried to hear all this from 'Raja Bhim Chand'. The Mughal army of 10 lakh soldiers was ordered to march against the Guru. Anandpur was besieged by the combined armies of the hill chiefs and the emperor. There were only 4,000 Singhs in Anandpur, but they were determined to fight. Mata Gujari wanted Guru Gobind Singh to trust the hill chiefs who offered safe evacuation. Guru Gobind Singh exposed their deceptive offer by sending out a party with bags full of old clothes and shoes. But the people still insisted that they should leave the town. Guru Gobind Singh asked them to give in writing that they were not his Sikhs and he was not their Guru. They had Mata Gujari's support and they wrote a disclaimer. Bhangu underlines that the Khalsa remained firm in its faith.[34] He makes a clear distinction between the Khalsa and the others in this situation.

On the whole, the eighteenth-century Sikh writers leave no doubt that the chief of Kahlur did not want Guru Gobind Singh to stay at Anandpur on his own terms. In the first battle of Anandpur, the Guru had the upper hand. But the chief requested him to leave Anandpur as the cow's feed (gau-bhat). Two battles were then fought outside Anandpur, one at Nirmoh and the other at Basoli. Guru Gobind Singh then returned to Anandpur. With the support of the Mughal authorities and the hill chiefs, the chief of Kahlur laid a long siege to Anandpur. Seeing no end to the armed conflict, the besiegers offered safe passage to Guru Gobind Singh for the evacuation of Anandpur. Aurangzeb's oath on the Qur'an was finally used for this purpose. Guru Gobind Singh decided to leave Anandpur against his own judgement. As he indicates in the *Zafarnama*, Prince Mu'azzam was taking interest in the matter.[35]

Notes

1. Jadunath Sarkar, *A Short History of Aurangzib (1618–1707)* (New Delhi: Orient Longman, 1979), p. 266.

2. Saqi Must'ad Khan, *Ma'asir-i Alamgiri*, edited by Jadunath Sarkar (Calcutta: Royal Asiatic Society of Bengal, 1947), pp. 255, 278, 295.

3. J. S. Grewal and Irfan Habib, eds, *Sikh History from Persian Sources: Translations of Major Texts* (New Delhi: Tulika/Indian History Congress, 2001), p. 113 n. 14.

4. Sri Ram Sharma, *The Religious Policy of the Mughal Emperors* (Bombay: Asia Publishing House, 1962, 2nd edn), p. 146 n. 79. Chetan Singh, *Region and Emperor: Panjab in the Seventeenth Century* (Delhi: Oxford University Press, 1994), p. 300 n. 129.

5. Sainapat, *Sri Gur Sobha*, edited by Shamsher Singh Ashok (Amritsar: Shiromani Gurdwara Prabandhak Committee, 1967), pp. 56–82.

6. Bhai Svarup Singh Kaushish, *Guru Kian Sakhian*, edited by Piara Singh Padam (Amritsar: Singh Brothers, 1999 [1986]), sakhis 66–72, 75, 78.

7. Sukha Singh, *Gurbilas Patsahi 10*, edited by Gursharan Kaur Jaggi (Patiala: Bhasha Vibhag, Punjab, 1989), pp. 186–380.

8. Sainapat, *Sri Gur Sobha*, pp. 56–7.

9. Sainapat, *Sri Gur Sobha*, pp. 57–9.

10. Sainapat, *Sri Gur Sobha*, pp. 60–2.

11. Koer Singh, *Gurbilas Patshahi 10*, edited by Shamsher Singh Ashok (Patiala: Punjabi University, 1968), pp. 140–4.

12. Koer Singh, *Gurbilas*, pp. 144–59.

13. Koer Singh, *Gurbilas*, pp. 160–9.

14. Kaushish, *Guru Kian Sakhian*, pp. 130–6.

15. Sukha Singh, *Gurbilas*, pp. 197–9.

16. Sukha Singh, *Gurbilas*, pp. 200–39.

17. Sainapat, *Sri Gur Sobha*, p. 62.

18. Sainapat, *Sri Gur Sobha*, pp. 63–9.

19. Kaushish, *Guru Kian Sakhian*, pp. 136–7.

20. Kaushish, *Guru Kian Sakhian*, pp. 138–41.

21. Sukha Singh, *Gurbilas*, pp. 265–72.

22. Sainapat, *Sri Gur Sobha*, pp. 70–4.

23. Kaushish, *Guru Kian Sakhian*, pp. 141–2.

24. Kaushish, *Guru Kian Sakhian*, p. 148.

25. Sainapat, *Sri Gur Sobha*, pp. 75–6.

26. Sainapat, *Sri Gur Sobha*, pp. 76–7.

27. Sainapat, *Sri Gur Sobha*, pp. 77–82.

28. Koer Singh, *Gurbilas*, pp. 178–89.

29. Koer Singh, *Gurbilas*, pp. 190–1.

30. Kesar Singh Chhibber, 'Bansavalinama Dasan Patshahian Ka', edited by Rattan Singh Jaggi, in *Parkh*, vol. 2, edited by S. S. Kohli (Chandigarh: Panjab University, 1972), pp. 148–50.

31. Sarup Das Bhalla, *Mahima Prakash*, edited by Gobind Singh Lamba and Khazan Singh (Patiala: Punjab Languages Department, 1972), part II, pp. 875–6.

32. Kaushish, *Guru Kian Sakhian*, pp. 152–3.

33. Sukha Singh, *Gurbilas*, pp. 287–310.

34. Ratan Singh Bhangu, *Sri Guru Panth Prakash*, edited by Balwant Singh Dhillon (Amritsar: Singh Brothers, 2004), pp. 43–6.

35. Christopher Shackle, *'Zafarnama'*, *Journal of Punjab Studies*, vol. 15, nos. 1 and 2 (Spring–Fall 2008): 172, 179, n. 48.

9

Negotiations with Aurangzeb
(1705–7)

After capturing the great forts of the Marathas before the end
of 1704, Aurangzeb began the siege of Wagingara, a stronghold
of the Berads, enclosed by the Krishna and the Bhima Rivers,
in February 1705. The fort was conquered towards the end
of April. Aurangzeb retreated to Ahmadnagar on 20 January
1706, but his retreat did not bring rest to his army or peace to the
empire. A vast Maratha army under all their great generals
appeared at 6 *kos* from the imperial encampment. On 20
February 1707, the emperor went through his morning prayers and
began to count his beads. Gradually, unconsciousness crept in, and
he died.[1]

The Sikh writers talk of the battle of Chamkaur, the martyrdom
of the four sons of Guru Gobind Singh, his disguise, his letter to
Aurangzeb and the emperor's response, the battle of Muktsar, his
stay at Damdama (Talwandi Sabo), his journey towards the South
through Rajasthan, the battle of Bagore, the news of Aurangzeb's
death, and Guru Gobind Singh's march towards Delhi with the
idea of meeting Bahadur Shah as Aurangzeb's successor. Guru
Gobind Singh's concern for a peaceful settlement with regard to
Anandpur appears to run through this phase of over two and a
half years.

From Anandpur to Dina-Kangar

Sainapat states that Guru Gobind Singh left Anandpur, like all other people. The Rajas of the hills and the Mughal commanders followed them. They stopped near Shahi Tibbi, close to Nirmoh, and Udai Singh (son of Bhai Mani Singh) challenged them; he fought for three hours and died fighting. Guru Gobind Singh continued his march and came to a garden outside the village of Chamkaur. Its zamindar requested the Guru to occupy his haveli in the village. The Guru went into the village. The zamindar informed the authorities.[2]

The troops of the hill chiefs and the Mughals laid siege to the village. Guru Gobind Singh had with him only a small number of Singhs. They were sent out one by one to die fighting. The Singh warriors used the sword, the dagger, the spear, the bow, and the musket with great effect. Sahibzada Ajit Singh (also called Ranjit Singh or Jit Singh) fought valiantly and killed many of the enemy, using his bow, spear, and sword. He drank the cup of love and Guru Gobind Singh remarked that he had proved to be a true Khalsa. Sahibzada Jujhar Singh killed a number of Pathans with his arrows, spear, and sword. Zorawar Singh (an adopted son of Guru Gobind Singh) used his arms effectively and was saved by God. Sant Singh took up the sword and engaged the enemy. He died with 'Vaheguru' on his lips. Finally, Guru Gobind Singh rode into the field, killed many of the enemy with his arrows, and left the field unseen.[3]

Koer Singh remains close to Sainapat, but gives more detail. For instance, the zamindar of Chamkaur informed the Raja of Kahlur first and then (the Mughal *faujdar* of) Sirhind. The number of Singhs in Chamkaur is mentioned as 40, while the strength of the Mughal forces is 10 lakh. The names of all the 40 Singhs are given with their sub-castes. The Singhs in general hope to establish Sikh Raj. Sangat Singh and Sant Singh were the last to leave the haveli. Bhai Mani Singh provides more information. At the same time, echoes of Sainapat are loud and clear. An interesting example is Koer Singh's use of the 'cup of love'.[4]

Kesar Singh Chhibber gives about 50 lines to the battle of Chamkaur, based on some different source. Guru Gobind Singh fought his way to Ropar before moving on to Chamkaur. Apart from Ajit Singh and Jujhar Singh, a few other warriors are named: Chandan Rao, Sangat Rai, Gulab Singh, and Sango Singh. They who die fighting in the battle go to heaven. All the 40 Singhs who died at Chamkaur came to be remembered as *mukte*. Guru Gobind Singh was accompanied by four men when he left Chamkaur for Machhiwara. Two of them were Singhs and two Sahajdhari Sikhs. They mixed with the 'Turks', shouting 'Hindu *bhaga*, Hindu bhaga' (The Hindu has fled). Four or five other Sikhs joined the Guru later.[5]

Sarup Das Bhalla talks only of the departure of Guru Gobind Singh from the 'fort' of Chamkaur. Ghani Khan and Nabi Khan took him to Machhiwara, dressed as the '*Pir* of Uch'. There, Guru Gobind Singh gave them a *hukamnama* addressed to the Sikhs, asking them to help the holders of the hukamnama. Their descendants were receiving thousands of rupees as *bhet* from the Sikhs in the time of Sarup Das Bhalla.[6]

Four *sakhi*s of the *Guru Kian Sakhian* relate to what happened immediately on Guru Gobind Singh leaving Anandpur, the battle of Chamkaur, the way in which the Guru left it, and the death of Bachittar Singh at Kotla Nihang. Udai Singh had fought near Shahi Tibbi till early morning to become a martyr. His head was cut off by Raja Ajmer Chand of Kahlur and was sent to Ropar, with the claim that he had killed Guru Gobind Singh. The hill Rajas returned to their homes, beating the drums of victory. Bachittar Singh fought on the bank of a stream called Sarsa, and all his companions were killed, including Bhai Jiwan Singh (a Ranghreta). Bachittar Singh went towards Ropar and was wounded in a fight with the Mughal troops. He managed to reach Kotla Nihang where Guru Gobind Singh happened to be at that time. Bachittar Singh died at Kotla Nihang after the Guru had left it for Chamkaur.[7]

The zamindar of Chamkaur, Chaudhari Buddi Raut, invited Guru Gobind Singh to stay at his haveli along with his Sikhs. Nahar Khan of Malerkotla marched against Chamkaur with the Mughal army. He was killed by an arrow shot by Guru Gobind Singh. Zorawar Singh (the adopted son of Guru Gobind Singh) fought his way out to Kotla Nihang where he had stayed in the house of Bagga Singh, a carpenter. Only Sant Singh and Sangat Singh were left with Guru

Gobind Singh. According to the *Guru Kian Sakhian*, Sant Singh was dressed in the Guru's clothes, with his *jigha* and *kalghi*, because of his resemblance with the Guru. Both of them were to fight unto death. Guru Gobind Singh left Chamkaur with Ghani Khan and Nabi Khan who were related to Chaudhari Nihang Khan of Kotla Nihang.[8]

Sukha Singh's account of the battle of Chamkaur remains close to the one given by Koer Singh in its broad outline and much of its detail. It is important to note that Sukha Singh places the evacuation of Anandpur (and consequently the battle of Chamkaur) in 1704, and looks upon the battle as *dharamyudh*.[9]

Linked closely with the battle of Chamkaur was the martyrdom of the younger Sahibzadas. Indeed, for Sainapat, it was a part of the battle of Chamkaur. In the last attack on Chamkaur, the Sahibzadas (Zorawar Singh and Fateh Singh) were captured by the enemy and taken to Sirhind. Zorawar Singh gave curt replies to all questions, and both the Sahibzadas went to God's abode. 'Praise be to the sons of the Guru,' says Sainapat, 'who did not care for their bodily existence, and gave up life in a manner manifest to the whole world'.[10]

In the account given by Koer Singh, Mata Gujari was in the *garhi* (fortress) after Guru Gobind Singh had left it. She was worried about the two younger Sahibzadas and went out in search of them. She was identified by some 'Turks'. They went into the garhi and saw one Sikh with the jigha and kalghi of Guru Gobind Singh. They killed him and claimed that they had killed Guru Gobind Singh. They took Mata Gujari and the younger Sahibzadas to Sirhind. They offered what they regarded as the most tempting offers, but the Sahibzadas did not care for them. They were asked to accept Islam, but they refused to do so. The Puri Khatri (Sucha Nand), Diwan of Sirhind, suggested their execution. A Pathan stood up in favour of the innocent children. But the Sahibzadas were bricked alive. The earth parted to serve as the final resting place of Mata Gujari.[11]

Kesar Singh Chhibber is very brief. Mata Gujari and the younger Sahibzadas (Zorawar Singh, aged nine years, and Fateh Singh, aged seven) were taken to Sirhind as prisoners, and Sucha Nand, a Puri Khatri relative of the Sahi Khatris of Lahore, got the Sahibzadas killed as potential traitors to the Mughal emperor. Mata Gujari took poison and died.[12] Earlier in his work, Chhibber mentions that Mata Gujari and the younger Sahibzadas had lost their way in the darkness of the night. They fell into the hands of some 'Ranghars' and 'Turks' who took them to Sirhind to be handed over to Wazir Khan. There, they were imprisoned.[13]

According to Sarup Das Bhalla, the people leaving Anandpur were attacked by the allied troops for plunder. The younger Sahibzadas got separated and lost their way. The Ranghars of a certain village reported to the officials of the government and they were taken to the *subadar* (actually, faujdar) of Sirhind whose intentions were not good. A Pathan of Malerkotla said that the Sahibzadas were innocent and it would be unjust to punish them. But Sucha Nand said that they would grow up to be refractory. When asked to salute the faujdar (called subadar), they indeed said that they saluted only the true king. The faujdar ordered the executioners to behead them. The *dehura*s of the Sahibzadas were there now. Bhalla adds that when 'Mata Sahib Devi' heard of their death, she fell from the tower and died. Her dehura was also there.[14]

Sukha Singh states at the outset that a Brahman had misguided Mata (Gujari) and taken her and the younger Sahibzadas to his village. He betrayed them to the enemy. An armed force took them to Sirhind. The curt replies of Zorawar Singh angered those low creatures. The Brahman mentioned above was a masand. It was near Ropar that Mata Gujari, Sahibzada Zorawar Singh, and Sahibzada Fateh Singh lost their way, and that butcher of a man took them to his place of residence. He was a greedy wretch. He deprived them of the cash they had and thought of getting a reward from the government by betraying them. The Sahibzadas were asked to show their submission by salutation (*taslim*), but Zorawar Singh said that they bowed only to the Lord of the universe. Sucha Nand said that they were the offsprings of a cobra, full of venom from head to foot. Despite the pleading of a Pathan, they were beheaded. Mata Gujari deliberately took poison and died. The accursed Brahman died due to his greed, shorn of all wealth.[15]

After leaving Chamkaur, Guru Gobind Singh became 'Ek Onkar' (one God), having abandoned wealth, a place of residence, sons, relatives, and spouse in a state of *nirban* (liberation). He began creation all afresh. He came to the country of the Brars, and all the Singhs came there for his *darshan*. He encamped near a large pool. His enemies found out where he was and came with a large army. But they left the field of battle in the hands of the Singhs. Guru Gobind Singh thought of writing to Aurangzeb.[16] The reference here is to the *Zafarnama*.

After leaving Chamkaur, Guru Gobind Singh, according to Koer Singh, composed the *chhand* starting with, 'To the beloved friend we talk of the state of his *murids*'. Nabi Khan and Ghani Khan were escorting him. The Guru wanted to give them a hukamnama, but they said that they had served the Guru in the name of God. Guru Gobind Singh told them that his hukamnama addressed to the Sikhs would be of great help to them under the Sikh rule, which was bound to be established. They understood the value of the hukamnama and accepted it with gratitude. The Guru stayed at Kangar in the Malwa *des* (country) for a considerable time (see Map 9.1). The Sikhs of Brar des became Khalsa in his *darbar*. Sikh *sangat*s used to come to Kangar every day. It was at Kangar that Guru Gobind Singh thought of writing the *Zafarnama* to be sent to Aurangzeb.[17]

Kesar Singh Chhibber says that Guru Gobind Singh went from Dina to Muktsar. There too came the 'Turks', and Guru Gobind Singh went to Kangar where he composed 1400 couplets of the *Zafarnama*.[18]

Sarup Das Bhalla makes a clear statement about Nabi Khan and Ghani Khan taking Guru Gobind Singh from Chamkaur to Machhiwara in the blue garb of the Pir of Uch, carrying his bed (*palang*) through the bazaar of the Lashkar. They reached Machhiwara in the evening. Nabi Khan and Ghani Khan received two studded bangles of gold from the Guru, and asked for a hukamnama addressed to the Sikhs in their favour. Bhalla adds that the descendants of Nabi Khan and Ghani Khan were receiving thousands of rupees in bhet. On the way from Machhiwara to Kot Kapura, Guru Gobind Singh stayed at a number of places, but no mention is made of Dina or Kangar. In fact, no reference is made to the *Zafarnama*.[19]

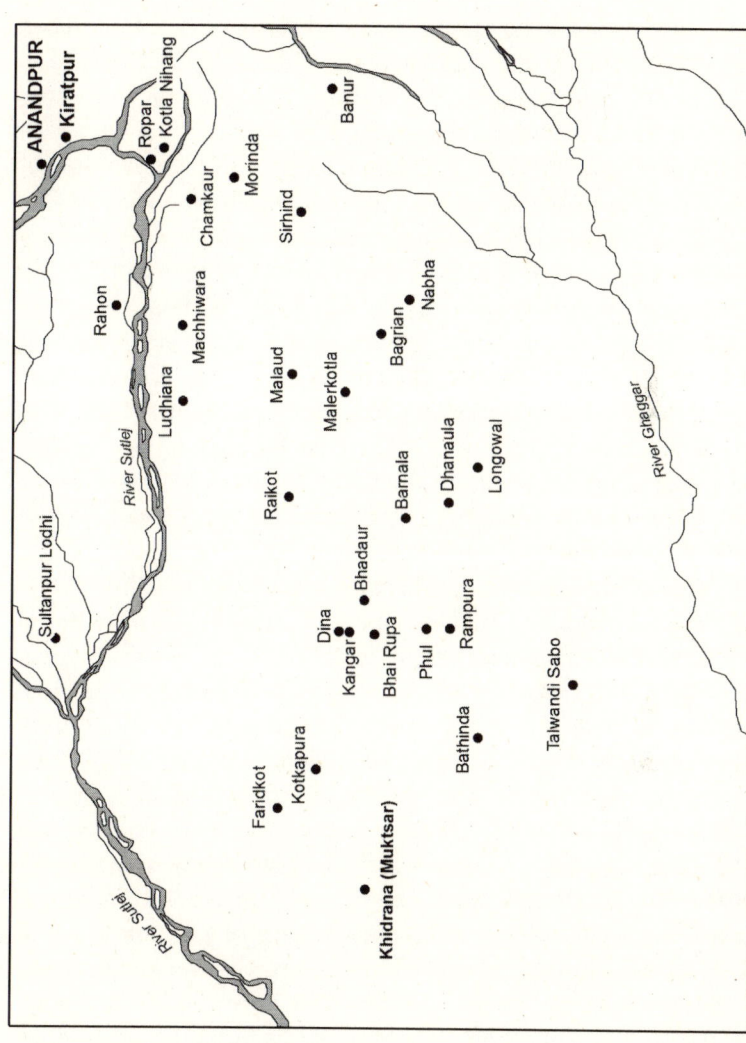

Map 9.1 The Malwa region
Source: Courtesy of the author.

In the *Guru Kian Sakhian*, Guru Gobind Singh's journey from
Machhiwara to Dina as the Pir of Uch is given in some detail.
The places where he stayed even for a short time are mentioned:
Ajmer, Kanech, Alamgir, Hehar, and Raikot. At Kanech, Haji
Charag Shah was a local pir. Guru Gobind Singh asked him to call
Chaudhari Fateh Chand, who knew the Guru. When Charag Shah
asked him to spare his mare, he said that it was not at his house.
When the Chaudhari returned home, he found the mare dead. At
Hehar, there was the *dera* of Mahant Kripal Das who had fought
in the battle of Bhangani on the Guru's side. The Mahant showed
great respect and served Guru Gobind Singh well. At Raikot, Guru
Gobind Singh told Rai Kallah that he would continue to rule over
his principality as long as he preserved the gifts given to him by
the Guru.[20]

In Sukha Singh's *Gurbilas*, Ghani Khan and Nabi Khan come to
the help of Guru Gobind Singh. They knew the Guru. They used
a *palaki* for carrying him to Machhiwara and then to other places
before they reached the des of the Brars. At Kanech, Guru Gobind
Singh wrote the hukamnama for them. The Pathans and Sayyids
who had been with them now returned to their homes. The Sikhs
of the Brar des became Khalsa. Bhai Dharam Singh and Bhai Param
Singh came for the Guru's darshan at Kangar. The decision to kill
the emperor was also taken there.[21]

In Ratan Singh Bhangu's account, the exodus from Anandpur
started in an orderly manner, with armed Singhs moving in front
and guarding both sides of the procession. The first stream was
in flood. Hard-pressed by the hill people at the rear, the people of
Anandpur followed their own inclination to seek safety. The elder
Sahibzadas remained with the Guru, but the younger Sahibzadas
and Mata Gujari got separated from them. Guru Gobind Singh went
towards Ropar, but he found no support. He was welcome at Kotla,
but there was no fortified place there. Guru Gobind Singh moved
to Chamkaur and occupied the fortified haveli of its zamindar.
The Pathans of Malerkotla surrounded Chamkaur. Nahar Khan
was killed in the field. Khuaja Khizar and Wazir Khan joined the
battle. The hill people also joined them. But the haveli did not
fall. Jujhar Singh and Zorawar Singh [sic] killed many Pathans
before they became martyrs. Guru Gobind Singh decided to give

Guruship to the Khalsa. He gave his dress and kalghi to Sant Singh and instructed him to die fighting. Sant Singh sat like the Guru and, thus, the true Guru gave *patshahi* to the Singhs.[22]

Bhangu goes on to say that Ghani Khan's brother (Nabi Khan) came to the Guru's help in a critical situation. When they came out of the haveli, they saw watchmen there. Guru Gobind Singh shouted '*Bhagio Hindu*' (the Hindu has fled). All the people who heard this came out shouting 'gone, gone, gone'. The Guru also did this and escaped through the crowd. On the way, they met a cattle-herd who recognized Guru Gobind Singh and threatened to disclose his identity. The Guru felt obliged to kill him. When they reached Machhiwara, the Pathan went into the town and brought Gulaba, a Khatri, with him. Guru Gobind Singh stayed in his haveli for 10 days. On one of these days, he got a goat slaughtered and cooked. When he ate the mutton, he threw the bones into the house of a Muslim neighbour. In order to keep him quiet, the Guru threw coins into his house. Dressed as a Haji and called 'Uch *ka* Pir', Guru Gobind Singh moved to the village Kanech. There, he asked Fatta, a former masand, to give him his mare for money. But he refused, saying, 'I do not wish to get hanged.'

'Get hanged you will all the same,' said the Guru. Fatta got hanged at Lahore. Passing through Sarai Doraha, Mohi, and Jatpura, the 'Uch ka Pir' reached the village Dina in Tappa Kangar. Rai Lakhmir (the Chaudhari of the Tappa) expressed his utter devotion to Guru Gobind Singh, who discarded his garb and the Sikhs began to come for his darshan.[23]

In Bhangu's story, Mata Gujari and her younger grandsons were separated from Guru Gobind Singh near Ropar. A Brahman cook from the village Saheri took them to his village. Tempted to misappropriate Mata Gujari's wealth, he asked the Ranghars of Morinda to take him to the Nawab (Wazir Khan) to get a reward for handing over to him the sons of Guru Gobind Singh. Jani and Mani, the Ranghar brothers, took the Sahibzadas to Wazir Khan. Sucha Nand advised Wazir Khan to get the snakes (the Sahibzadas) killed to make himself safe from their bite. Sher Muhammad of Malerkotla, whose brother Nahar Khan had been killed at Chamkaur, was strongly opposed to the idea. The Sahibzadas were told to accept

Islam, but they refused and were slaughtered. Mata Gujari fell from the tower and died.[24] Guru Gobind Singh wrote:

> To the Beloved Friend the state of his devotees is submitted. To lie under a quilt is painful like a disease, and to live in mansions is like living with cobras. The pot of wine is a cross and the cup of wine a dagger. (To remain away from you) is to bear a thrust of the crooked knife of the butcher. Far better for us is the bare earth (to sit with the Friend) than to live in a habitation.[25]

The *Zafarnama*

According to Sainapat, Guru Gobind Singh thought of writing to Aurangzeb after the victory of the Singhs in the battle near the pool (of Khidrana). The duty of carrying this document was entrusted to Daya Singh with the instruction that it should be delivered to Aurangzeb personally. Disguised as an Ahadi, Daya Singh had five other Singhs with him. The Sikh sangat in Delhi gave him money for his travel expenses. Passing through Agra, Gwalior, Ujjain, Burhanpur, and Aurangabad, he reached Ahmadnagar. There, he stayed with Jeth Singh for the night and went to the *dharamsal* in the morning. The purpose of Daya Singh's visit was discussed by the sangat and the matter was seriously taken up. But there was some opposition too, and Daya Singh's efforts did not bring about the desired effect. He sent a message to Guru Gobind Singh to seek his aid. The Guru sent five orders. Consequently, the letter was delivered to Aurangzeb.[26]

Guru Gobind Singh told Aurangzeb that all his men had broken their promise and attacked (the Guru and his followers). Many Rajas and Rais had entered the battle. There was now a great burden over Aurangzeb's head, and he was accountable to God. A man of God keeps his promise and means what he says. Aurangzeb was expected to discharge his duty without delay. He should send a *farman* so that Guru Gobind Singh could meet him personally, marching through various provinces with a thousand horsemen. Aurangzeb sent a farman with a *gurz-bardar* (mace bearer), giving freedom to Guru Gobind Singh to go wherever he liked. Guru Gobind Singh started for the South.[27]

Writing at about the same time as Sainapat, Sewadas gives a different account of the *Zafarnama*. He links it with the martyrdom of Guru Tegh Bahadur. The Sikhs were mourning his death. Guru Gobind Singh told them that life and death on earth made no difference to Guru Tegh Bahadur who was *nirankar* (the formless one) in life and after death. It was wrong to mourn for him. His objective had been to expose the falsehood of the 'Turks'. Now, it was the turn of the Sikhs to destroy the 'Turks'. Guru Tegh Bahadur had given no offence to Aurangzeb, but he killed him because of his own religious bias. The Khalsa should fight the 'Turks' now to destroy them. The Khalsa said that the 'Turks' commanded 10 lakhs of cavalry. The Guru said that he would kill the 'Turk' by writing a letter. He wrote a letter to Aurangzeb. It was called the *Zafarnama*.[28]

Sewadas proposed to give only the essence of the letter and not its detail. The Guru wrote many couplets and quatrains, and many sakhis of kings. He wrote something about himself too. God had given kingship to Aurangzeb to do justice, but he had done gross injustice to the Guru. First of all, he had killed the Guru's father, Guru Tegh Bahadur, who had done nothing wrong. Then, he sent armies against the Guru, joining hands with the hill Rajas. They too were unjust, like the emperor. The combined forces of the 'Turks' and the Rajas killed the Guru's sons and the women of his household. His property was plundered. All this happened because the emperor was unjust. God would ask the emperor about his misdeeds and if no satisfactory answer is given, he would be sent to hell. A king and a worm are equal in the divine court. In fact, God responded to the worm's complaint first, and the king was heard only afterwards. Injustice on the part of a king was unpardonable.[29]

Aurangzeb was told in no uncertain terms that he possessed no merit that could save him from punishment. If he thought that his hard labour to subsist on barley would save him, he was mistaken. Even horses laboured hard and lived on barley, but acquired no spiritual merit. If he thought that he would be forgiven because he used to read the Qur'an regularly, he was mistaken. Merely the reading of the scripture without any good deeds to one's credit did not lead to redemption. If he believed that his *bandagi* would save him, he was mistaken because real bandagi was not in reciting a few traditions of the Prophet but in controlling one's egoistic and earthly desires. Aurangzeb had killed his father and brothers to gratify his own earthly ambition. This was no bandagi. To obey the commandments of the Prophet was meritorious. He who loved earthly things was dubbed by the Prophet as a dog. Aurangzeb called himself an idol-breaker, but he had failed to stop idol-worship. If anything, idol-worship had increased. Therefore, he could not claim any merit on this account either. To break oneself, and to control the self, was true idol-breaking. Similarly, to follow the *shari'at* had no intrinsic merit. Even if people praised him, he could not be forgiven. Finally, if he banked on the mercy of God, he was mistaken because God was merciful only to those who had shown mercy to others. Aurangzeb had no such merit.[30]

According to Sewadas, Aurangzeb was informed that the Khalsa had been created as the real idol-breaker to take revenge. The emperor asked Daya Singh whether the Khalsa had indeed been created. Daya Singh said, 'Yes, the Khalsa has come into existence.' Aurangzeb's face turned pale, and he died.[31]

Koer Singh repeats nearly all the hypothetical assumptions attributed to Aurangzeb by Sewadas, along with their refutation, but places them in a different context. Guru Gobind Singh stayed at Kangar for a considerable length of time and the Sikhs, especially the Brars, flocked to him to take *pahul* of the double-edged sword. The Guru suggested that the Khalsa could now destroy the Turk. They responded by pointing to the huge army of the emperor. Then, the Guru wrote a letter to Aurangzeb. It was known as the *Zafarnama*. It consisted of 12 *hikayat*s (stories) about kings and the *'umara* (nobles). The Guru charged the emperor with a false oath on the Qur'an, followed by the evacuation of Anandpur and the battle of Chamkaur. Aurangzeb had done gross injustice to the Guru and was bound to receive punishment in the divine court. It was still open to him to see the Guru at Kangar with 1000 horsemen to have talks and resolve all issues. The letter called *Bijaynama* (Epistle of Victory) referred to these matters.[32]

Koer Singh's account of how Daya Singh carried the letter to Aurangzeb and gave it to him personally after facing some difficulty remains very close to the account given by Sainapat. According to Koer Singh, Aurangzeb himself helped Daya Singh to meet him because, in his dream, he was told by Guru Gobind Singh to receive the *Zafarnama*. Daya Singh was armed with five weapons when he went into the presence of the emperor and greeted him with '*Vaheguru ji ki fateh*' (Victory of God). He placed the order (*hukam*) of Guru Gobind Singh before Aurangzeb. On reading the *Zafarnama*, his face went pale. He never recovered from the shock and died within a month.[33] At this time, Guru Gobind Singh was marching through Rajasthan to meet Aurangzeb. Daya Singh met him near Bagore and gave him an account of Aurangzeb's death on reading the *Zafarnama*.[34]

Kesar Singh Chhibber's account of the *Zafarnama* is different from the accounts considered so far. In his account, the *Zafarnama*, written at Kangar after the battle of Muktsar, consisted of 1,400 couplets. To carry the *Zafarnama* to Aurangzeb involved great risk, even the risk of life. Daya Singh, mentioned as a munshi, volunteered himself. He was instructed to give the *Zafarnama* personally to Aurangzeb. In the guise of a haji, Daya Singh placed the *Zafarnama* over his head as if it were a copy of the Qur'an. As a well-read munshi, he could argue with the Muftis and the mullas. He was easily admitted into the presence of the emperor as a haji who had brought a copy of the Qur'an from Mecca. Aurangzeb received the document with reverence, kissed it, and placed it over his eyes and forehead, showing great respect. On reading the *Zafarnama*, his face became pale, realizing that he had kissed the book of a Hindu. He died while reading the *Zafarnama*. Chhibber introduces here a mythical anecdote of a supernatural character to demonstrate Guru Gobind Singh's spiritual superiority over Aurangzeb. When the emperor wanted to know if the Khalsa had been created, Daya Singh said, 'Yes.' Aurangzeb asked again if this was true. Daya Singh said, 'A Khalsa is standing before you.' Aurangzeb said, 'I shall kill it.' But he died within 40 days.[35]

According to Sarup Das Bhalla, Guru Gobind Singh told Daya Singh to deliver his letter to Aurangzeb and bring back his reply. Daya Singh was instructed to go fully armed into the presence of the emperor and greet him with '*Guru ki fateh*' and not '*salam*'. It took him many days to arrive at the emperor's gate. There, he insisted that he would not handover the documents to the *chobdar* (mace bearer) but deliver it personally to the emperor. The chobdar told Aurangzeb that a messenger from Guru Gobind Singh was insisting at the gate to see the emperor for favourable orders. The chobdar was told to bring in the messenger. Daya Singh went in, greeted Aurangzeb with *'Guru ki fateh'*, and handed over the *Zafarnama* to him. On reading the document, he felt the fear of God. He went into the palace in a sad state. The ladies of the palace asked him why he was so morose, and he told them that the letter of Guru Gobind Singh had created a difficult situation for him. The Guru was asking for four *'lals'* (sons). 'Nur Jahan' offered to spare four *'lals'* (rubies) from her necklace. The emperor explained that the Guru was asking for his four sons who had become martyrs, two of them on the field of battle and two at the hands of the executioner. The *begam* kept quiet. The emperor could not sleep during the night. On the following day, he called Daya Singh to the court and said that he had seen the Guru in a dream. Symbolic of his personal regard for the Guru, the emperor thought of sending for him a garment with a grey hair of the emperor. Aurangzeb's health began to deteriorate, and he died. Daya Singh returned to the Guru and related the whole story.[36]

Sarup Singh Kaushish states that Guru Gobind Singh wrote his letter to Aurangzeb from Dina-Kangar in response to the emperor's letter he had received at Anandpur before its evacuation. The lines quoted from the *Zafarnama* indicate that Kaushish was familiar with its text. After a few couplets in praise of God, Guru Gobind Singh related his story (*dastan*). The *Zafarnama* was sent to Aurangzeb through Daya Singh and Dharam Singh, both of them in the guise of Ahadis. They left Dina-Kangar for the South.[37] Meanwhile, Guru Gobind Singh had reached Talwandi Sabo and decided to stay there to wait for news from Daya Singh and Dharam Singh.[38] There was no news for five months. Then, Bhai Dharam Singh and Desa Singh came to Talwandi Sabo with a letter from Daya Singh. They submitted that they had failed to see Aurangzeb despite great effort. Guru Gobind Singh wrote five orders and handed them over to Dharam Singh. They returned to Ahmadnagar.[39] Bhai Daya Singh, Dharam Singh, Shiv Singh, and Desa Singh could now meet Aurangzeb, and he listened to them very attentively. On hearing the *Zafarnama*, he nodded his head several times and said that the administrators in Delhi had kept him in the dark. Otherwise, a God-loving person such as Guru Gobind Singh would not have been treated so badly. He told his munshi that, as desired by the Guru, he would meet him personally and help him. He issued a farman on a copy of the Qur'an and sent it to Delhi with the Qazi of the empire. He was accompanied by two gurz-bardars. Having an inkling that Aurangzeb's end was near, Guru Gobind Singh left Talwandi Sabo for the South with the idea that he would meet Daya Singh and Dharam Singh on his way.[40] They met the Guru in Rajasthan near Bagore and informed him of the action taken by Aurangzeb on the *Zafarnama*. Guru Gobind Singh smiled and said that the emperor would not survive meeting the Guru. After his death, Guru Gobind Singh saw no point in going any further.[41]

The account of the *Zafarnama* given by Sukha Singh is so close to what we find in the works of Sewadas and Koer Singh that there seems to be no need to give any detail.[42] Ratan Singh Bhangu refers to the *ba'its* written at Dina in which Guru Gobind Singh said something about his war (with the hill chiefs and the Mughal faujdars) and gave some advice (to the Mughal emperor). Daya Singh took these ba'its to Aurangzeb, who died before he had heard the whole composition.[43] Bhangu does not use the term '*Zafarnama*', or any other term for the ba'its.

A *hasb al-hukm* of Aurangzeb to Mun'im Khan, the *naib* subadar of Lahore, throws further light on the situation. It refers to a petition (*arzdasht*) received from Guru Gobind Singh for the issuance of an imperial order in his favour. The emperor had granted a farman. It was being sent to Mun'im Khan with Muhammad, the mace-bearer, and Yar Muhammad, the mansabdar. Mun'im Khan was to give Guru Gobind Singh assurance, to summon him to his presence, and to send a trustworthy person to convey him to the imperial court, along with the mace-bearer and the mansabdar.[44] This confirms the statement made by Sainapat.

Furthermore, a hasb al-hukm sent to Wazir Khan, the faujdar of Sirhind, repeats the content of the order to Mun'im Khan and adds:

Whenever the said Gobind reaches the environs of Sirhind, [Wazir Khan] should provide him with an escort to let him pass through the limits of his own jurisdiction. Should he express some fears, either in absentia or on personal appearance, he should reassure him. Should he solicit expenses for the journey, he should be given money, in accordance with the requirements, out of his effects that [Wazir Khan] has seized from him.[45]

In retrospect, we can see that soon after the death of Guru Gobind Singh, two very different versions of the *Zafarnama* were presented by Sainapat and Sewadas, the former stating that Aurangzeb responded by sending a farman with a mace-bearer, and the latter talking of Aurangzeb's death on reading the *Zafarnama*. Most of our writers refer to the *Zafarnama* as causing the death of Aurangzeb immediately on, or shortly after, reading it. Koer Singh introduced the element that Daya Singh, and his companions, went fully armed into the presence of Aurangzeb and greeted him with '*Vaheguru ji ki fateh*'. He also refers to the *Zafarnama* as consisting of 12 hikayats. There are some other minor variants. On the whole, all the writers give due importance to the *Zafarnama* as a work of Guru Gobind Singh.[46]

From Dina-Kangar to Talwandi Sabo (Damdama)

Koer Singh states that Guru Gobind Singh went to Kot Kapura to see the country of the Brars. He was well served by Kapura. When Guru Gobind Singh asked him to hand over the fort (*kot*) so that he was able to destroy the *mlechh*, Kapura did not like the suggestion because it would amount to revolting against the Mughal emperor. 'You want to ruin me,' he said, 'I treated you well as a guest.' He was ruined later due to the Guru's displeasure.[47]

Guru Gobind Singh went to Muktsar. Kapura informed the Mughal authorities of it. Armed forces came from Sirhind. The emperor also sent his army. Guru Gobind Singh was now supported by the Singhs who had disowned him at Anandpur. They fought for about four hours to repulse the enemy. Most of the Singhs who had joined Guru Gobind Singh at the time of the battle died fighting to redeem themselves. They became *mukta*s, the liberated ones. The pool near which the battle was fought was now called 'Mukt Sarovar' or Muktsar. A shahidganj was built at the place of martyrdom of the redeemed Singhs. The merit of bathing at Muktsar was no less than that of bathing in *amritsar* at Ramdaspur.[48]

Guru Gobind Singh crossed the 'Lakhi Jungle' to go to Talwandi Sabo. On the way, he came across a wilderness with an abundance of lions, pigs, *nilgao*s, and deer. It took him three days to cross the wilderness. He came upon the fort of Bathinda which was originally built during the *satjug*. At Talwandi Sabo, Dalla and other Brar sardars of varying importance had Guru Gobind Singh's darshan. The place where Guru Gobind Singh used to give open darshan came to be known as 'Damdama'. There were two *sarovar*s there, known as 'Gurusar' and 'Jandiana'. At another spot, Guru Gobind Singh planted his pen (*kalam*) to make the Guru's Kashi [a centre of Sikh learning] manifest. Talwandi Sabo was meant to be an eminent place for Sikh learning and scholarship.[49]

Guru Gobind Singh was happy with the services performed by Dalla and told him thrice to ask for a boon. Dalla asked for (*a*) rain, (*b*) pulse and grain, and (*c*) pulse, grain, and milk. 'Why didn't you ask for rulership?' asked the Guru. Or, he could have asked for a productive territory like Sirhind which yielded 52 crores of *dam*s as the yearly revenue. Guru Gobind Singh went on to remark that the people of the hills were raw; the people of Majha were hard like pieces of stone; and the people of Malwa were mentally unsound. They gave preference to *moth* (pulses) and *bajri* (millets) over rice and wheat. Then the Guru began to talk about the South. Darbari and Gharbari said that the wilderness was better than the South. They mentioned several things in favour of Malwa and its people. But the Guru said that he had to go for the sake of the Khalsa. Preparations were made for Guru Gobind Singh's departure. Koer Singh quotes Sainapat on the majestic appearance of Guru Gobind Singh.[50]

In the *Guru Kian Sakhian*, the Khalsa who had left Anandpur during its last siege now came from Majha on the initiative of Mai Bhag Kaur (Mai Bhago). Their leaders suggested that Guru Gobind Singh could patch up peace with the emperor at any cost. Guru Gobind Singh told them to sign a declaration of their disaffiliation. Only three of them signed this paper. The remaining 37 men and Mai Bhago were unhappy about this situation. Meanwhile, the army of Sirhind came in sight, and the Sikhs of Majha decided to fight. Only three of them survived. They implored the Guru to tear up their letter. This was done before they died. All 40 were declared to be martyrs.[51]

On the invitation of Rai Dalla, Guru Gobind Singh went to Talwandi Sabo and named it Damdama. Mata Sundari and Mata Sahib Devi, who were in Delhi, were brought there. On the Baisakhi of the new year, Sikh sangats converged on Talwandi Sabo. Soon, a sarovar was dug up in 11 days; it was named 'Gurusar'. Waiting for Aurangzeb's reply to the *Zafarnama*, Guru Gobind Singh sent hukamnamas to all Sikh sangats that they could come to Talwandi Sabo. Bhai Mani Singh came from Ramdaspur. Rama and Taloka came from Phul. Five months had passed at Talwandi Sabo when Bhai Dharam Singh and Desa Singh came from the South with a letter from Daya Singh. It said that he had been unable to meet Aurangzeb and needed the Guru's help. Guru Gobind Singh gave them a hukamnama, saying that Daya Singh would now be successful.[52]

Guru Gobind Singh exhorted the Sikhs to take pahul of the double-edged sword. He declared that he would withdraw his support from any Sikh or Sikhni who did not take pahul. Among many others, three important individuals took pahul, personally administered by Guru Gobind Singh: Rai Dalla, the chief of Talwandi Sabo and Rama and Taloka (last two from Phul). Evidently, the epithet 'Singh' was added to their names. They became Dalla Singh, Ram Singh and Talok Singh.[53]

The account of Guru Gobind Singh's activity after leaving Kangar and before leaving Talwandi Sabo, given by Sukha Singh, is close to the one given by Koer Singh. Sukha Singh talks of Kot Kapura, the battle of Khidrana (Muktsar), the great forest crossed by Guru Gobind Singh, the fort of Bathinda, his arrival in Talwandi Sabo, naming it Damdama, the Gurusar, Guru ki Kashi, the message of Daya Singh, and finally his departure from Talwandi Sabo towards Marwar. Rai Dalla figures most prominently in Sukha Singh's account.[54]

In Bhangu's *Sri Gur Panth Prakash*, Guru Gobind Singh is unhappy with Rai Lakhmir who did not eat the Guru's *prasad* because of his fidelity to Sakhi Sarwar. Guru Gobind Singh was also unhappy with Kapura who did not become a Khalsa for fear of the Mughals. He did not wish to be hanged, he said. 'You will surely be hanged,' said the Guru. Kapura was later hanged by Isa Khan Manjh.[55]

The Majhail Singhs who had forsaken Guru Gobind Singh at Anandpur met him in the wilderness (*rohi*) and expressed their wish to be forgiven. Meanwhile, informed by Kapura of Guru Gobind Singh's location, the 'Turks' came from Sirhind to attack him. The Majhail Singhs fought desperately to repulse them. Only two of them were left alive when Guru Gobind Singh arrived at the place. He told them to ask for anything they wanted. On their request, the Guru tore the piece of paper on which they had written their disclaimer.[56]

Guru Gobind Singh went to Talwandi Sabo, which was declared to be the Guru's Kashi to become a centre of learning. Several important Sikhs took pahul to become Khalsa, such as Dalla (the Chaudhari of Talwandi Sabo), Bhai Fateh Singh (the grandson of Bhai Bhagtu), Dharam Singh and Karam Singh (the grandsons of Bhai Rupa), and Ram Singh and Talok Singh (the sons of [Chaudhari] Phul). On a request from the sangat, Guru Gobind Singh prayed for rain. He wanted Malwa to become fertile like (the Sarkar of) Sirhind and to grow sugarcane, wheat, and rice. Dalla Singh said that they were happy with moth and bajri. Guru Gobind Singh did not appreciate this attitude.[57]

On 21 October 1706, Guru Gobind Singh wrote a hukamnama to the *sarbat* (whole) sangat of the Brars to the effect that he had started his journey for the South, and anyone who wished to join him could do so. Four persons are named for sending a bullock each for the Guru (see Image 9.1). Among them was Bhai Dharam Singh of Rupa.[58]

From Talwandi Sabo to Bagore in Rajasthan

Sainapat refers to the preparation made by Guru Gobind Singh's armed Singhs to travel towards Marwar. He presents an impressive picture of Guru Gobind Singh riding a Turki horse with a golden saddle, and wearing a studded necklace and a bright kalghi in his turban. A formal ardas was performed by the *ardasia* of the darbar. Guru Gobind Singh was armed with a bow and arrows, a *barchha*

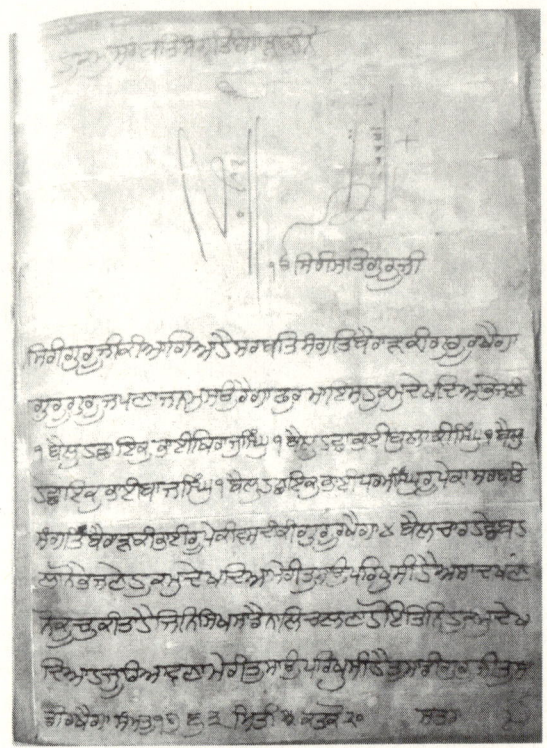

Image 9.1   Guru Gobind Singh's *hukamnama*, dated 21 October 1706, (document 62) addressed to the *sangat* of Bhai Rupa and the Brars. Four persons are mentioned by name to send a bullock each, indicating the importance of the *sangat* of Bhai Rupa. *Source*: Ganda Singh ed., *Hukamname*.

(a large spear), a sword and a shield, and a *jamdhar*. He said farewell with 'Vaheguru ji ki fateh'. The drum was beaten and Guru Gobind Singh left Talwandi Sabo as an image of power.[59]

In the country of the Rajputs, many a Raja came to meet Guru Gobind Singh as he moved on. Among them were great warriors and powerful rulers. On a request from the Singhs and the Sikhs present with him, the Guru agreed to get married and the ceremony was performed. Guru Gobind Singh was near Bagore, associated with Bhim of the *Mahabharat* for killing Kichak (who had misbehaved with Dropadi), when Daya Singh met him with the news of Aurangzeb's death.[60]

Guru Gobind Singh wanted to see Bagore. The people of the city got frightened, thinking that the Guru had halted near the city to attack it. Dharam Singh clarified the position to their leaders and they felt reassured. Guru Gobind Singh started exploring the city and it took him several days. He was encamped in a garden lying on the outskirts of the city. His camels ate the leaves of all the trees and the gardener informed the Rai who owned the garden of this. This led to a serious battle which lasted for more than two days. Sainapat describes the battle in some detail. It is surely of interest, but not an important battle historically. Guru Gobind Singh was victorious and marched towards Shahjahanabad.[61]

In Koer Singh's account, the Rajput Rajas met Guru Gobind Singh as he passed through Rajasthan. Koer Singh refers to the Guru's marriage too. Daya Singh met the Guru and told him of the death of Aurangzeb. Guru Gobind Singh decided to go and watch the war of succession (*sultani jang*). However, he thought of see-ing the sites of Bagore first. A situation arose to result inevitably in battle, which is described in some detail. Thus, the outline and order of events given by Koer Singh is similar to what is given in the *Gur Sobha*. There is one important difference, however. Koer Singh makes it very clear that Guru Gobind Singh was strongly in favour of Prince Mu'azzam (Bahadur Shah).[62]

In the *Guru Kian Sakhian*, Sikh sangats came for the Guru's darshan on the eve of his departure for the South. Among them were Gurbakhsh Singh (the son of Baba Buddha), Bhai Mani Singh, Gurdas Singh, Bhai Dharam Singh of the village Bhai Rupa, and Ram Singh and Talok Singh of Phul. An Akhand Path was arranged. Its merit equaled that of 101 *Asumedh Jaggs* (*Aswamedh yajnas* [horse sacrifice]). Guru Gobind Singh was in Kalait when Bhai Daya Singh and Dharam Singh met him. Near Bagore, the Guru heard the news of Aurangzeb's death. Guru Gobind Singh was victorious in a battle fought with the Sardars of Bagore. After the battle, he marched toward Shahjahanabad.[63]

In Sukha Singh's *Gurbilas*, the first important happening in Rajasthan is Guru Gobind Singh's meeting with the Mahant of Dadu Dwar (Naraina). Their conversation related to the use of physical force by a spiritual leader. After a two-day stay at Dadu Dwar, Guru Gobind Singh marched on. The Rajput Rajas met him

all along the way. Sukha Singh refers to Guru Gobind Singh's marriage. Daya Singh met him on the way. Sometime later, the news of
Aurangzeb's death was received. Guru Gobind Singh made it clear
that he was in favour of Bahadur Shah's succession to the throne,
since he had performed many services for the Guru. To watch the
war of succession (sultani jang), he marched toward Delhi.[64]

Ratan Singh Bhangu says that Guru Gobind Singh heard the
news of Aurangzeb's death at Talwandi Sabo and thought of
going to the South. He asked Dalla Singh to go with him and to
become the ruler of Delhi. Dalla's younger brother remarked that
the Guru would give them a rulership of the kind he had given to
his sons. Guru Gobind Singh said that all his sons had not died,
for the Khalsa were his sons. Having stayed at Talwandi Sabo for
nine months and nine days, Guru Gobind Singh started his march
towards the South. Bhangu points out that four families of Singhs
remained loyal to Guru Gobind Singh: the descendants of Mohan,
Bhagtu, Behlo, and Rupa. Bhangu refers to the *Gurbilas* of Sukha
Singh for details, pointing out that it was an enlarged version of
the narrative of Bhai Mani Singh (Koer Singh's *Gurbilas*).[65]

It can be seen in retrospect that Guru Gobind Singh was in
favour of a peaceful settlement. Aurangzeb gave some kind of
assurance to him at Anandpur. After leaving Anandpur, his first
concern was to pick up the old thread. The *Zafarnama* suggested a
personal meeting between Guru Gobind Singh and Aurangzeb. The
response from the emperor was positive. Guru Gobind Singh left
Talwandi Sabo to march towards the South. He was near Bagore
in Rajasthan when he heard the news of Aurangzeb's death. He
decided to meet Bahadur Shah.

Notes

1. Jadunath Sarkar, *A Short History of Aurangzib (1618–1707)* (New
Delhi: Orient Longman, 1979), pp. 309–21.

2. Sainapat, *Sri Gur Sobha*, edited by Shamsher Singh Ashok (Amritsar:
Shiromani Gurdwara Prabandhak Committee, 1967), pp. 83–5.

3. Sainapat, *Sri Gur Sobha*, pp. 85–94.

4. Koer Singh, *Gurbilas Patshahi 10*, edited by Shamsher Singh Ashok
(Patiala: Punjabi University, 1968), pp. 195–203.

5. Kesar Singh Chhibber, 'Bansavalinama Dasan Patshahian Ka', edited by Rattan Singh Jaggi, in *Parkh*, vol. 2, edited by S. S. Kohli (Chandigarh: Panjab University, 1972), pp. 151–2.

6. Sarup Das Bhalla, *Mahima Prakash*, edited by Gobind Singh Lamba and Khazan Singh (Patiala: Punjab Languages Department, 1972), part II, pp. 879–80.

7. Bhai Svarup Singh Kaushish, *Guru Kian Sakhian*, edited by Piara Singh Padam (Amritsar: Singh Brothers, 1999 [1986]), pp. 152–4, 158.

8. Kaushish, *Guru Kian Sakhian*, pp. 154–7.

9. Sukha Singh, *Gurbilas Patsahi 10*, edited by Gursharan Kaur Jaggi (Patiala: Bhasha Vibhag, Punjab, 1989), pp. 310, 320.

10. Sainapat, *Sri Gur Sobha*, p. 94. Sainapat mistakenly mentions Jujhar Singh instead of Zorawar Singh.

11. Koer Singh, *Gurbilas*, pp. 209–16.

12. Chhibber, *Bansavalinama*, p. 153.

13. Chhibber, *Bansavalinama*, p. 150.

14. Bhalla, *Mahima Prakash*, pp. 877–8.

15. Sukha Singh, *Gurbilas*, pp. 329–34.

16. Sainapat, *Sri Gur Sobha*, pp. 95–7.

17. Koer Singh, *Gurbilas*, pp. 205, 217–18.

18. Chhibber, *Bansavalinama*, p. 153.

19. Bhalla, *Mahima Prakash*, pp. 879–82.

20. Kaushish, *Guru Kian Sakhian*, pp. 159–64.

21. Sukha Singh, *Gurbilas*, pp. 337–43.

22. Ratan Singh Bhangu, *Sri Guru Panth Prakash*, edited by Balwant Singh Dhillon (Amritsar: Singh Brothers, 2004), pp. 46–52.

23. Bhangu, *Sri Guru Panth Prakash*, pp. 52–5.

24. Bhangu, *Sri Guru Panth Prakash*, pp. 55–7.

25. *Sri Dasam-Granth Sahib*, edited by Ratan Singh Jaggi and Gursharan Kaur Jaggi (New Delhi: Gobind Sadan, 1999), part III, p. 354.

26. Sainapat, *Sri Gur Sobha*, pp. 97–8.

27. Sainapat, *Sri Gur Sobha*, pp. 99–100.

28. Kharak Singh and Gurtej Singh, trans. and eds, *Episodes from Lives of the Gurus: Parchian Sewadas* (Chandigarh: Institute of Sikh Studies, 1995), p. 133.

29. *Parchian Sewadas*, p. 133.

30. *Parchian Sewadas*, pp. 133–4.

31. *Parchian Sewadas*, p. 135.

32. Koer Singh, *Gurbilas*, pp. 218–20.

33. Koer Singh, *Gurbilas*, pp. 221–4.

34. Koer Singh, *Gurbilas*, pp. 238–9.

35. Chhibber, *Bansavlinama*, pp. 153–5.

36. Bhalla, *Mahima Parkash*, pp. 886–90.

37. Kaushish, *Guru Kian Sakhian*, p. 165.

38. Kaushish, *Guru Kian Sakhian*, p. 180.

39. Kaushish, *Guru Kian Sakhian*, p. 183.

40. Kaushish, *Guru Kian Sakhian*, pp. 185–6.

41. Kaushish, *Guru Kian Sakhian*, p. 189.

42. Sukha Singh, *Gurbilas*, pp. 343–50, 375–7.

43. Bhangu, *Sri Guru Panth Prakash*, pp. 58–9.

44. J. S. Grewal and Irfan Habib, eds, *Sikh History from Persian Sources: Translations of Major Texts* (New Delhi: Tulika/Indian History Congress, 2001), p. 98.

45. *Sikh History from Persian Sources*, pp. 98–9.

46. See Appendix 9.1 on the *Zafarnama*.

47. Koer Singh, *Gurbilas*, pp. 224–5.

48. Koer Singh, *Gurbilas*, pp. 225–8.

49. Koer Singh, *Gurbilas*, pp. 229–33.

50. Koer Singh, *Gurbilas*, pp. 233–4.

51. Kaushish, *Guru Kian Sakhian*, pp. 170–3.

52. Kaushish, *Guru Kian Sakhian*, pp. 180–3.

53. Kaushish, *Guru Kian Sakhian*, pp. 184–5.

54. Sukha Singh, *Gurbilas*, pp. 350–70.

55. Bhangu, *Sri Guru Panth Prakash*, pp. 59–60.

56. Bhangu, *Sri Guru Panth Prakash*, pp. 60–4.

57. Bhangu, *Sri Guru Panth Prakash*, pp. 65–8.

58. *Hukamname Guru Sahiban, Mata Sahiban, Banda Singh ate Khalsa Ji De*, edited by Ganda Singh (Patiala: Punjabi University, 1967), document 62.

59. Sainapat, *Sri Gur Sobha*, pp. 103–5.

60. Sainapat, *Sri Gur Sobha*, pp. 105–6.

61. Sainapat, *Sri Gur Sobha*, pp. 106–12.

62. Koer Singh, *Gurbilas*, pp. 234–44.

63. Kaushish, *Guru Kian Sakhian*, pp. 186–9.

64. Sukha Singh, *Gurbilas*, pp. 376–7.

65. Bhangu, *Sri Guru Panth Prakash*, pp. 68–9. This is the only piece of external evidence on the issue. It supports the view that Koer Singh had written his *Gurbilas* first to be folloed by the *Gurbilas* of Sukha Singh. See Appendix 1.3.

Appendix 9A

Perspectives on the *Zafarnama*

In an article on the *Zafarnama* of Guru Gobind Singh, written half a century ago, I had suggested that the significance of the *Zafarnama* should be looked for in its ideas and its general argument rather than in the factual information it contained. Guru Gobind Singh took his stand essentially on moral grounds. The officials of Aurangzeb had forced an unjust war on Guru Gobind Singh and had broken their oaths on the Qur'an. If all this was done with the Emperor's approval, then the Emperor could not boast of being a believer of God. He should have remembered the True Lord if he wished Him to remember the Emperor in the life hereafter. By ignoring the dictates of justice, Aurangzeb had shown himself to be a stranger to real statesmanship as well as to God. In possession of immense power, he should not have forgotten that power was entrusted to the ruler for protecting the innocent people and not for spilling their blood. The *Zafarnama* was thus 'the epistle of moral victory'.[1]

Christopher Shackle refers to this article as 'short but magisterial'. It showed 'how little the *Zafarnama* actually adds in the way of hard historical data to the evidence of contemporary Sikh and Mughal sources'.[2] Shackle points out that the *Zafarnama* is one of the very few examples of an Indo-Persian text being regularly reprinted in India, though in an Indian script—the Gurmukhi. He also observes that the *Zafarnama* has become 'effectively compressed within the living tradition' to the single well-known verse 22: 'When matters pass all other means, it is allowed to take up arms'. The style of the *Zafarnama* recalls the Persian poetic models. The *Zafarnama* is the first of the 12 *hikayats* (tales) placed at the end of the *Dasam Granth*. But its tone is quite different from that of the 11 tales which follow. Shackle suggests that the original letter of Guru Gobind Singh was in prose. The present *Zafarnama* appears to have been composed as 'a deliberate literary exercise'. It is an imitation of the *Shahnama* of Firdausi, composed in the same epic metre; it contains a direct allusion to one of the episodes of the *Shahnama*: 'How well had the sweet-tongued Firdausi said: Haste is the devil's work.' The style and language of the *Zafarnama* are aligned with the chief purpose of its contents: appropriation of the values of Islamic kingship to undermine the moral authority of Aurangzeb in its own terms.[3]

In a felicitous and apt rendering of the *Zafarnama* into English, Shackle divides the text informally into five sections: the invocation of God, the loss of Anandpur, the battle of Chamkaur, the address to Aurangzeb, and the conclusion. The first four couplets (*ba'its*) of the invocation read as follows:

> Eternal, gracious, wonderful,
> Kind Comforter, Deliverer,
> Protector, Giver who supports,
> Sustainer who fulfils desires,
> Giver of goodness, King and Guide,
> Unequalled and unparalleled,
> Who needs no royal pomp and show,
> The Lord whose grace grants heaven's bliss[4]

Before the evacuation of Anandpur, solemn promises of safety were given by the *bakhshi*s and diwans of Aurangzeb by oaths on the Qur'an, but not fulfilled. Nevertheless, the brave Singhs fought their way out under divine protection:

> The lion's cover keeps him safe,
> Goats, sheep and dear are kept at bay.[5]

In the battle of Chamkaur, 40 starving men resisted the onslaught of thousands.

> They broke their oath and suddenly
> Attacked with arrows, swords and guns.
> Surrounded, with no choice, in turn
> I too attacked with bow and gun.
> When matters pass all other means,
> It is allowed to take up arms.[6]

It is clear that ba'it 22 relates to a specific situation, but the choice of words makes it a potential generalization.

In the address to Aurangzeb, the emperor is reminded of his oath on the Qur'an:

> Be true to your Koran-sworn oath,
> Perform the promise which you made.

After six lines, the emperor is told:

> Do not forget, for else God will
> Most certainly forget you too.[7]

In the last four lines of the section, it is revealed that Prince Mu'azzam was also keen for some kind of settlement, and Guru Gobind Singh was persuaded by his call rather than the oaths of Aurangzeb.

In the concluding couplets, 'Great Aurangzeb, world-emperor' is compared with the unrighteous Darius who was 'far from faith'. The Guru was 'the idol-breaker' who had slain the 'hill-idolators'.[8] The emperor is told:

> See too the holy power of God
> Which lets one man defeat whole hosts.[9]

There is a great emphasis laid on divine protection for Guru Gobind Singh. God blinds the foe before he acts and brings the helpless forth unhurt.

> Attacked by many thousands, he
> Rests safe in the creator's care.

Aurangzeb is advised not to use his strength to harm the weak. In any case,

> However many troops he leads,
> No foe harms him whom God befriends.
> Nor will a thousand arts allow
> His foe to harm one hair of his.[10]

Louis E. Fenech, in his preface to *The Sikh Zafar-Namah of Guru Gobind Singh*, says that the *Zafarnama* could be treated as

a product of the India-Timurid courtly culture.[11] The first chapter, on diplomacy at the court of Guru Gobind Singh, ends with
the relevance of the Persian language. A diplomatic letter to the
Mughal court, addressed to the emperor in Persian, was most
likely to produce a quick result.[12] In the second chapter, Fenech
suggests that the *Fateh-namah* (an incomplete composition similar to the *Zafarnama*) was a draft or a first attempt. If not, it would
be a highly questionable text. The hikayats were an inextricable
part of the *Zafarnama*.[13] In the third chapter, Fenech discusses the
text of the *Zafarnama* in relation to Firdausi and Sa'di. There is a
direct reference to Firdausi in one couplet. Ba'it 22 is an adaptation
of a couplet by Sa'di. No singular attention was paid to this ba'it
in the eighteenth century. Fenech suggests that the *Zafarnama*
itself was the sword used by Guru Gobind Singh.[14] The authorship
of the *Zafarnama* is discussed in the fourth chapter. The term
'arzdasht' (a written request) could be used for the *Zafarnama* at the
Mughal court. Therefore, the use of this term for a communication
from Guru Gobind Singh did not mean that his communication
could not be the *Zafarnama*. Nevertheless, Fenech does not come
to a specific conclusion.[15] In Chapter 5, he makes a case for the
Zafarnama being 'purposefully crafted as a Sikh *Shah-namah'*.[16]

Fenech takes up the historiography of the *Zafarnama* in a separate chapter. He talks of Anandpur as a place of great importance
for the Khalsa. There was nostalgia, and there was hope of return to
it in triumph. For a Sikh understanding of the *Zafarnama*, Fenech
turns to the Sikh works of the eighteenth and nineteenth centuries: Sainapat, Kesar Singh Chhibber, Sewadas Udasi, Kirpal Das
Bhalla (*Mahima Prakash Vartak*), Sarup Das Bhalla, Sukha Singh,
Koer Singh, Santokh Singh, Ratan Singh Bhangu and the *Guru Kian
Sakhian* of Sarup Singh Kaushish. The earliest written Sikh
source to mention the letter was by Sainapat. The account given
by him was to 'continue with very little change for the next 100
years'. Fenech takes notice of the minor changes. In Chhibber's
Bansavalinama, there is an exchange between Bhai Daya Singh and
Aurangzeb that had first appeared briefly in Sewadas's *Parchian*,
followed some years later by Kirpal Das Bhalla's *Mahima Prakash
Vartak*. This exchange in the later works becomes more dramatic
and more heated, and ultimately demonstrates the sovereignty

of Guru Gobind Singh. The example of the *Mahima Prakash Kavita* (1776) is given by Fenech. The entry of Daya Singh into the court of Aurangzeb, as presented by Sukha Singh and Koer Singh, reinforces the idea of the sovereignty of Guru Gobind Singh and his Khalsa.[17]

Fenech's analysis is affected by his assumption about the date of the composition of some works, notably the *Parchian* of Sewadas (placed in 1741). Kharak Singh and Gurtej Singh, who have edited and translated the text of the *Parchian*, place it in 1708.[18] Gurinder Singh Mann places it in 1709.[19] Sewadas presents not merely a variation upon Sainapat but a totally different account of the *Zafarnama*, including the death of Aurangzeb on reading the *Zafarnama*. These two parallel accounts were used by the later Sikh writers to produce their own mixed or unmixed accounts. There is a sort of evolution, but not of the kind presented by Fenech. The position of eighteenth-century writers becomes clear when we place their works in a correct chronological order. Fenech emphasized the importance of the *Parchian* of Sewadas, accepting a later date for its composition. On the whole, Sewadas appears to have been more influential than Sainapat. Fenech recognizes his importance, but does not see it in the right chronological perspective.

Fenech gets the impression that Sikh texts appearing after the *Parchian* of Sewadas and the *Mahima Prakash* (*Vartak*) continue to suffuse their *Zafarnama* narratives with the extraordinary power of the Guru and his words. In almost all of these, it is the Guru's letter and the words within it that result in Aurangzeb's death. This is the case in Sarup Das Bhalla's text and Sukha Singh's late eighteenth-century *Gurbilas*. However, in the *Parchian* of Sewadas already, Guru Gobind Singh presents two options to the Khalsa: to kill Aurangzeb by a writing on paper or in the field of battle, face to face.[20]

For his conclusion, Fenech turns to the popular Sikh art. It appears to depict Guru Gobind Singh's 'kingly and soldierly status', his moral victory over Aurangzeb, and his spiritual status. 'Put simply, what we have here is the visualization of the Guru as the master of *miri* [temporal authority] and *piri* [spiritual authority].' The *Zafarnama*, thus, is very much a testament to Sikh independence and gives textual form to the fulfilment of the popular Sikh refrain, *'Raj karega Khalsa'* (the Khalsa shall rule). Fenech points out that the *Zafarnama* was completely shorn of its miraculous content due to the tireless campaigns of the Singh Sabha movement.[21]

Notes

1. J. S. Grewal, 'The Zafarnama of Guru Gobind Singh', in *From Guru Nanak to Maharaja Ranjit Singh: Essays in Sikh History* (Amritsar: Guru Nanak (Dev) University, 1972), pp. 62–6. A slightly revised version was published as *'Zafarnama*: Declaration of Moral Victory', in *Sikh Ideology, Polity and Social Order* (New Delhi: Manohar, 2007), pp. 96–100, n. 5.

2. Christopher Shackle, *'Zafarnama'*, in *Journal of Punjab Studies*, vol. 15, nos. 1 and 2 (Spring–Fall, 2008): 163.

3. Shackle, *'Zafarnama'*, pp. 161–5.

4. Christopher Shackle, 'Zafarnama', *Journal of Punjab Studies*, vol. 15 nos. 1 and 2 (Spring–Fall 2008): 168.

5. Shackle, *Journal of Punjab Studies*, (Spring–Fall 2008): 169.

6. Shackle, *Journal of Punjab Studies*, (Spring–Fall 2008): 169.

7. Shackle, *Journal of Punjab Studies*, (Spring–Fall 2008): 172.

8. Shackle, *Journal of Punjab Studies*, (Spring–Fall 2008): 173.

9. Shackle, *Journal of Punjab Studies*, (Spring–Fall 2008): 173.

10. Shackle, *Journal of Punjab Studies*, (Spring–Fall 2008): 173.

11. Louis E. Fenech, *The Sikh Zafar-Namah of Guru Gobind Singh* (New York: Oxford University Press, 2013), pp. xii–xiii.

12. Fenech, *The Sikh Zafar-Namah*, pp. 16–17.

13. Fenech, *The Sikh Zafar-Namah*, pp. 23, 31–2.

14. Fenech, *The Sikh Zafar-Namah*, pp. 42, 46, 54–5, 60, 66, 68.

15. Fenech, *The Sikh Zafar-Namah*, pp. 71–3, 77–8.

16. Fenech, *The Sikh Zafar-Namah*, pp. 81, 84, 88–9, 96, 100.

17. Fenech, *The Sikh Zafar-Namah*, pp. 101–13.

18. Kharak Singh and Gurtej Singh, trans. and eds, *Episodes from Lives of the Gurus: Parchian Sevadas* (Chandigarh: Institute of Sikh Studies, 1995), p. 3.

19. Gurinder Singh Mann, 'Sources for the Study of Guru Gobind Singh's Life and Times', *Journal of Punjab Studies* (Special Issue on Guru Gobind Singh), vol. 15, nos. 1 and 2 (Spring–Fall 2008): 252.

20. Fenech, *The Sikh Zafar-Namah*, p. 119.

21. Fenech, *The Sikh Zafar-Namah*, p. 132.

10

Failure of Negotiations with Bahadur Shah (1707–8)

In the war of succession after the death of Aurangzeb, his eldest son, Muhammad Mu'azzam Shah Alam, declared himself to be the ruler as Bahadur Shah. In a battle fought at Jajau in June 1707, Azam Shah, the younger brother of Bahadur Shah, was killed. Bahadur Shah had to go to Rajasthan to pacify the Rajput chiefs of Jodhpur (Marwar) and Udaipur (Mewar). Having patched up peace with them, he moved towards the Deccan to fight his brother, Kam Bakhsh. He stayed at Burhanpur for some time in the summer of 1708. Then he moved towards Hyderabad. Kam Bakhsh was defeated and killed on 3 January 1709.

Guru Gobind Singh met Bahadur Shah at Agra in July 1707. He was hopeful of a satisfactory settlement, but Bahadur Shah had to go to Rajasthan and Guru Gobind Singh was persuaded to go with him. He remained close to Bahadur Shah's camp even when he decided to go to Hyderabad. At Burhanpur, Guru Gobind Singh decided to go to Nanded. He did not accompany Bahadur Shah when he marched towards Hyderabad. It was at Nanded, early in September 1708, that Guru Gobind Singh commissioned Banda Singh to go to Punjab and lead the Khalsa in revolt. All other means had failed, and it was decided to resort to the sword.

Exploring a Peaceful Settlement

Sainapat gives a simple account of Guru Gobind Singh's activities after the death of Aurangzeb. Prince Mu'azzam heard the news of his father's death and marched towards Delhi. Before reaching Delhi, he wrote to Guru Gobind Singh for support in the war of succession. Guru Gobind Singh told him to regard the Raj as his own. In the battle fought at Jajau, Azam Shah and his sons died fighting with extraordinary courage and bravery. Bahadur Shah was happy over his victory and thanked God for his success. He went to Agra and spent the four months of the rainy season there.[1]

Meanwhile, Guru Gobind Singh reached Delhi. The Sikhs of Delhi received him with great joy and enthusiasm. After some days, he left Delhi and, on his way to Agra, saw Mathura and Bindraban. He encamped in a garden at two kos from Agra. The Khan-i Khanan (Mun'im Khan) invited Guru Gobind Singh to his residence. He was happy to receive the Guru and showed great respect and regard for him. Some days later, Bahadur Shah invited Guru Gobind Singh to his court. The Guru met the emperor fully armed and with aigrette in his turban. Bahadur Shah praised Guru Gobind Singh and thanked him for establishing his Raj on a firm footing, saying that he owed his throne to the Guru. The emperor presented to him a *kalghi* and a *dhukh-dhukhi* with a *khil'at*.[2]

During the rainy season at Agra, Guru Gobind Singh enjoyed an elephant fight. After the rains, Bahadur Shah decided to go to Rajasthan and Guru Gobind Singh decided to go with him. He remained close to the camp of the emperor when he went to Ajmer, Jodhpur, and Udaipur where Raja Jit Singh submitted to him. Another incident of this time was the death of Zorawar Singh (an adopted son of Guru Gobind Singh) at Chittor where he had picked up a fight with the guards of the fort. Sainapat describes the battle briefly. Bahadur Shah decided to go to the South, and Guru Gobind Singh accompanied him. After they had crossed the Narbada, the Singhs had to fight for fodder, and a few skirmishes took place. Guru Gobind Singh advised them to exercise restraint. Reaching Burhanpur, Guru Gobind Singh decided to stay there for some time. Bahadur Shah left Burhanpur, asking the Guru to join him soon. They crossed the Tapti. Guru Gobind Singh had a personal meeting with Bahadur Shah and returned to his camp. Finally, he decided to stay behind at Nanded.[3] Sainapat remains silent about the purpose of Guru Gobind Singh in meeting Bahadur Shah and what transpired in their meeting at Agra, why Guru Gobind Singh followed Bahadur Shah, and finally why he decided to stay at Nanded.

According to Sewadas, Bahadur Shah sat on the throne after the death of Aurangzeb, but he was removed from it by his brothers. He was running before them when Guru Gobind Singh told him not to run away. 'I have come for your support,' he said. 'Come with me. I shall enable you to fight against your brothers and shall get *patshahi* for you.' Bahadur Shah agreed. The Guru created the appearance of such a huge army in his support that his brothers were frightened. He sat on the throne again. A Sikh asked Guru Gobind Singh why he was so kind to Bahadur Shah. He was told that Bahadur Shah had served the Guru in a previous birth in the hope of getting rulership. That was why the Guru supported him now.[4] Bahadur Shah, in turn, had great respect and affection for Guru Gobind Singh and used to send fruit to him. Often, he wrote loving letters to the Guru, expressing his ardent wish to have his *darshan*. 'Guru Gobind Singh wanted to go east and Bahadur Shah, at Agra, was on the way. That was how he met the emperor.[5]

Bahadur Shah gave costly presents to Guru Gobind Singh. His diwan asked the Guru whether Islam or his own faith was better. The Guru said, 'Your religion is good for you and our religion is good for us.' Then, the diwan said that in his religion, people embraced the converts and ate with them without any hesitation. Would the people of his religion do this? Guru Gobind Singh said that the Muslims would have this freedom 'under our rule'. The diwan kept quiet. The Qazi wanted to know about *bandagi*, as God had created *banda* for bandagi. He was told that he who was free from sin, yet regarded himself as a sinner was a true banda. In reply to further questions by the Qazi, Guru Gobind Singh explained that God would judge His devotee on the basis of his genuine conviction and not merely on verbal profession. Purity was of two kinds. The purity of the body was to remain free from sin. But the purity of the mind was to get rid of the self (*khudi*). This depended on God's grace and not merely on the effort of the individual. However, God's grace (*lutf-i Subhani*) was not possible if a devotee was proud of his sinlessness. The Qazi was satisfied with the Guru's responses.[6]

The emperor's pir happened to stay in a garden close to a city in which lived a large number of Khatri Sikhs. When the pir came to meet the Guru, he observed that the Sikhs brought him offerings of cloth and arms (*bastar, shastar*) and the ardasia performed ardas for them. The pir suggested that ardas couldn't possibly change anything because everything was predetermined by God the Almighty. Guru Gobind Singh explained the position by using the seal in the ring he was wearing. It contained an inscription that by itself made no sense, but when ink was applied to it for getting an impression on paper, its sense became absolutely clear. God's will was thus realized partly due to human effort in the form of submission to a perfect murshid and the service of the people. The pir was satisfied.[7] The ideas of Guru Gobind Singh appeared to be in harmony with the Islamic thought, both orthodox and Sufi.

According to Koer Singh, on hearing the news of Aurangzeb's death, Guru Gobind Singh wanted to know who had succeeded him. He was told that Azam was trusted by the people and appeared to have greater merit than others. Bahadur Shah was afraid of challenging Azam. In this situation, Azam ascended the throne with the consent of the people. Guru Gobind Singh remarked that he had given Raj to Mu'azzam and none would be able to stop him. He had served the Guru very well. Therefore, the Guru now gave his support to Mu'azzam. Moreover, Raj was given to him in accordance with God's will. Guru Gobind Singh wrote a letter to Mu'azzam that Delhi was a wilderness without him. He should be bold enough to obtain the throne for himself: 'Collect an army and fight. Regard me as your companion in this venture.' After writing this letter, Guru Gobind Singh moved on to see the battle for succession (sultani jang).[8]

Koer Singh gives a separate chapter to the battle. After ascending the throne, Azam marched towards Delhi. Bahadur Shah collected his army, but found it unsatisfactory. He wrote to Guru Gobind Singh for help. He was reassured: 'Do not entertain the slightest doubt in your mind that the Raj is yours.' He was advised to go ahead and fight as if the Guru was present with him. It was a grim battle. Azam fought like a great warrior. Bahadur Shah lost courage. His face went pale and he began to tremble. He prayed to the Guru to come to his aid now. When he opened his eyes, he saw Guru Gobind Singh in full battle regalia and the Khalsa facing Azam. The critical moment came when Azam attacked Bahadur Shah with his sword. Guru Gobind Singh used his shield to save Bahadur Shah. Then, the Guru killed Azam with an arrow. The army of Azam Shah fled from the field. 'Who killed Azam?' was the question in the minds of all. The arrow that had killed Azam did not belong to anyone in Bahadur Shah's camp. At last, Bahadur Shah said, 'I know the person from whose quiver the arrow came.' The victorious Bahadur Shah went to Agra. Guru Gobind Singh had reached Delhi by this time.[9]

The Sikh *sangat* of Delhi received Guru Gobind Singh with enthusiasm and reverence. He went to the dharamsal in the city and also visited Sisganj, the place of Guru Tegh Bahadur's martyrdom. After some days, the servants of Bahadur Shah came to Delhi and Guru Gobind Singh left the city for Agra. On his way, he saw many places in Mathura, Gokul, and Bindraban—all associated with Krishna. At four kos from Agra, Guru Gobind Singh encamped in a garden. The Khan-i Khanan (Mun'im Khan) invited Guru Gobind Singh to his house and thanked him for his gracious visit. The Guru moved to Agra. Bahadur Shah's men came to say that the emperor wanted to see Guru Gobind Singh. When the Guru entered the palace, he was fully armed and had his kalghi and jigha in place. Bahadur Shah presented a dhukhdhukhi to the Guru, apart from a new kalghi and a new jigha.[10] Bahadur Shah paid a visit to Guru Gobind Singh sometime later and said that he had heard that the Guru wanted to go to the South. The Guru confirmed this. Bahadur Shah requested him to stay in Agra during the rainy months, after which he would accompany the Guru to the South. Guru Gobind Singh agreed to stay on.[11]

Koer Singh repeats the questions posed by Bahadur Shah's diwan, the Qazi of the empire, and Bahadur Shah's pir, and the replies given by Guru Gobind Singh. A significant point added by Koer Singh is a reference to the *Masnavi* (presumably of Jalaluddin

Rumi) for the idea that God is present in every living being, from the ant to the elephant. Koer Singh says emphatically that all the three—the diwan, the Qazi, and the pir—were so impressed by Guru Gobind Singh's responses that they went to Bahadur Shah to sing praises of the Guru.[12]

Another incident of the rainy season at Agra mentioned by Koer Singh is the hunting of a lion. Bahadur Shah was accompanied by Guru Gobind Singh on a hunting expedition. Many animals and birds were hunted, but a lion defied every warrior. In fact, this lion killed several brave men of the emperor. Bahadur Shah requested Guru Gobind Singh to send one of his Sikhs to face the lion. Guru Gobind Singh indicated to a Sikh named Roshan Singh that he should go forward. Roshan Singh killed the lion with his sword. Bahadur Shah was so happy that he told Roshan Singh to ask for anything as a reward. He said that he had received everything from the Guru.[13]

It is interesting to find the Sikhs asking the Guru when the Sikh Raj would be established. Guru Gobind Singh had to travel with Bahadur Shah in Rajasthan. He was encamped near a village close to Jaipur. There was a *jand* (a hardy tree) and a *karir* (a hardy bush), and under them was a small pipal tree. A Singh suggested that the pipal should be replanted away from the jand and the karir. The Guru said that this pipal tree would never be destroyed in its present place. In fact, it was meant to overshadow the jand and the karir, which would become extinct sooner or later. When that happened, the Sikh Raj would be established. All the Singhs present asked Guru Gobind Singh when the Khalsa Raj would be established. He replied, 'When these trees become extinct.' They said that the jand and the karir would be revived by the rains and would never become totally dry. Then, the true Guru said that he would destroy the 'Turks'. The Guru would remain present in the Khalsa and they would destroy the 'Turks'.[14]

There is a lot of confusion in Koer Singh's account at this stage. Guru Gobind Singh saw many places in Rajasthan, such as Ajmer, Jodhpur, Jaisalmer, and Chittor (Udaipur), and took leave of Bahadur Shah. The Guru marched towards Patna and stayed at Patna for over four years before he stayed at Burhanpur for a considerably long period. Hathi Singh (son of Ajit Singh, the adopted son of Mata Sundari) came to pay homage to the Guru. Bahadur Shah also came for the Guru's darshan and made offerings (bhet). After many days, Guru Gobind Singh went to Nanded.[15]

Kesar Singh Chhibber presents Guru Gobind Singh's support for Prince Mu'azzam somewhat dramatically. In his *hukamnama*s to the Sikhs in the army of Prince Mu'azzam, the Guru used to address them as 'the sangat of the *lashkar* (army) of the Prince', but now he addressed them as '*sarbat Khalsa wasi lashkar Badshah*' (the entire Khalsa of the camp of the emperor). They congratulated Bahadur Shah because they had no doubt that their Guru had given *badshahi* (rulership) to him. In the battle between the two sons of Aurangzeb, one killed the other. Bahadur Shah moved from Kabul, killed his victorious brother, and became the emperor. He said that Ramdas (Guru Gobind Singh) had given badshahi to him and he was the Guru's servant (*khadim*).[16]

Sarup Singh Kaushish gives a short and clear account of the activity of Guru Gobind Singh in relation to Bahadur Shah in 1707–8. After the news of Aurangzeb's death, Guru Gobind Singh left Bagore for Delhi (Shahjahanabad). On his way, he received a letter from Bahadur Shah, asking for help in the battle between him and his brother Azam to be fought at Jajau on the banks of the Chambal river. Immediately, on receiving this letter, Guru Gobind Singh sent 25 Singhs under Daya Singh, while he himself, with the rest of the Singhs, arrived at Jajau in the afternoon to join the battle. The fight between the two brothers was grim. Azam and his son were killed on the battlefield. With the support and blessings of Guru Gobind Singh, Bahadur Shah gained victory. He went to Agra and, before ascending the throne, invited Guru Gobind Singh and showed great respect to him. After his coronation, Bahadur Shah gave him a robe of honour, a *jarau* (studded with jewels) kal-ghi, and 101 gold coins.[17]

At Naraina in Rajasthan, Guru Gobind Singh had shown respect to the *samadh* of Dadu. Daya Singh pointed out that this was an infringement of the Khalsa *rahit*. Guru Gobind Singh smiled and said that the Khalsa had come of age. He paid Rs 125 by way of *tankhah* (penance). Mahant Jait Ram (Dadu's successor at Naraina) was surprised to see that Guru Gobind Singh accepted 'punishment' from his followers. Jait Ram asked the Guru why he had taken up arms. Guru Gobind Singh referred to the martyrdom of Guru Arjan, the imprisonment of Guru Hargobind, and the martyrdom of Guru Tegh Bahadur, and then quoted the well-known couplet from the *Zafarnama* which justifies the use of the sword when all other means fail. At the time of Guru Gobind Singh's departure from Naraina, Mahant Jait Ram warned him against meeting Madho Das (Banda). But Guru Gobind Singh said that he would certainly meet Madho Das. He had an important matter to settle with the 'Bairagi'.[18]

Zorawar Singh, an adopted son of Guru Gobind Singh, joined the Guru's camp. When Bahadur Shah was near Chittor, Sahibzada Zorawar Singh went to see the fort with 20 to 25 warriors. The guards did not allow Zorawar Singh to enter the fort. This led to a fight in which the Sahibzada died as a martyr. The dead bodies of Zorawar Singh and his companions were cremated on the bank of a stream near Chittor.[19]

The author of the *Nairang-i Zamana*, who was in the camp of Bahadur Shah at that time, gives an ornate account of the occurrence. The imperial camp was pitched near the fort of Chittor for some time when Bahadur Shah was on his way to the Deccan from Ajmer. The son of Guru Gobind Singh was seized by the desire to visit the fort of Chittor. He rode out along with some friends. When he approached the fort, the guards of the gate barred him from fulfilling his wish. They said that from the time of the conquest of this great fortress by the sword of the victorious armies of Islam, during the reign of Jalaluddin Muhammad Akbar Padshah Ghazi, it had been firmly established that no Hindu or Muslim could come into this strong fort. The son of Guru Gobind, like a fierce tiger, with a sword that cut through the armour, sent many persons to death to join his own companions, and then he too, falling, lay dead by their side.[20]

Bahadur Shah sought Guru Gobind Singh's advice with regard to the revolt of his brother Kam Bakhsh and the unrest in Punjab. He was advised that he should first deal with Kam Bakhsh and then he could take necessary action against the Punjab hill Rajas. The emperor was happy to hear this. He added that he could not leave Guru Gobind Singh alone and requested the Guru to accompany him. The Guru made up his mind to go with the emperor.

Both Bahadur Shah and Guru Gobind Singh reached Burhanpur in due course. The Sikh sangat in Burhanpur was jubilant to see the Guru and showed great respect to him.[21]

Sukha Singh, on the whole, remains close to Koer Singh in his account of Guru Gobind Singh's activity in relation to Bahadur Shah. Indeed, the works of Sainapat and Sewadas appear to be the common sources for Koer Singh and Sukha Singh. After receiving the news of Aurangzeb's death, Guru Gobind Singh wanted to know who had succeeded him. He was told that Prince Azam had ascended the throne. 'But we have given Raj to Bahadur Shah,' said Guru Gobind Singh. Bahadur Shah had performed many services for the Guru. After this, Guru Gobind Singh marched towards Delhi to see the 'sultani jang'.[22]

Sukha Singh gives a separate chapter to the 'sultani jang' at Jajau. On the suggestion given by Nand Lal, Bahadur Shah wrote a letter to Guru Gobind Singh, seeking his blessings and help. Guru Gobind Singh's response was strong and positive. He reassured Bahadur Shah of his victory and his Raj. He also deputed five Singhs, equal to five lakhs, to fight on Bahadur Shah's side. Led by Dharam Singh, they played a crucial role in the battle. Azam was a valiant warrior and no one could face him on the battlefield. Bahadur Shah's army was hard pressed and he was in despair. Dharam Singh asked him to look behind. He saw Guru Gobind Singh approaching with a huge army. The tide was turned. After the battle, everyone wanted to know who had killed Azam. The arrows collected from the field of battle did not belong to any Mughal warrior. Bahadur Shah knew, but he simply said that the Guru had given the Raj to his servant. Bahadur Shah then went to Agra and Guru Gobind Singh reached Delhi.[23]

Sukha Singh gives a separate chapter to Bahadur Shah's stay in Agra during the rainy months. His stay was marked by (*a*) Guru Gobind Singh's meeting with him, (*b*) Guru Gobind Singh's conversation with the diwan, the Qazi of the empire, and Bahadur Shah's pir, and (*c*) the hunting expedition of Bahadur Shah. The treatment of all the three is similar to the one by Koer Singh.[24] In a separate chapter on Bahadur Shah's campaign in Rajasthan, Sukha Singh gives an account of Sahibzada Zorawar Singh's union with Guru Gobind Singh, and his death in a fight with the guards of the fort of Chittor.[25] Both Bahadur Shah and Guru Gobind Singh then left Rajasthan and reached Burhanpur. Finally, Guru Gobind Singh decided to stay at Nanded, though Bahadur Shah tried to persuade him to go to the north.[26]

Guru Gobind Singh's meeting with Bahadur Shah was recorded on 4 August 1707 in the *Akhbarat-i Darbar-i Mu'alla* in courtly language: 'Gobind the Nanaki came armed, in accordance with orders, and presented himself, making an offering of 100 *ashrafi*s [gold coins]. A robe of honour and *padak* [medallion], set with precious stones, was given to him, and he was permitted to leave.'[27]

A hukamnama of Guru Gobind Singh, addressed to the sangat of Khara (district Amritsar) on 2 October 1707 (see Image 10.1), provides a clue to the purpose for which Guru Gobind Singh wanted to meet Aurangzeb and for which he later met Bahadur Shah. The sangat was informed that the Guru had met the emperor and received a dhukhdhukhi worth Rs 60,000 with a robe of honour. All other matters were in order, and he would return to Kahlur in a short time; the entire Khalsa sangat should then come, armed with all the weapons.[28]

It is safe to infer that Guru Gobind Singh hoped to go back to Anandpur on the basis of a peaceful settlement for which negotiations had taken place. Even if Bahadur Shah was not sincere or steadfast, Guru Gobind Singh had surely been in favour of a peaceful settlement since the beginning of his negotiations with Aurangzeb. When Bahadur Shah decided to go to Rajasthan to deal with a serious revolt there and then to the South to do battle with Kam Bakhsh, Guru Gobind Singh went with him. Eventually, however, he was not very hopeful of a peaceful settlement and decided to stay behind in Nanded.

Koer Singh and Sukha Singh indicate in their own ways that Bahadur Shah was not trusted by some of the Sikhs of Guru Gobind Singh. According to Koer Singh, when the leading Sikhs asked Guru Gobind Singh about his successor, he said that he would remain present with them. They said that Bahadur Shah did not do what he had promised to do. Guru Gobind Singh told them that he did not beg for anything: he got with his own strength whatever he wanted. The Khalsa should avenge the death of the Sahibzadas. According to Sukha Singh, a Pathan noble came to Nanded with

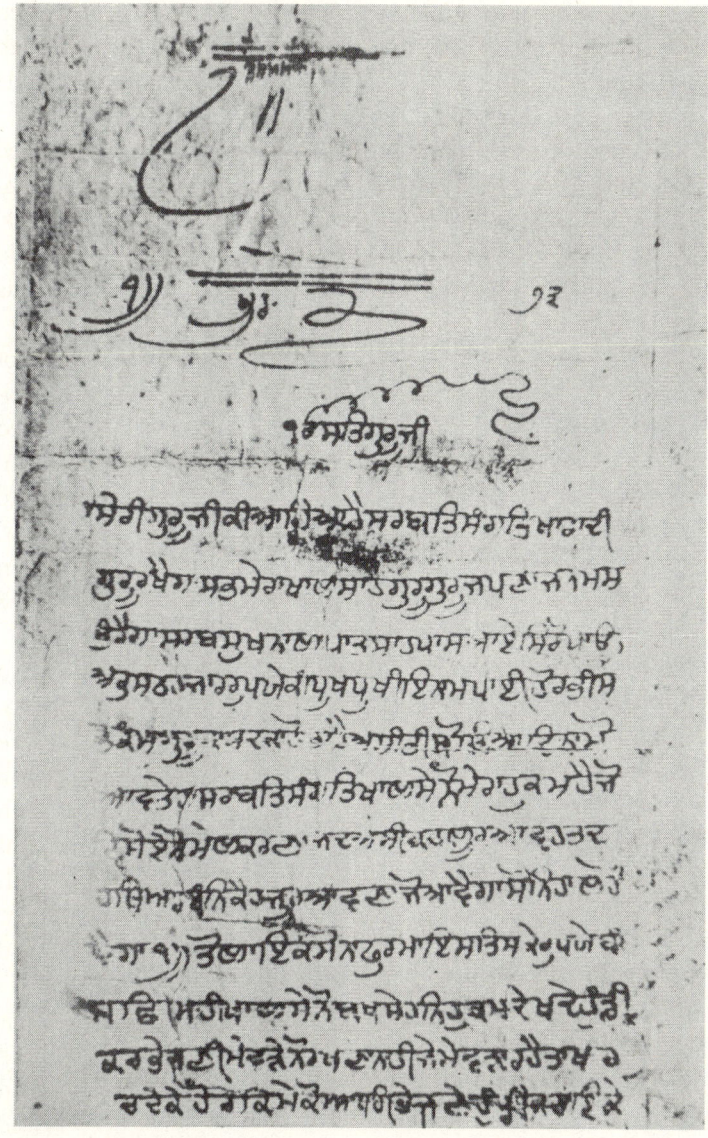

Image 10.1   Guru Gobind Singh's *hukamnama*, dated 2 October 1707 (document 64), addressed to the *sangat* of Khara. This document refers to the meeting of Guru Gobind Singh with Bahadur Shah, which was exceptionally good, and Guru Gobind Singh expected to return to Anandpur before long.

Source: Ganda Singh ed., *Hukamname*.

a large army and a message from Bahadur Shah that he wanted
to move forward and Guru Gobind Singh should accompany him.
Guru Gobind Singh made it clear that he could not leave Nanded
because he had something important to do there. The Pathan
noble failed to persuade Guru Gobind Singh and Bahadur Shah had
to move on without the Guru.[29]

Negotiations No More

Guru Gobind Singh's encounter with Banda on the day of the solar
eclipse (3 September 1708) on the River Godavari near Nanded
turned out to be an event of vital importance. As witnessed by
Dhadi Nath Mal, the Guru visited the *dera* of an ill-tempered
renunciate, believed to have been endowed with supernatural
powers. In his absence, his goats were killed by the Guru's Singhs.
He sent five of his *Bir*s to kill the Guru, but they were no match
for the Khalsa. They reported to their master what had happened.
The renunciate went into the town and collected a large number
of people for support against the Guru for having killed his
goats on the auspicious day of the solar eclipse. They approached
the emperor for justice. Among the advisers of the emperor was
Nand Lal who advised him to discuss the matter with Guru
Gobind Singh. The complainants maintained that the eclipse was
caused by the seizure of the sun by two demons to whom the sun
was indebted. The Guru suggested that the emperor could relieve
the suffering of the sun by clearing their debt. The complainants
saw the absurdity of their argument and returned to their homes.
The renunciate fell at the Guru's feet and begged for mercy. Guru
Gobind Singh ordered him to go to Punjab. Five Singhs were to
accompany him.[30]

Koer Singh underlines that Guru Gobind Singh wanted the
Khalsa to take revenge for the death of the Sahibzadas. He commanded 'Banda' to perform this task without fear. Banda became
a Sikh and was given arms by the Guru. Four brave warriors were
sent with him. The Singhs had been taught how to fight and with
their support, Banda could take revenge. Koer Singh goes on to add
that Banda waged war as he liked. He became somewhat proud and

infringed some of the rahit. The support given by the Guru was withdrawn, and soon Banda went to the other world.[31]

Much more sympathetic to 'Banda Sahib Ji', Kesar Singh Chhibber gives much greater detail. Before meeting Guru Gobind Singh, he was known as Madho Das Bairagi. He had lived at Firozanagar in the east as a sanyasi for two years before coming to Haripur in the south, where he lived for 60 years. From there, he came to the country of the Chauhan Jatts under the name of Lachhman Das in the garb of a *bairagi*. In fact, he could change his form at will, having been endowed with supernatural powers by God. Known as Wali Ravali (a yogi), he had built a Thakurdwara which he looked after as a renunciate (*udasi*).[32]

Chhibber refers to an earlier meeting in which Banda had been persuaded by the Guru to undertake a task for which he was initially reluctant. The time for undertaking the task assigned to Banda had arrived. Chhibber talks of the manner in which Banda got the Labana Sikh traders ready to take up arms for action under Banda's leadership. Among the Sikhs who joined Banda were Kaur Singh, Baj Singh, and Bhagwant Singh. All the three were made 'sardars' by 'Banda Sahib'.[33]

Sarup Das Bhalla talks of Banda's meeting with Guru Gobind Singh on his way to the south. At that time, Banda's name was Madho Das. At his place of residence, there was a cot which turned upside down when anyone other than him sat on it. The cot was guarded by four unseen persons who were under Banda's power. This was the *siddhi* which Banda demonstrated to his visitors. When Guru Gobind Singh sat on the cot, it did not move. The four guards of the cot went to Banda and told him how they proved to be helpless. This came to Banda as a great surprise, and he came hurriedly to meet Guru Gobind Singh. Immediately upon seeing the Guru, Banda submitted to him completely and fell at his feet. Banda asked many questions, but he was fully gratified in the end. Then, the Guru said, 'Are you now a *banda* of Akal Purkh? I will send you to Punjab to take revenge from the *mlechh*.' He said that he would start his own faith (*matt*) and the Khalsa Panth would be badly affected. Guru Gobind Singh said that his Panth would not be affected in any way. Banda said, 'Then, I am your banda. I shall do whatever you command me to do.' Banda was told to remain celibate. Baba Binod Singh and Baba Kahn Singh, the father and the son, and the Trehan Sahibzadas in addition to the eminent Singhs such as Baj Singh, who had taken *pahul* from Guru Gobind Singh, were told to accompany Banda, to remain obedient to him, and to support him. Guru Gobind Singh gave five arrows from his own quiver to Banda for use in a crisis. With those, Banda went to Punjab.[34]

According to Sarup Singh Kaushish, Madho Das Bairagi had stayed with Lunia Siddh for three years and regarded him as his guru. Kaushish says that Guru Gobind Singh met Madho Das Bairagi at Nanded on 3 Assu, Sammat 1765 (CE 1708). When the Guru went to the dera of Madho Das, he was not there. Guru Gobind Singh sat on his cot to wait for him. After midday, the cook (*langari*) asked what he should cook for the langar. 'Whatever is available in the dera,' said the Guru. There was a deer, a goat, and its two kids. All four were slaughtered for the langar. The disciples of Madho Das raised objections, but a few of them were beaten by the Singhs and they all went to Madho Das to narrate what had happened. He was extremely angry and sent his 'Birs' to throw down the intruder from the cot, but the cot remained unmoved like the Sumer Mountain. The birs returned and said that they could not even cast a look at the cot. Madho Das now began to think who could possibly be so powerful a person. He recalled what a Siddh had told him of a Raj-jogi (one who combines temporal authority with the spiritual) who would be more powerful than he and would make him a disciple to give him more power. Madho Das went to his dera. Guru Gobind Singh smiled when he saw him. In the conversation that followed, Guru Gobind Singh told Madho Das that he had come to awaken the bairagi to the larger dera called 'Hind' in which thousands of innocent people were being victimized. Madho Das said, 'I am your banda [slave].'[35]

Madho Das entrusted his dera to Hari Das Dakhani and accompanied Guru Gobind Singh to his place. On the following day, pahul of the double-edged sword was administered to him personally by Guru Gobind Singh and his name was changed to 'Banda Singh'. As Jathedar (leader) of the Panth, he was sent with five eminent Sikhs: Bhagwant Singh, Koer Singh, Baj Singh, Binod Singh,

and Kahn Singh. He was instructed to request all the five to perform ardas in a crisis.[36]

In Bhangu's *Sri Gur Panth Prakash*, Mahant Jait Ram, Dadu's
successor at Naraina, warns Guru Gobind Singh against 'Narain
Das' Bairagi who took delight in humiliating sants. He had played
a prank on Jait Ram, throwing him off a cot. He recognized no guru
or pir, but appropriated these epithets for himself. Jait Ram advised
Guru Gobind Singh to avoid Narain Das. But Guru Gobind Singh
said that he would overcome his supernatural power and show him
the right path. He would be made a Sikh of Guru Gobind Singh.
Mahant Jait Ram talked of the supernatural powers of Narain Das
in detail to underline that he could do everything against the natural order. He was the master of all the eight siddhis. Mahant Jait
Ram repeated his warning and Guru Gobind Singh reiterated his
resolve: 'I would show him the power of Guru Nanak and oblige
him to touch my feet.'[37]

At the place of Narain Das, Guru Gobind Singh saw a Persian
wheel working without bullocks, and the cot of Narain Das
remained a yard and a quarter above the earth. Only he could bring
it down to the earth to sit on it. Guru Gobind Singh sat on the
cot and it came down to the earth. No agent of Narain Das could
move the cot. The Birs of Narain Das were helpless against the
Sikhs of Guru Gobind Singh and Narain Das himself made his
submission to him. 'I am your banda,' he said, 'I am your Sikh and
you are my Guru.' Guru Gobind Singh told him that the path of
Sikhi is hard. It is narrower than the width of a hair and sharper
than a double-edged sword. A Sikh has to lose his 'self' (*api*). Banda
was keen to serve. He was then assigned the task of destroying
the Mughal empire. Guru Gobind Singh gave him arrows to be
used in a critical situation. It was made clear to him that Guruship
belonged to the Khalsa, and there was no difference between the
Guru and the Khalsa.[38]

The Punjabi Singhs who knew the enemies of the Sikhs and
were well versed in matters of the Khalsa rahit were sent with
Banda. Baj Singh Bal of Mirpur near Patti and his four brothers
are specifically mentioned. The Majhail Sikhs were asked to join
Banda. Bajida (Wazir Khan) was to be their first target. The Khalsa
present at Nanded wanted Guru Gobind Singh to clarify the issue

of rulership (*patshahi*). If Banda wanted patshahi for himself and not for the Khalsa, they would not join him. Guru Gobind Singh told Banda that he would not be able to go against the wishes of the Khalsa. Banda accepted all these terms. Letters were written for the Sikhs to join Banda. He who joined the Khalsa would have a share in patshahi and those who remained aloof would be the subject people. Banda wanted to have something from the Guru and was told that he had become a part of the Khalsa and was entitled to a share in whatever was acquired by the Khalsa. He could ask five Singhs to pray for anything he wanted. Banda was ready to leave for Punjab.[39] The revolt of the Khalsa under Banda's leadership was nothing short of a bid for sovereign rule.

All the writers agree that Banda was commissioned by Guru Gobind Singh to go to Punjab and lead the Khalsa in revolt against the Mughal authorities. Some of the writers explicitly state that he was initiated through *khande ki pahul* and was made a Singh. Evidently, he was bound by the Khalsa rahit and a special injunction was to remain celibate. His purpose was to take revenge, shatter the Mughal power, and establish Sikh rule. The Sikh writers of the eighteenth century looked upon Banda as a failure, and attributed this failure to an infringement of the rahit or the injunction of celibacy. The only exception was Kesar Singh Chhibber. He admired 'Banda Sahib' for three main reasons: Banda took revenge, he ensured justice, and he died as a martyr. Significantly, all Sikh writers looked upon Banda as commissioned for a certain purpose on certain terms, and they judged him in that framework. They regarded Banda Singh's activity as a projection of Guru Gobind Singh's intentions.

In retrospect, we can see that Guru Gobind Singh met Bahadur Shah in Agra in July 1707. On 4 August 1707, it was recorded in the *Akhbarat-i Darbar-i Mu'alla* that Guru Gobind Singh went fully armed into the presence of Bahadur Shah and received a medallion set with precious stones. On 2 October 1707, Guru Gobind Singh wrote to the sangat of Khara that he had received a dhukhdhukhi worth Rs 60,000; other matters were taken care of; and he would return to Kahlur in a short time. Evidently, he hoped to return to Anandpur. However, Bahadur Shah had to go to Rajasthan first and then to Hyderabad. Guru Gobind Singh remained close to his camp. At Burhanpur, in the summer of 1708, he decided to go to Nanded. Disillusioned by the evasive attitude of Bahadur Shah, the first thing he did in Nanded was to commission Banda to go to Punjab and lead the Khalsa in revolt in a bid to establish Khalsa Raj.

Notes

1. Sainapat, *Sri Gur Sobha*, edited by Shamsher Singh Ashok (Amritsar: Shiromani Gurdwara Prabandhak Committee, 1967), pp. 113–16.

2. Sainapat, *Sri Gur Sobha*, pp. 119–21.

3. Sainapat, *Sri Gur Sobha*, pp. 121–8.

4. Kharak Singh and Gurtej Singh, trans. and eds, *Episodes from Lives of the Gurus: Parchian Sewadas* (Chandigarh: Institute of Sikh Studies, 1995), p. 135.

5. *Parchian Sewadas*, p. 135.

6. *Parchian Sewadas*, pp. 135–6.

7. *Parchian Sewadas*, pp. 137–8.

8. Koer Singh, *Gurbilas Patshahi 10*, edited by Shamsher Singh Ashok (Patiala: Punjabi University, 1968), pp. 239–40.

9. Koer Singh, *Gurbilas*, pp. 245–51.

10. See Appendix 10.1 on Guru Gobind Singh and Bahadur Shah.

11. Koer Singh, *Gurbilas*, pp. 281–2.

12. Koer Singh, *Gurbilas*, pp. 262–6.

13. Koer Singh, *Gurbilas*, pp. 267–9.

14. Koer Singh, *Gurbilas*, pp. 270–1.

15. Koer Singh, *Gurbilas*, pp. 271–3.

16. Kesar Singh Chhibber, 'Bansavalinama Dasan Patshahian Ka', edited by Rattan Singh Jaggi, in *Parkh*, vol. 2, edited by S. S. Kohli (Chandigarh: Panjab University, 1972), pp. 155–6.

17. Bhai Svarup Singh Kaushish, *Guru Kian Sakhian*, edited by Piara Singh Padam (Amritsar: Singh Brothers, 1999 [1986]), pp. 189–90.

18. Kaushish, *Guru Kian Sakhian*, pp. 191–3.

19. Kaushish, *Guru Kian Sakhian*, pp. 190–1, 194.

20. J. S. Grewal and Irfan Habib, eds, *Sikh History from Persian Sources: Translations of Major Texts* (New Delhi: Tulika/Indian History Congress, 2001), pp. 101–3.

21. Kaushish, *Guru Kian Sakhian*, pp. 190, 195.

22. Sukha Singh, *Gurbilas Patsahi 10*, edited by Gursharan Kaur Jaggi (Patiala: Bhasha Vibhag, Punjab, 1989), pp. 377, 381–2.

23. Sukha Singh, *Gurbilas*, pp. 383–4.

24. Sukha Singh, *Gurbilas*, pp. 395–412.

25. Sukha Singh, *Gurbilas*, pp. 413–18.

26. Sukha Singh, *Gurbilas*, pp. 419–25.

27. *Sikh History from Persian Sources*, p. 106.

28. *Hukamname Guru Sahiban, Mata Sahiban, Banda Singh ate Khalsa Ji De*, edited by Ganda Singh (Patiala: Punjabi University, 1967), document 64.

29. Koer Singh, *Gurbilas*, pp. 281–6. Sukha Singh, *Gurbilas*, pp. 424–31.

30. Gurtej Singh, 'Amarnamah, An Important Document of Sikh History', in his *Chakravyuh: Web of Indian Secularism* (Chandigarh: Institute of Sikhs Studies, 2000), pp. 9–12.

31. Koer Singh, *Gurbilas*, pp. 281–2.

32. Chhibber, *Bansavalinama*, p. 170.

33. Chhibber, *Bansavalinama*, pp. 170–1.

34. Sarup Das Bhalla, *Mahima Prakash*, edited by Gobind Singh Lamba and Khazan Singh (Patiala: Punjab Languages Department, 1972), part II, pp. 883–4.

35. Kaushish, *Guru Kian Sakhian*, pp. 196–200.

36. Sukha Singh, *Gurbilas*, p. 445.

37. Ratan Singh Bhangu, *Sri Guru Panth Prakash*, edited by Balwant Singh Dhillon (Amritsar: Singh Brothers, 2004), pp. 69–74.

38. Bhangu, *Sri Guru Panth Prakash*, pp. 74–7.

39. Bhangu, *Sri Guru Panth Prakash*, pp. 77–9.

Appendix 10A

How to Account for Guru Gobind Singh's Presence Near Bahadur Shah in 1707–8

The eighteenth-century Sikh writers talk of Guru Gobind Singh remaining close to the court of Bahadur Shah for his own purposes, not suggesting in any way that he accepted service. But the British writers of the late eighteenth and the early nineteenth century explicitly state that he accepted service in the Mughal army. George Forster was the first writer to make such a statement:

> After his late disaster, Govind Singh found a secure retreat in the Lacky [Lakhi] Jungle, which its natural defence, a scarcity of water, and the valour of its inhabitants had rendered at that day impregnable. But when the resentment of government abated, he returned without molestation to his former residence in the Punjab. The Sicques say, he even received marks of favour from Bhahauder Shah, who, being apprised of his military abilities, gave him a charge in the army which marched into the Decan to oppose the rebellion of Rambuchsh [Kam Bakhsh].[1]

John Malcolm virtually reiterated Forster's statement:

> Guru Gobind Singh after remaining sometime in the Lak'hi Jungle, to which he had fled, returned without molestation to his former residence in the Punjab; and ..., so far from meeting with any persecution from the Muhammedan government, he received favours from the emperor, Bahader Shah; who, aware of his military talents, gave him a small military command in the Dek'hin.[2]

W. L. M'Gregor gives his own interpretation of the situation, without a reference to any source: 'Seeing that he was not yet prepared to compete with Alumgeer, or wrest from his grasp the territories lying on both sides of the Sutlej, as well as the different Doabs, Govind humbled himself, and even accepted employment from his powerful rival.'³ J. D. Cunningham gives his own meaning to the same evidence:

> While engaged in this last campaign, Bahadur Shah summoned Govind to his camp. The Gooroo went; he was treated with respect and he received a military command in the valley of the Godavery. The emperor perhaps thought that the leader of insurrectionary Juts might be usefully employed in opposing rebellious Mahrattas, and Govind perhaps saw in the imperial service a ready way of disarming suspicion and of reorganizing his followers.⁴

Cunningham adds a footnote: 'The liberal conduct of Bahadur Shah is confirmed by the contemporary historian, Khafee Khan, who states that he received rank in the Moghul army (see Elphinstone, *History of India*, ii. 566, note), and it is in a degree corroborated by the undoubted fact of the Gooroo's death, on the banks of the Godavery.'⁵

The modern Sikh historians Teja Singh and Ganda Singh categorically reject the idea of service:

> The moving of the Guru along with the royal camp has been misinterpreted by some writers, like Forster, Cunningham and Elphinstone who allege that the Guru was given a military command in the expeditionary force led by the Emperor. The allegation began with Forster who says that 'the Sikhs say', and Cunningham goes further in saying that 'the Sikh writers seem unanimous in giving to their great teacher a military command in the Daccan'. Who are these Sikh writers? Nobody knows. Khafi Khan only says that during Bahadur Shah's march to the Deccan, Guru Gobind Singh, with 200 or 300 spear-men, came to the Emperor and accompanied him (*dar rakab rafaqat namud*). *Tarikh-i-Bahadurshahi*, however, leaves no ground for ambiguity. It says that 'Guru Gobind, one of the descendants of Nanak, had come into these districts to *travel* and accompanied the royal camp. He was in the habit of constantly addressing assemblies of worldly persons, religious fanatics and all sorts of people' (E. & D., vii. 566). This could not have been allowed to a man in government service, much less to a military commander proceeding on an important expedition.⁶

The idea of service refuses to disappear. A book written in 1994 by a well-known professor of History for schools hammers the point that Bahadur Shah tried to conciliate 'the rebellious Sikhs' by making peace with Guru Gobind Singh and giving him a *mansab*. He goes on to add: 'After Aurangzeb's death, Guru Gobind Singh joined Bahadur Shah's camp as a noble of the rank of 5000 *Zat* and 5000 *Savar*.' This view has been refuted by another professor of History. Among other things, he refers to my paper to the Indian History Congress which argues against the idea of service. He also quotes Khafi Khan's text to show that the crucial word used in it is '*rafaqat*'. This word cannot be interpreted as 'service'. Thus, there was no basis for the statement that Guru Gobind Singh accepted service.[7]

In the paper on Guru Gobind Singh's relations with Bahadur Shah presented at the Indian History Congress in 1966, I had pointed out that William Irvine, basing himself on the statements of some early writers such as Warid, had suggested that Guru Gobind Singh 'must have received some rank' from the emperor.[8] This appeared satisfactorily to explain Guru Gobind Singh's presence at or near the court and camp of Bahadur Shah for over a year. It is important to note, however, that there are explicit and implicit statements in near-contemporary writers which mention only the presence of Guru Gobind Singh near the court and camp of Bahadur Shah.

To some modern historians of the Sikhs, the acceptance of a mansab appears to be in flagrant contradiction with Guru Gobind Singh's character and earlier career. Indubhusan Banerjee, for instance, argued at length against the service theory in his *Evolution of the Khalsa*. Banerjee does not say so, but if Warid's whole account of Guru Gobind Singh is carefully examined in the light of what is now known of Guru Gobind Singh, Warid appears to be a very superficial and 'distant' observer of the events. His isolated statement lacks credibility.

Nevertheless, the rejection of the service theory obliges the historian to offer a better explanation of Guru Gobind Singh's presence near the imperial camp for more than a year before his death in October 1708. Banerjee was quite alive to this obligation and suggested that Guru Gobind Singh had met Bahadur Shah to seek redress against certain Mughal officials, notably Wazir Khan, the *faujdar* of Sirhind, who had inflicted heavy losses on Guru Gobind

Singh. Curiously enough, the motivation of revenge had suggested itself to Muhammad Qasim Lahauri.[9]

Guru Gobind Singh had instituted the Khalsa in 1699 and, soon afterwards, the chief of Kahlur was obliged to take notice of the growing numbers and activities of the Khalsa, who appeared to threaten not only the jealously guarded authority of the chief but also the integrity of his not very large dominions. His aim was to expel Guru Gobind Singh and the Khalsa from Anandpur on the plea that they lived within his territories without acknowledging his authority. But he soon realized that his own limited resources were not enough for achieving that aim. In fact, he failed to take the well-fortified Anandpur even with the aid of neighbouring chiefs. The only alternative left for him was to request his suzerain, Emperor Aurangzeb, for help. It was with the aid of the Mughal faujdar of Sirhind that the chief of Kahlur succeeded in taking Anandpur finally in 1704.

In 1705–6, Guru Gobind Singh negotiated with Aurangzeb. Sainapat's account of Guru Gobind Singh's life and mission gives briefly the contents of a letter he wrote to the Emperor. Guru Gobind Singh refers to the perjury of Mughal officials and underlines the moral obligation of the Emperor to pay immediate attention to this matter. He was willing to see the Emperor to discuss the matter in person. That his letter had the desired effect on Aurangzeb is evident from one of his orders in which Mun'im Khan at Lahore is asked to try reconciliation.[10] Before the end of 1706, Guru Gobind Singh had decided to see the Emperor. But Aurangzeb died while Guru Gobind Singh was on his way to Ahmadnagar. He then decided to see Bahadur Shah.

Guru Gobind Singh was given a reception by Bahadur Shah at Agra in July 1707. He went fully armed into the royal presence and was given a costly present along with a *khil'at*.[11] His appreciation of what passed between himself and the Emperor was soon conveyed to the Khalsa in Punjab. This letter is most significant for its allusion to the purpose of the meeting. After mentioning the jewelled medallion and the khil'at presented to him, Guru Gobind Singh expresses his satisfaction with 'other matters'. He then informs the Khalsa that he would return to them in a few days. He asks the Khalsa to maintain friendly association, and to come fully armed to the Guru's presence on his return to Kahlur.[12] It is evident that Anandpur was very much on his mind, now as before. This is what a careful study of Guru Gobind Singh's whole career would lead one to expect. Anandpur, which had remained the cause of a protracted dispute between Bhim Chand and Guru Gobind Singh, was always regarded by Guru Gobind Singh as his ancestral inheritance and his 'home'. Guru Gobind Singh's argument with the Mughal Emperor was basically a moral argument: In the initial conflict of the Guru with the hill chief, the Mughal officials had interfered on behalf of the party that had been in the wrong.

Guru Gobind Singh's presence near the imperial court suited Bahadur Shah's purpose. As Prince Mu'azzam, Bahadur Shah had been sent towards Punjab in 1696. He was appointed to the governorship of Kabul as well, with Mun'im Khan as his deputy in Lahore. Thus, Bahadur Shah was aware of the political situation in Punjab. If the hill chiefs could be a source of trouble to the local faujdars, the popularity of Guru Gobind Singh with his Sikhs scattered nearly all over Punjab made him equally important from a political point of view. Bahadur Shah also knew that Aurangzeb had eventually decided upon reconciliation. In 1707, with the issue of the succession to the Mughal throne not yet finally settled, it was in Bahadur Shah's interest to secure peace and order in the northwest; for his part, it was highly politic to offend neither the hill chiefs nor Guru Gobind Singh. Guru Gobind Singh's awkward presence near the court was preferable to his dangerous freedom in Punjab. The Emperor's gestures of goodwill and kindness were expected to keep the Guru in good humour and hopeful suspense.

When Bahadur Shah started on his campaign in Rajasthan, Guru Gobind Singh accompanied the imperial army and remained near the camp for 10 more months. His continued presence with or near the camp could easily be interpreted by distant or superficial observers as his acceptance of service with Bahadur Shah, especially because Guru Gobind Singh and his Khalsa used to carry arms wherever they went. To many a contemporary and near-contemporary writers, Guru Gobind Singh's presence with Bahadur Shah meant no more than his presence.[13] On several occasions, Guru Gobind Singh left the camp to spend his time elsewhere in his own way. He continued preaching to all kinds of people. When Bahadur Shah moved towards Hyderabad, Guru Gobind Singh moved with him; he was probably encouraged to hope that the Emperor would soon be free to attend to the Punjab affairs. When Guru Gobind Singh sensed that Bahadur Shah was evading the issue, he commissioned Banda to lead direct action in the north-west. Within two years of Guru Gobind Singh's death, Bahadur Shah was obliged to face a formidable revolt of the Khalsa.

On Guru Gobind Singh's death, it had been represented to Bahadur Shah that the Guru's property should be considered for escheat. This has been regarded as proof of his having accepted service with the Mughals. This, however, is no proof. In the first place, Bahadur Shah ordered that his property was not to be touched as it was the property of a darvesh.[14] Second, the question of escheat had come up because Guru Gobind Singh had died without a legal heir.[15]

Notes

1. George Forster, *A Journey from Bengal to England through the Northern Part of India, Kashmire, Afghanistan and Persia and into Russia by the Caspian Sea* (Patiala: Punjab Languages Department, 1970 [1798]), vol. 1, pp. 302–3.

2. John Malcolm, *A Sketch of the Sikhs* (New Delhi: Asian Educational Services, 1986 [1812]), pp. 70–1.

3. W. L. M'Gregor, *The History of the Sikhs* (Patiala: Punjab Languages Department, 1970 [1846]), p. 102.

4. Joseph Davey Cunningham, *History of the Sikhs: From the Origin of the Nation to the Battles of the Sutlej* (New Delhi: Rupa & Co., 2002 [1849]), p. 79.

5. Cunningham, *History of the Sikhs*, p. 79n.

6. Teja Singh and Ganda Singh, *A Short History of the Sikhs (1465–1765)* (Patiala: Punjabi University, 1999 [1950]), p. 76n.

7. Dalbir Singh Dhillon, 'Bipan Chandra's View About Guru Gobind Singh's Relations with Bahadur Shah – A Historical Analysis', in *Guru Gobind Singh and Creation of the Khalsa*, edited by Madanjit Kaur (Amritsar: Guru Nanak Dev University, 2000), pp. 90–7.

8. J. S. Grewal, 'Zafarnama: Declaration of Moral Victory', *Sikh Ideology, Polity and Social Order* (New Delhi: Manohar, 2007), pp. 96–100.

9. Muhammad Qasim Lahauri, '*Ibratnama*', extract in *Sikh History from Persian Sources*, edited by J. S. Grewal and Irfan Habib (New Delhi: Tulika/Indian History Congress, 2001), p. 115.

10. *Makhaz-i Tawarikh Sikhan*, edited by Ganda Singh (Amritsar: Sikh History Society, 1949), p. 75. *Sikh History from Persian Sources*, pp. 98–9.

11. *Makhaz-i Tawarikh Sikhan*, p. 82. *Sikh History from Persian Sources*, p. 106.

12. *Hukamname Guru Sahiban, Mata Sahiban, Banda Singh ate Khalsa Ji De*, edited by Ganda Singh (Patiala: Punjabi University, 1967), pp. 186–9.

13. For instance, Khafi Khan, *Muntakhab al-Lubāb* (Calcutta: 1984), pp. 651–2.

14. *Sikh History from Persian Sources*, p. 107.

15. All the four sons of Guru Gobind Singh died in his lifetime. Contemporary sources refer to his adopted sons, Zorawar Singh and Ajit Singh. See *Nairang-i Zamana*, in *Sikh History from Persian Sources*, pp. 101–3, 107. Sainapat, *Sri Gur Sobha*, edited by Shamsher Singh Ashok (Amritsar: Shiromani Gurdwara Prabandhak Committee, 1967), pp. 123–6. *Chahar Gulshan*, in *Sikh History from Persian Sources*, p. 166.

11

The Last Commandment

Sikh writers of the eighteenth century make interesting statements about the last days of Guru Gobind Singh at Nanded. They were concerned with the way in which Guru Gobind Singh departed from the world. Sainapat records that a Pathan came to see the Guru in order to assess the situation for a suitable time to assassinate him. He came several times before he attacked Guru Gobind Singh with a dagger. The Pathan was killed by the Guru. The wounds of Guru Gobind Singh were dressed. Three or four days later, many Singhs came to have his *darshan* and Guru Gobind Singh held a *diwan*. Many days later came his end. He said farewell to the Singhs after midnight with '*Vaheguru ji ki fateh*'. His light mingled with the divine light on 7 October 1708. His body was cremated that very night.[1]

Sewadas strikes a different note. The Pathan who attacked Guru Gobind Singh was a grandson of Painde Khan, who had been killed in battle by Guru Hargobind, and Guru Gobind Singh deliberately incited him to attack. Bahadur Shah sent his hakims for treatment and the wounds healed in a week. The Guru stretched a strong bow and the wounds reopened. Guru Gobind Singh announced that he would leave his body at this place (Nanded) which was sanctified by gods, *siddh*s, and sants. Preparations for his cremation were made. Guru Gobind Singh sat on the funeral pyre, fully dressed and armed. When the ashes were searched later for the remains of the Guru's body, nothing was found of his body or his arms. Everyone believed that Guru Gobind Singh had bodily (*san-deh*) gone to his heavenly abode. A *dehura* was built at the spot of cremation.[2]

According to Koer Singh, the Pathan who came to see the Guru was the son of a Pathan who had been killed by Guru Gobind Singh in the territory of Sirhind for using derogatory language for the Guru. Guru Gobind Singh took the responsibility of looking after the young Pathan who, however, thought of taking revenge. Finding the Guru alone on a quiet evening, he struck the Guru with a dagger three times, causing deep wounds. Bahadur Shah was surprised at the news and sent English surgeons for his treatment. The wounds healed in 10 days. A short time later, the Guru stretched two bows together till they broke. The wounds reopened, but the Guru refused to have any treatment. On the 16th day, he announced that he would leave the world on the day of Guru Tegh Bahadur's martyrdom. Koer Singh says that no weapons or bones were found in the ashes. The Sikhs were mourning his passing away when an Udasi came from outside and told them that he had seen the Guru sitting fully armed in a *palaki* in his formal attire.[3] The implication was clear: Guru Gobind Singh had gone bodily to the other world.

Sukha Singh remains close to Koer Singh in his account of the last days of Guru Gobind Singh. Two Pathans came to the diwan. Guru Gobind Singh treated them with cordiality, and they came again after a few days. Their visit became a daily routine and the Guru gave them *in'am* (reward) at parting. One of them was a grandson of Painde Khan. Guru Gobind Singh had killed his father. One day, Guru Gobind Singh gave him a dagger and also said that the son who did not avenge his father was a contemptible wretch. Repeatedly incited, the Pathan attacked Guru Gobind Singh with the dagger and wounded him. But he was killed by the Guru. His companion was killed by the Singhs. Bahadur Shah sent his vaids who remained in attendance on the Guru for 10 days, and the wounds were healed. The hakims were generously rewarded for their services. However, Guru Gobind Singh stretched a bow and the wounds reopened. He knew that the time for his departure had come. He told the Singhs not to mourn, but to perform *kirtan* and *katha*, and to hold diwan for 40 days so that everyone could have his sight (*didar*). Later, when his ashes were searched for his remains, nothing was found, not even the weapons. This led to a common belief among the Sikhs that Guru Gobind Singh had bodily gone to the other world.[4]

Kesar Singh Chhibber, Sarup Das Bhalla, and Sarup Singh Kaushish have little to add. Chhibber says that Guru Gobind Singh thought of discarding his mortal frame, knowing that the time fixed for his departure from the world had come. He began to taunt Painde Khan's sons and grandsons, who were in his service, saying that a person who did not avenge the death of his father and grandfather was a contemptible wretch. Two of the young Pathans were given the duty of watching over the Guru's bedroom. One of them attacked him with a dagger. The Guru killed the assailant. Bahadur Shah heard the news and sent hakims for dressing the Guru's wounds. They were generously rewarded before they went back to Burhanpur. However, the wounds reopened when Guru Gobind Singh stretched a bow. His end now seemed to be inevitable. For over half an hour, the Sikhs went on conversing with the Guru before his light mingled with the light of Akal Purkh.[5]

Sarup Das Bhalla says that Guru Gobind Singh thought of leaving the world. A Pathan whose father had been killed by the Guru was employed to play *chaupar* (a board game) with him. His daily allowance was eventually raised to five *ashrafi*s (gold coins). While playing chaupar, the Guru used to incite him to avenge his father's death. One day, the Pathan took up the dagger which the Guru had placed on his side and struck the Guru a few times. The Pathan was cut into pieces by a Sikh. The Guru's wounds healed, but he deliberately stretched a bow made in Lahore. He told the Sikhs to prepare the funeral pyre. When it was ready, he lay down on it, covering himself with a sheet. He was absorbed in *nirban* (liberation), and his body was cremated.[6]

Sarup Singh Kaushish says that two Pathans came to see Guru Gobind Singh after Banda had left Nanded with the caravan of Bhagwant Singh. After nightfall, one of the Pathans went out of the tent and the other, Jamshed Khan, remained with the Guru. He attacked the Guru with a dagger and struck him twice. He tried to run away, but was killed by the Sikh watchman. The Sikhs were surprised to find that the Guru had been wounded. Guru Gobind

Singh told them that all this was in accordance with the will of God. The time had come for him to go to the *dargah* of Nirankar.[7]

Koer Singh records a significant incident. Mata Sahib Devi wanted to burn herself with Guru Gobind Singh. This would not be good, he said. She must live to die a natural death. A *kalal* (vintner) Singh, with five others, was deputed to escort Mata Sahib Devi to Delhi. Guru Gobind Singh cited a verse from the *Sukhmani*. According to Kaushish, Mata Sahib Kaur was utterly dejected over the prospect of separation from her husband. Guru Gobind Singh consoled her and said that she now had the entire Khalsa placed in her lap as their mother.[8]

Far more important was the question of Guruship. According to Sainapat, when the Singhs asked Guru Gobind Singh about his successor, he named 'the Khalsa'. He was concerned with the Khalsa, he said, and had bestowed his robe upon the Khalsa. 'Khalis [pure] is my form and I am with the Khalis. From the beginning to the end, my abode is the Khalsa.' Equally emphatically, the true Guru was essentially the *shabad*, the *bani*, which led to the state of liberation (nirban). This enunciation meant the end of personal Guruship, and the vesting of Guruship in the Panth and the Granth.[9]

Koer Singh, Kaushish, and Sukha Singh also refer to the issue of Guruship. According to Koer Singh, Guru Gobind Singh underscored that no person but the Granth was to be the Guru. He offered five paise and a coconut to the *Granth Sahib* and told the Sikhs to read the *Granth Sahib* when they wanted to speak to the Guru. After dwelling on the Khalsa rahit, Guru Gobind Singh said that the entire sangat was his form (*rup*), and he would always be present in the Khalsa who followed the rahit.[10]

In the account given by Kaushish, the Sikhs ask Guru Gobind Singh about his successor, and he says that the Panth had been created in accordance with the divine command and God would come to its aid in all crises. He asked Daya Singh to place five paise and a coconut before the *Granth Sahib*. Daya Singh did that and Guru Gobind Singh declared the Granth and the Khalsa to be the Guru after him.[11]

Sukha Singh says in his *Gurbilas* that when the Khalsa asked Guru Gobind Singh about his successor, he said that they were entrusted to Akal Purkh. The writer refers also to the injunction that the Khalsa should read the bani of the Gurus and observe the rahit. By using the term 'Guru-Khalsa' for the Guru, Sukha Singh leaves no room for ambiguity.[12]

The doctrines of Guru Granth and Guru Panth became current among the Khalsa during the eighteenth century as the last commandment of Guru Gobind Singh.

In the entries made in the *Akhbarat-i Darbar-i Mu'alla* in November 1708, the name of the Pathan who attacked Guru Gobind Singh is Jamshed Khan. A 'mourning robe' was given to his son on 8 November. The nature of Jamshed Khan's link with the court of Bahadur Shah is not known. It has been conjectured by some twentieth-century Sikh historians that he was a hired assassin sent by Bahadur Shah. The eighteenth-century writers provide no clue. But the question remains: Why was Jamshed Khan's son given a mourning robe?

On 10 November, it was ordered that 'the son of Guru Gobind Rai' be given a mourning robe 'on account of his father's death'. The reference is to the adopted son of Guru Gobind Singh, named Ajit Singh. On 22 November, it was reported that Guru Gobind Singh had left much property behind and orders were sought on its disposal. Bahadur Shah observed: 'The king's treasury does not get affluent by seizing such property. Let them not interfere with the property of dervishes.'[13]

Finally, Sainapat gives expression to his conviction that the Khalsa would establish their rule in the future. The last *savvayya* in Chapter 19 of his *Sri Gur Sobha* has the refrain:

> *Bhal bhag bhaya tum tahe kaho*
> *Garh Anand pher basavenge.*[14]
> [It is our good fortune to declare: 'we shall establish Anandgarh one again'.]

There can hardly be any doubt that the re-establishment of Anandgarh is symbolic of the establishment of Khalsa rule. Sainapat does not use the phrase '*Raj karega Khalsa*' (the Khalsa shall rule), but this is precisely the idea that he projects:

> All of the masters, kings, and emperors of the world, seeing your splendor they will be frightened,

Very frightened, the warriors and kings will abandon the country, all of them will flee,

In their worried minds, without any recourse, they will achieve liberation from Hari,

It is our good destiny, we promise this to you, we will re-establish Anandgarh.[15]

Notes

1. Sainapat, *Sri Gur Sobha*, edited by Shamsher Singh Ashok (Amritsar: Shiromani Gurdwara Prabandhak Committee, 1967), pp. 128–31.

2. Kharak Singh and Gurtej Singh, trans. and eds, *Episodes from Lives of the Gurus: Parchian Sewadas* (Chandigarh: Institute of Sikh Studies, 1995), pp. 161–2.

3. Koer Singh, *Gurbilas Patshahi 10*, edited by Shamsher Singh Ashok (Patiala: Punjabi University, 1968), pp. 273–9.

4. Sukha Singh, *Gurbilas Patsahi 10*, edited by Gursharan Kaur Jaggi (Patiala: Bhasha Vibhag, Punjab, 1989), pp. 430–7, 439–45. It may be pointed out that Ganda Singh has written a whole monograph on the death of Guru Gobind Singh, using all the available sources in Gurmukhi and Persian, to establish the fact that Guru Gobind Singh had not 'ascended to heaven bodily'. Ganda Singh rightly traces this idea to the *Parchian* of Sewadas (then placed in 1741). This idea had a bearing on the belief of the Kukas (Namdharis) that Guru Gobind Singh lived for a long time after 1708 to nominate Baba Balak Singh as his successor who, in turn, nominated Baba Ram Singh as the Guru. This made him the 12th Guru of the Sikhs, in line with the 10 Gurus from Guru Nanak to Guru Gobind Singh. Ganda Singh, *Guru Gobind Singh's Death at Nanded: An Examination of Succession Theories* (Patiala: Punjabi University, 2008 [1972]).

5. Kesar Singh Chhibber, 'Bansavalinama Dasan Patshahian Ka', edited by Rattan Singh Jaggi, in *Parkh*, vol. 2, edited by S. S. Kohli (Chandigarh: Panjab University, 1972), pp. 162–4.

6. Sarup Das Bhalla, *Mahima Prakash*, edited by Gobind Singh Lamba and Khazan Singh (Patiala: Punjab Languages Department, 1972), part II, pp. 891–2.

7. Bhai Svarup Singh Kaushish, *Guru Kian Sakhian*, edited by Piara Singh Padam (Amritsar: Singh Brothers, 1999 [1986]), pp. 195–200.

8. Koer Singh, *Gurbilas*, pp. 286–7. Kaushish, *Guru Kian Sakhian*, pp. 200–1. For the role of Mata Sundari and Mata Sahib Devi, see Appendix 11.1.

9. Sainapat, *Sri Gur Sobha*, p. 132.

10. Koer Singh, *Gurbilas*, pp. 281–6.

11. Kaushish, *Guru Kian Sakhian*, pp. 200–1.

12. Sukha Singh, *Gurbilas*, pp. 178–80.

13. J. S. Grewal and Irfan Habib, eds, *Sikh History from Persian Sources: Translations of Major Texts* (New Delhi: Tulika/Indian History Congress, 2001), p. 107.

14. Sainapat, *Sri Gur Sobha*, pp. 136–8.

15. Ami P. Shah, 'In Praise of the Guru: A Study and Translation of Sainapati's Gursobha', PhD diss. (University of California, Santa Barbara, 2010), p. 224.

Appendix 11A

Mata Sundari, Mata Sahib Devi, and the Khalsa Panth

Rai Chaturman Saksena in his *Chahar Gulshan* takes notice of the Hindu sects, including the Nanak Panthis. After a brief statement on Guru Nanak and his nine successors, he talks of Guru Ajit Singh and his son Hathi Singh, Mata Sundari, and Mata Sahib Devi. After the death of Guru Gobind Singh, his followers took permission from Bahadur Shah for enthroning Ajit Singh, the adopted son of Guru Gobind Singh, on the spiritual seat. In the reign of Farrukh Siyar (1713–19), Mata Sundari established a separate seat. Some Sikhs deserted Ajit Singh to join the followers of Mata Sundari. When she died, her followers turned to Mata Sahib Devi, known as the 'Virgin Bride' (*Kunwara Dola*). She too died after a year. Meanwhile, Ajit Singh was unjustly killed in 1721–2 on the false accusation that he had killed a Muslim dervish. His son, Hathi Singh, was taken by his well-wishers to Mathura, which was considered as a safer place. He was still there in 1759–60, with a following of a 100 to 200 persons.[1]

According to Kesar Singh Chhibber, Mata Sundari and Mata Sahib Devi came to Delhi in 1707 and brought Jit Singh, the adopted son of Guru Gobind Singh, with them. After Guru Gobind Singh's death, Ajit Singh was made the Guru. He did not treat Mata Sundari with respect and 'Uncle Kirpal Singh' brought him back to obedience. Chhibber talks of the death of a Muslim fakir due to Jit Singh's order to punish him for his insolence. In reaction, the Muslims plundered the *dera* of Mata Sundari, and Jit Singh died of fear. His family shifted to Mathura with his son, Hathi Singh. The Guruship of Jit Singh lasted for 16 years, and he had a large number of followers called 'Jit Mallias'. For two years after his death, the Sikh sangat did not visit Mata Sundari's dera. She was served by a large number of male and female *tehalia*s (attendants).[2]

After Mata Sundari's death, Mata Sahib Devi began to look after both the deras, Mata Sundari's and her own. Sikhs began to come to her presence in large numbers, particularly at the time of Baisakhi and Diwali. Mata Sahib Devi began to feel that large gatherings of Sikhs in Delhi could lead to some unpleasant happening. She discussed this matter with the prominent Sikhs of Delhi and the women of the dera. A *gurmata* was passed to the effect that the Baisakhi and Diwali festivals be held in Ramdaspur rather than in Delhi.[3]

Kirpal Singh, the maternal uncle of Guru Gobind Singh, with seven other persons, came to Ramdaspur in 1727 and met the *panch*s of the town, mostly Khatris. All matters related to the management of the sacred space and the town were divided into four departments, and a '*masandi*' (follower of a masand) was appointed for each. Kesar Singh's father, Gurbakhsh Singh Chhibber, was appointed as *darogha* of the *karkhana*, the treasury, and the *gao-khana* (cowshed). It is quite clear that Ramdaspur was an autonomous town. Kesar Singh Chhibber mentions the important Sikhs who came to the town and stayed there for a long or short period of time, such as Bhai Mani Singh and Tara Singh, both of whom became martyrs later. The conflict between the followers of Banda (Bandais) and the Akal Purkhias (the Khalsa) is described by Chhibber. Ultimately, the Akal Purkhias alone survived to take control of the Harmandar and the Akal Bunga. Chhibber looks upon the attacks of the 'Turks' on Ramdaspur as a serious problem.[4] The prolonged concern of the Mughal administrators with Ramdaspur and their atrocities are underlined by Chhibber in his chapter on the 'contemporary Sikhs'.[5]

The *hukamnama*s of Mata Sundari and Mata Sahib Devi follow the pattern of the hukamnamas of Guru Gobind Singh. The first hukamnama of Mata Sundari, dated 12 October 1717 (Image 11A.1), is addressed to the sangat of Patna as 'Sri Akal Purkh ji ka Khalsa'. Two of the 23 persons named are not Singhs. They are asked to send for the *langar* Rs 200 by a *hundi*.[6]

The hukamnama of 29 March 1721 also asks for Rs 200.[7] In the hukamnama of 20 September 1722, Chet Singh is the *mewara* (messenger) sent for the collection of Rs 200 for the *langar*, in addition to a six-monthly contribution by way of *kar-bhet, sukh-mannat, dasaundh (dasvandh), chaliha,* and *golak.* Bhai Gurbakhsh Singh was sent so that he may get things done by the Mughal administration.[8] In the hukamnama of 18 October 1723, the Khalsa are asked to resolve impartially a dispute between Bhai Lal Pala and

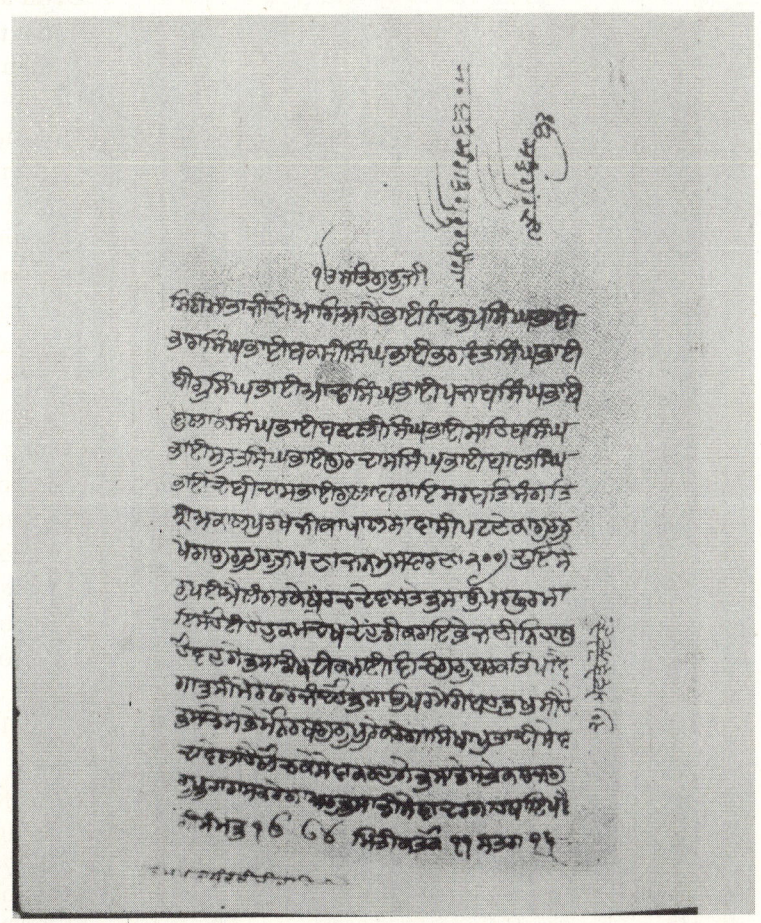

Image 11A.1 Mata Sundari's *hukamnama* dated 12 October 1717 (document 68), addressed to the *sangat* of Patna. Among the persons named there are 12 Singhs and 2 non-Singhs. The *sangat* is addressed as 'Sri Akal Purakh ji ka Khalsa'. They are called 'my sons', and asked to send Rs 200/- for the *langar* established by Mata Sundari in Delhi.

Source: Ganda Singh ed., *Hukamname*.

Bhai Sango Lal.[9] The sangat of Ghazipur was asked to send Rs 50 for the langar on 2 June 1722.[10] The hukamnama of 13 September 1728 (Image 11A.2) is addressed to Bhai Duna, Bhai Bighamal, Bhai Gurdas, and Bhai Rama, informing the *qabila* (tribe/clan)

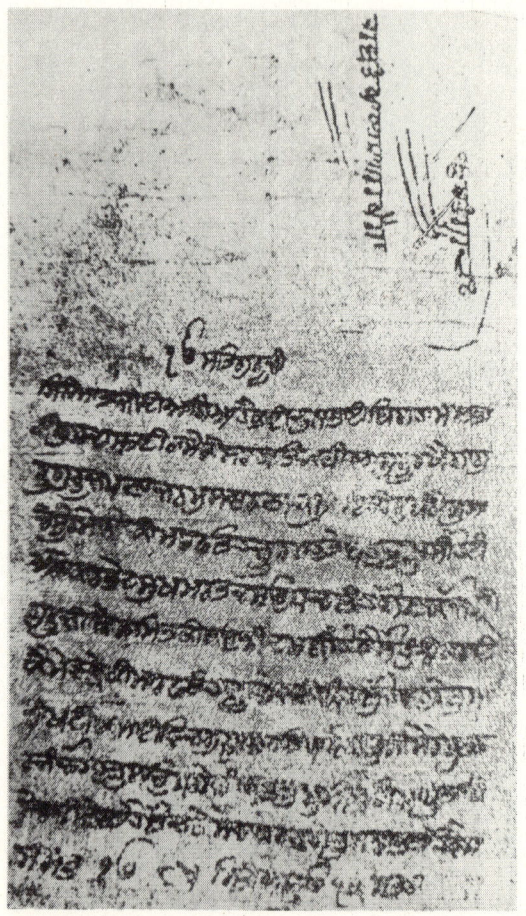

Image 11A.2 Mata Sundari's *hukamnama*, dated 13 September 1728 (document 76), addressed to the clan of Bhai Rama. The other members named are Bhai Duna, Bhai Bighamal, and Bhai Gurdas. The receipt of Rs. 21/- is acknowledged and it is expected that they would continue to send *kar, bhet, sukh, mannat, dasvandh, chaliha,* and *golak.*

Source: Ganda Singh ed., *Hukamname.*

that Rs 23 sent with the mewara had been received.[11] Another hukamnama acknowledges the receipt of Rs 21.

The last hukamnama of Mata Sundari, dated 10 August 1730, acknowledges the receipt of Rs 25 for the marriage of the daughter of Bebe Nufi.[12]

The hukamnamas of Mata Sahib Devi are no less interesting or significant. A hukamnama is addressed to Bhai Duna, Bhai Sabha, Bhai Ala, Bhai Bakhta, and Bhai Laddha—the entire qabila of Bhai Rama, son of Phul. It is underlined that the addressee should make no difference between Mata Sahib Devi and Mata Sundari in sending their offerings for the langar.[13]

The hukamnama dated 10 September 1726 (Image 11A.3), addressed to Bhai Alam Singh Jama'itdar, wishes for him *deg, teg,* and *fateh,* and asks him to collect offerings from the Singhs (of his unit) for the langar and send the entire amount with the mewara Gurbakhsh Bhagta.[14]

The hukamnama of 27 March 1729 asks the sangat of Patna to send contributions for the langar.[15] The Khalsa of Benares are asked to send Rs 50 for the langar in March 1929.[16] The '*Sarbat Khalsa Sri Akal Purkh ji ka*' at Naushehra Pannuan are asked to send Rs 11 for the langar through the mewara Bhai Ram Singh.[17] In the hukamnama of 17 November 1732 the receipt of Rs 14 though Bhai Mann Singh is acknowledged.[18] In the hukamnama of 30 December 1734, Bhai Mann Singh is told to dig up a well in Pattan Shaikh Farid for drinking water at the cost of the establishment of Mata Sahib Devi (see Image 11A.4 for another hukamnama referring to the Pattan Shaikh Farid residents).[19]

Karamjit K. Malhotra has looked at these hukamnamas from the viewpoint of the issue of gender. She observes that Mata Sundari and Mata Sahib Devi assumed leadership of the Sikh community on their own. Their authority was acceptable to the Sikhs because of their personalities. They exercised their authority primarily on moral grounds. They maintained two separate establishments. Mata Sahib Devi did not succeed Mata Sundari, but showed initiative to have an establishment of her own.[20] It may be added that for their active participation in the affairs of the Khalsa Panth, their widowhood was of no consequence.

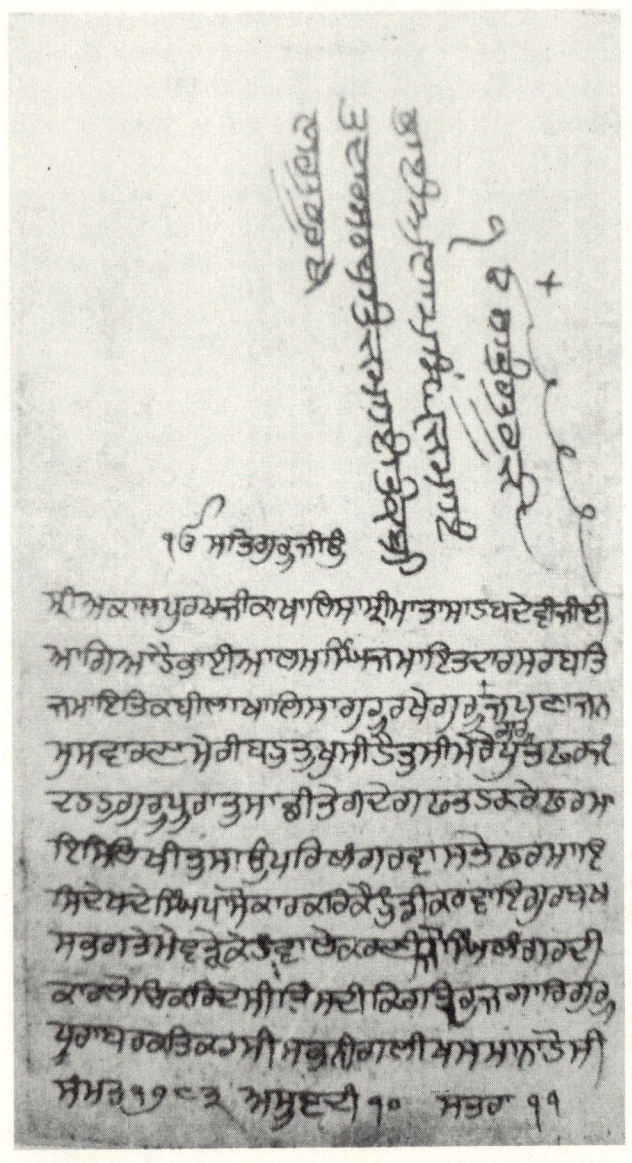

Image 11A.3 Mata Sahib Devi's *hukamnama*, dated 10 September 1726 (document 75), addressed to Bhai Alam Singh, the *Jama'atdar*. The *Jama'at* is addressed as 'Sri Akal Purkh ji ka Khalsa' and as 'my sons'. Mata Sahib Devi prays for the blessings of *deg, teg,* and *fateh* for them.

Source: Ganda Singh ed., *Hukamname.*

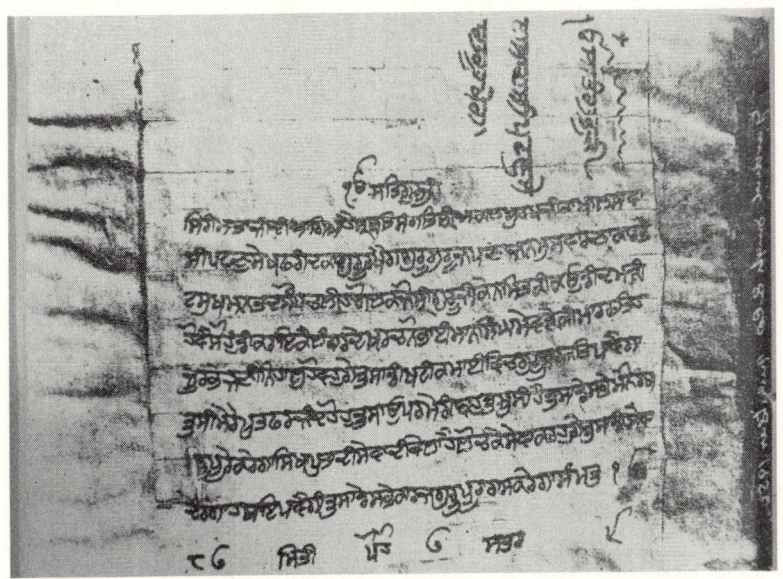

Image 11A.4   Mata Sahib Devi's *hukamnama*, dated 7 December 1730 (document 81), addressed to the residents of Pattan Shaikh Farid, who are addressed as 'Sarbat Sangat Sri Akal Purkh ji ka Khalsa'.
Source: Ganda Singh ed., *Hukamname*.

Notes

1. J. S. Grewal and Irfan Habib, eds, *Sikh History from Persian Sources* (New Delhi: Tulika/Indian History Congress, 2001), pp. 164–7.

2. Kesar Singh Chhibber, 'Bansavalinama Dasan Patsahian ka', edited by Ratan Singh Jaggi, in *Parkh*, vol. 2, edited by S. S. Kohli (Chandigarh: Panjab University, 1972), pp. 178–81.

3. Chhibber, *Bansavalinama*, p. 182.

4. Chhibber, *Bansavalinama*, pp. 182–5.

5. Chhibber, *Bansavalinama*, pp. 190–3.

6. *Hukamname Guru Sahiban, Mata Sahiban, Banda Singh ate Khalsa ji de*, edited by Ganda Singh (Patiala: Punjabi University, 1967), document 68.

7. *Hukamname*, document 69.

8. *Hukamname*, document 70.

9. *Hukamname*, document 73.

10. *Hukamname*, document 72.

11. *Hukamname*, document 76.

12. *Hukamname*, document 80.

13. *Hukamname*, document 74.

14. *Hukamname*, document 75.

15. *Hukamname*, document 77.

16. *Hukamname*, document 78.

17. *Hukamname*, document 83.

18. *Hukamname*, document 84.

19. *Hukamname*, document 85.

20. Karamjit K. Malhotra, *The Eighteenth Century in Sikh History: Political Resurgence, Religious and Social Life, and Cultural Articulation* (New Delhi: Oxford University Press, 2016), pp. 217–19.

12

Political, Social, and Cultural Legacies

The most striking legacy of Guru Gobind Singh was the long struggle for political power that culminated in the establishment of the Khalsa Raj in the third quarter of the eighteenth century. The century was marked also by literary activity, resulting in a wide range of literature being produced by Sikh writers in new and old literary forms. The *Dasam Granth* emerged as a text of considerable importance. The doctrines of Guru Granth and Guru Panth crystallized to influence the religious, social, and political life of the Khalsa. Sikh identity was sharpened to make the Khalsa visibly the 'third community' (*tisar panth*).

Sovereign Rule

Early in September 1708, Guru Gobind Singh deputed Banda to mobilize the Khalsa against the Mughal authorities to establish the Khalsa Raj (see Images 12.1 and 12.2).[1] A coin was struck after the conquest of Sirhind in the summer of 1710 to mark their sovereign status. The inscription on the coin contained a reference to the sword of Guru Nanak. The victory of Gobind, the king of kings, was a manifestation of God's grace.[2] It was a realization of the ideal of *Raj Karega Khalsa* (the Khalsa shall rule). The inscription on the seal used by Banda proclaimed that Guru Gobind Singh

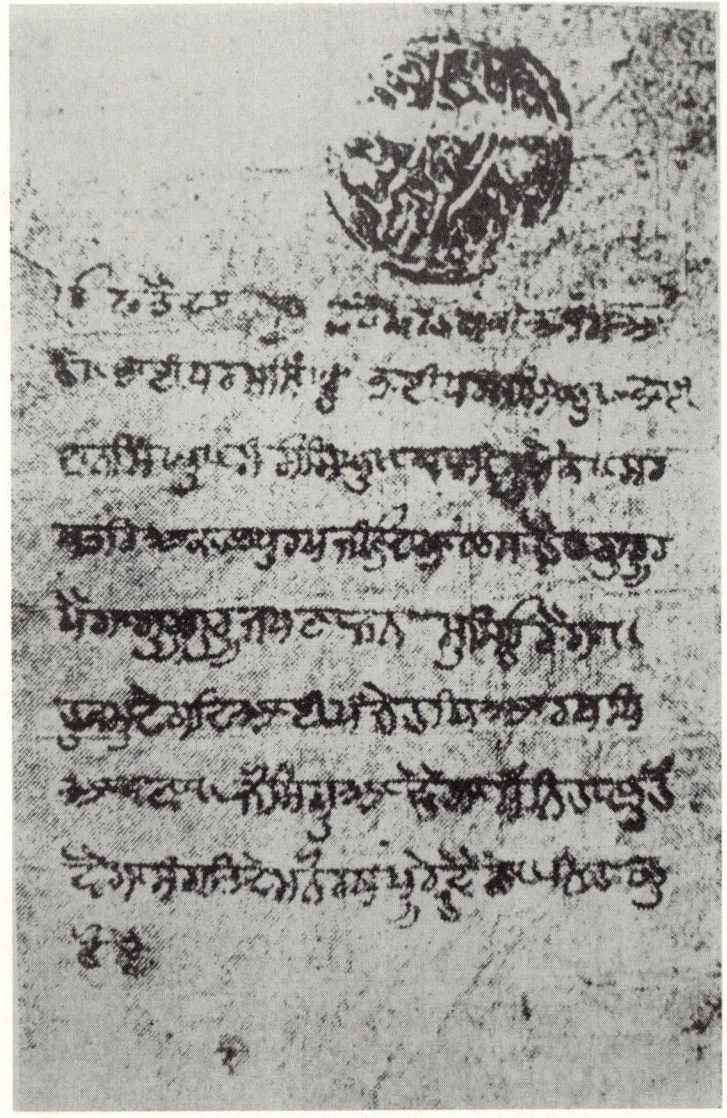

Image 12.1 This *hukamnama* is undated (document 66). It is addressed to Bhai Dharam Singh, Bhai Param Singh, Bhai Dhan Singh, and Bhai Sangu Singh, residents of Rupeke. They are addressed as the Khalsa of Akal Purakh Jio, and asked to come fully armed. This document bears the seal impression, stating that *deg, teg, and fateh* were the gifts received by Guru Gobind Singh from Guru Nanak.
Source: Ganda Singh ed., *Hukamname*.

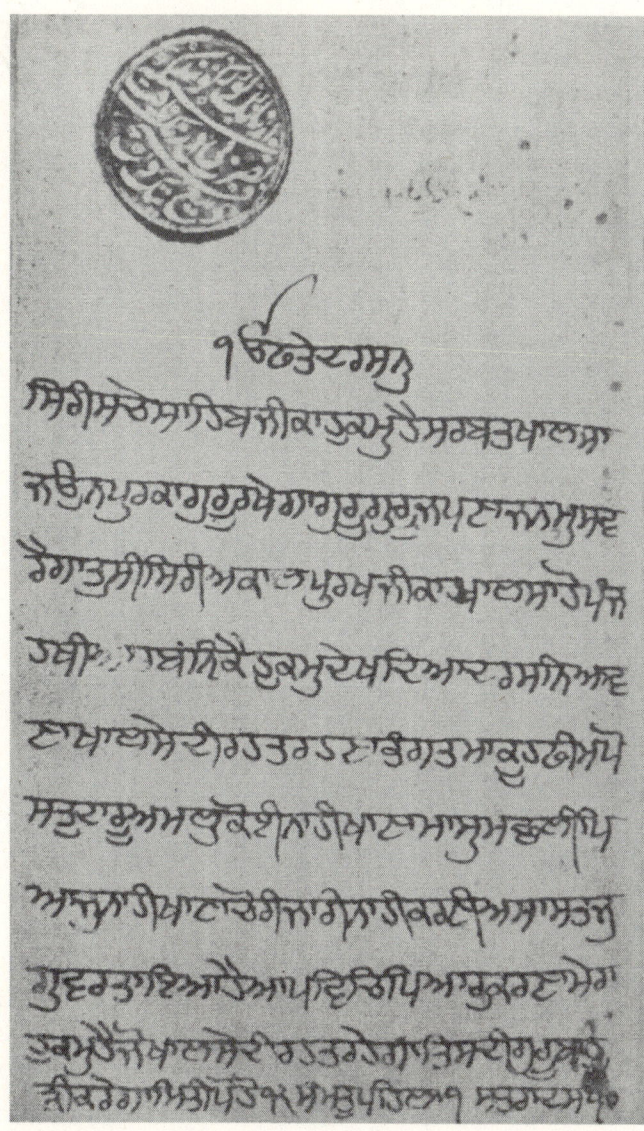

Image 12.2 This document 67 is similar to document 66 but it is dated 12 December 1710, the time of Banda Singh. The document refers to the rahit of the Khalsa and claims to have established *satjug*. It also refers to vegetarian diet. More significantly, the salutation used in the document is 'fateh darshan' and not 'Vaheguru ji ka Khalsa'. There is reference also to the first (regnal) year.
Source: Ganda Singh ed., *Hukamname*.

received from Guru Nanak '*deg, teg* and *fateh*'.[3] The foundation of a sovereign Sikh state is attributed to the grace of the True Master.

The contemporary Persian historians revile Banda, but they recognize that under his leadership the Khalsa established their own government and administration. They also recognize their bravery and spirit of sacrifice. Though eventually defeated, they were not demoralized.

Seated on the back of an elephant in a cage and followed by 740 other Sikh prisoners on camels, Banda entered Delhi in a procession that was meant to humiliate them. But 'there was no sign of humility and submission on their faces. Rather, most of them, riding on the camels' backs, kept singing and reciting melodious verses'.[4] Khafi Khan records the story of 'a youth in fresh bloom' among the Sikh prisoners whose mother had obtained the order of his release from the emperor, Farrukh Siyar, on the plea that her son had been forced to join the rebels. 'My mother lies,' said the young man, 'I am, heart and soul, a life-sacrificing believer and devotee of my guide [*murshid*].' He urged the executioner to send him to his companions already beheaded.[5]

The news reports of the time of Abd us-Samad Khan, governor of Punjab, indicate that Sikh outlaws were committing highway robbery and murder in defiance of the government. In 1721, they made a night attack on a Mughal detachment in pargana Pasrur. In 1726, they plundered an imperial caravan and killed some Mughal officials on the highway between Lahore and Sirhind. This was the year of Abd us-Samad Khan's transfer to Multan.[6]

In the time of Zakariya Khan (1726–45), son of Abd us-Samad Khan, Kesar Singh Chhibber was an eyewitness to the events at Ramdaspur: (*a*) ascendancy of the Akal Purkhia Khalsa and downfall of the followers of Banda, (*b*) organization of the affairs of Ramdaspur by Kirpal Singh, the maternal uncle of Guru Gobind Singh, on the advice of Mata Sahib Devi, and (*c*) establishment of a Mughal *thana* close to Ramdaspur to keep a watch over the activities of the Khalsa and to intervene for a virtual control of the place.[7] Thus, Ramdaspur became a rallying centre for the Khalsa and a target of the Mughals at the same time.

Chhibber refers to three well-known Sikh martyrs of the second quarter of the eighteenth century: Bhai Tara Singh, Bhai Mani

Singh, and Bhai Taru Singh. Tara Singh used to cultivate land and serve the Sikhs. A force of 900 men was sent against him, and he died fighting valiantly. Bhai Mani Singh, a pious Sikh, established his *dera* at Chohla Bagh in Ramdaspur. He was arrested by an army of 'Turks' and taken away. He remained firm in his faith even when he was cut into pieces, limb by limb. Taru Singh was another Sikh who was taken to Lahore and his scalp was removed from his head with the hair intact, while he sat calmly reciting the *Japu*.[8] The Sikh martyrs of the second quarter of the eighteenth century bear witness to both the persecution and the survival of the Khalsa as a political entity.

The province of Lahore was 'the Balkh and Bukhara of the Mughals where they had their mansions, orchards and graveyards'. The Mughal nobles of the empire looked upon it as their personal domain, like the *watan* [jagir] of an autonomous chief.[9] When Zakariya Khan died in July 1745, his eldest son, Yahiya Khan, was made the Deputy Governor of Punjab on 3 January 1746. His tenure was marked by the massacre of several thousand Sikhs, known as *chhota ghallughara* (the lesser massacre). His younger brother, Shahnawaz Khan, was made the Deputy Governor of Multan. There was a war between the two brothers in 1746–7 in which Yahiya Khan was worsted. Shah Nawaz Khan invited Ahmad Shah Abdali to invade India.

Ahmad Shah Abdali had succeeded to the eastern dominions of Nadir Shah to whom the Mughal emperor ceded the trans-Indus territories and the province of Thatta in 1739. Ahmad Shah Abdali obliged the Mughal emperor in 1752 to cede the provinces of Lahore and Multan to him. In 1757, the sarkar of Sirhind was added to his possessions. The Marathas occupied Punjab on behalf of the Mughal emperor in 1758. But they retreated before Ahmad Shah Abdali returned in 1759, and suffered a crushing defeat at Panipat in 1761. Ahmad Shah Abdali was at the height of his power in the early 1760s.

It is important here to note that individual Sikhs had begun to occupy pockets of territory by 1750. An order of Hukumat Singh issued in 1752 tells the 'amils (administrators of revenue) and zamindars of the town of Kahnuwan not to interfere in the affairs of the market and the land given as madad-i ma'ash to the Mahants of Pindori.[10] The seal of Jai Singh, who later became the ruler of Batala, bears the date 1750. This carries the implication that he had begun to issue orders in his name in 1750.[11] For 15 years then, the Sikhs continued to occupy pockets of territory despite all measures of suppression taken by Ahmad Shah Abdali.

Tahmas Khan was a witness to the severe repression of the Sikhs by Muin ul-Mulk, popularly called Mir Mannu, as the 'Afghan' governor. Mir Mannu used to pay 10 rupees for a Sikh head. He had to restore order in Punjab 'which had undergone a small revolution' on account of the tumult caused by Ahmad Shah Abdali in 1751–2. In the territory around Batala, a large number of Sikhs had caused a disturbance. An army was sent against them. They took to their heels and 900 of them took shelter in the fort of Ram Rauni near Ramdaspur (Amritsar). They were besieged. They came out and died fighting. Mir Mannu continued to persecute the Sikhs. When caught alive, they were put under the nail press (*mekh-chu*).[12]

Tahmas Khan narrates two events from the year 1757 which suggest that the Sikh resurgence was gaining ground. Qasim Khan got himself appointed as the *faujdar* of Patti, but he was not allowed to join his post by the Sikhs. The ill treatment of a Sikh sardar (actually Sodhi Badbhag Singh of Kartarpur near Jalandhar) by the Afghan soldiers led to a great loss of repute for the government and 'the administration of the country was thrown into disorder' (see also Image 12.3).[13]

In 1760 when Ahmad Shah Abdali was in India but away from Punjab, the Sikhs occupied much of the province. The news report of 11 October 1760 states that the Sikhs had brought under their control the territories of the province and established a system of tax collection over the country, sharing it with Ahmad Shah Abdali. When Ahmad Shah returned to Afghanistan in May–June 1761, the administration could not be restored because the tumult of the Sikhs in the province was quite considerable.[15]

In the 'great carnage' (*vadha ghallughara*) of February 1762, according to Tahmas Khan who was fighting on the Afghan side, about 25,000 Sikhs were slain in a single day.[16] A year later, however, Ahmad Shah Abdali suffered the humiliation of defeat 'at the

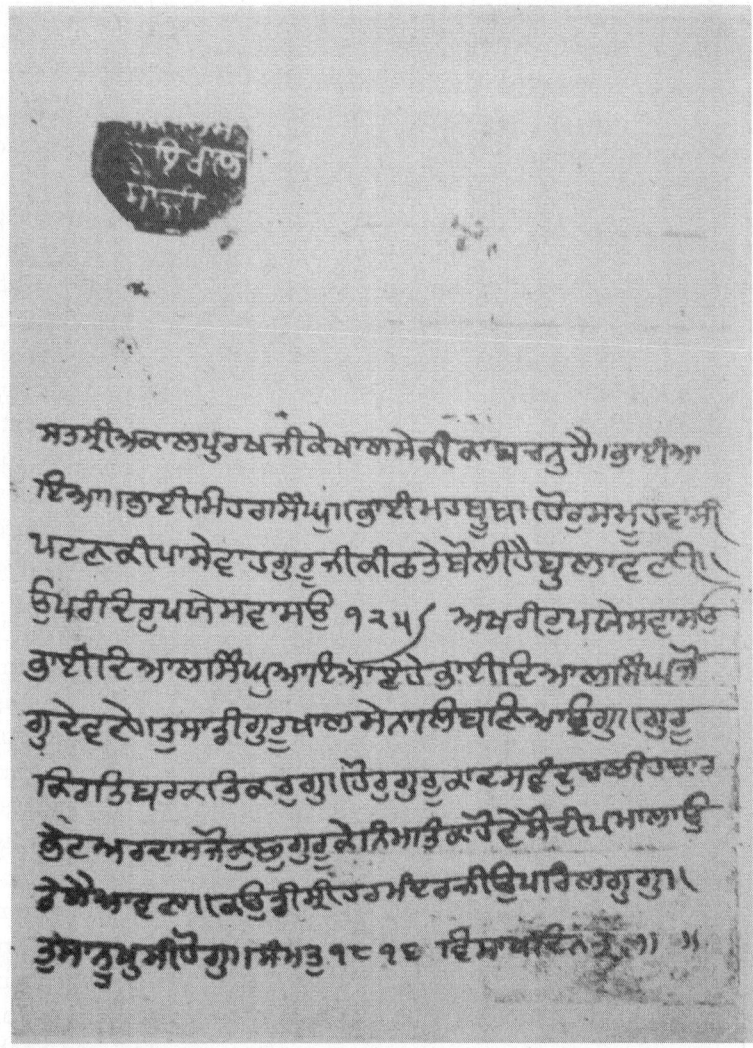

Image 12.3 *Hukamnama* of Sri Akal Purkh ji ka Khalsa, dated 12 April 1759 (document 86), addressed to the residents of Pattan. The salutation used in this document is 'Vaheguruji ki Fateh'. Three persons are named and only one of them is a Singh. They are asked to send Rs 125/- for the repair of Sri Harmandar ji. There is an explicit reference to 'Guru Khalsa' for the authority issuing this *hukamnama*. This document bears a seal impression which is partly deleted. The words 'Akal Sahai' (also used by Sikh rulers on their seals) are clear enough.[14]
Source: Ganda Singh ed., *Hukamname*.

hands of the Sikh chiefs' who took possession of the territory up to the river Jhelum.[17] Tahmas Khan refers to a meeting of the 'Sikh chiefs' at Ramdaspur at the time of Baisakhi in 1763 for 'deliberation and consultation' among them to divide and distribute the territories conquered.[18]

In the news report of 9 July 1763, the term 'Gurmata' is used for a meeting of the Sikh chiefs, explicitly stating that 'whatever is decided after mutual consultation will be acted upon'.[19] Indeed, a Gurmata was morally binding for all the Sikhs. According to the news report of 2 August 1763, the Sikh chiefs met at Ramdaspur again for deliberation and consultation.[20]

Qazi Nur Muhammad wrote in 1765 that no one could stand up to the Sikhs in battle. They were good at the sword, the spear, the bow, and the battle-axe. They used the musket as if it were their own invention. The Qazi talks of the exceptional moral traits of the Sikhs in war and in peace. From Sirhind, Lahore, and the territory of Multan up to the Derajat, they had divided the country among themselves. They feared no one.[21] When Ahmad Shah Abdali went to Ramdaspur to destroy it once again, there were 30 Sikhs in the Akal Bunga. They did not show any fear of being killed, fought the Afghan army, and died fighting.[22]

The Khalsa declared their sovereignty by striking a coin at Lahore in 1765. It bore the same inscription as the one on the seal of Banda. It refers to deg, teg, and fateh received from Guru Nanak by Guru Gobind Singh. These three terms had first appeared on the seal of Guru Gobind Singh. Thus, there can be little doubt that the Khalsa looked upon these gifts as a legacy of Guru Nanak mediated by Guru Gobind Singh. It is also obvious that they had never forgotten the ideal of 'Raj Karega Khalsa'.

Distinct Identity, Doctrines, and Literary Articulation

The ideal of equality was reflected in the Khalsa social order. The caste system was discarded: There was no restriction on one's choice of occupation and no denial of spiritual life to a Sikh; the basic beliefs and practices were the same for all. There was a remarkable equality in congregational worship (sangat) and the community meal (langar). In theory, there was no bar on inter-caste marriage. The idea of equality was built into the doctrine of the Guru Panth. The doctrine of the Guru Granth ensured religious equality in principle. Both these doctrines had a close bearing on the Khalsa social order. Commensality was extended to all except the former outcastes, and conjugality within the Khalsa order was underscored as the norm. The ideal norms were compromised, but never discarded.

The most visible legacy of Guru Gobind Singh was the iden-tity of the Khalsa.[23] In the beginning, the followers of the masands were sought to be persuaded to discard the mediacy of the masands and become directly linked with the Guru. With the introduction of khande ki pahul, the Khalsa were divided into 'Kesdhari Singhs' and 'Sahajdhari Sikhs'. Their rahit was largely common, but the differences between them were more glaring. The Sahajdharis were not supposed to keep unshorn hair, bear arms, and add the suffix 'Singh' to their names. They remained in existence in the time of Guru Gobind Singh and in the early decades of the eigh-teenth century. They were still there in the late eighteenth cen-tury, but the category 'Sahajdhari' became more inclusive. Guru Gobind Singh had excommunicated the Minas, Dhir Mallias, and Ram Raiyas. Some of them joined the Khalsa in the late eighteenth century, creating a more complex pattern. But the Kesdhari Singhs overshadowed all of them at the end of the eighteenth century. Sikh identity came to be equated with the Singh identity. They appeared to represent the '*tisar panth*', the Third Panth, different from both the Hindu and the Muslim.

The Kesdhari Singhs believed in one God, subscribed to the doctrines of the Guru Granth and the Guru Panth, and strength-ened the Gurdwara as the socio-religious institution of the Sikhs. Gradually, they evolved the norms of rites and ceremonies in which the Brahman had no important role to play. The ceremonies of birth, marriage, and death were sought to be made character-istically Sikh. The Rahitnama of Daya Singh, which is generally placed in the early nineteenth century, stipulates that there should be no marriage without the *Anand*. There should be no mourning on death. He who has taken amrit should not associate with the

Brahmans. He should not eat food cooked by a Brahman who had not taken pahul.[24] The core of *kirya-karam* in the *Sakhi Rahit Patshahi 10* are the Anand and the ardas.[25]

In the cultural legacy of Guru Gobind Singh, the *Dasam Granth* occupies an important place. Kesar Singh Chhibber advocated that the book of the 10th king should be regarded as the Guru, like the *Granth Sahib*. In the eighteenth century, the Granth of Guru Gobind Singh was not regarded as the Guru, but in several other ways it was given parity with the *Granth Sahib*. In the eighteenth century, the Sikh writers generally tended to assume that the compositions included in the *Dasam Granth* were written by Guru Gobind Singh. This could be the main reason for the myth of the Goddess being introduced in Sikh works of the eighteenth century in connection with the institution of the Khalsa.

Like the *Dasam Granth*, a number of Rahitnamas were part of the literary efflorescence of the time of Guru Gobind Singh. At least three important Rahitnamas were added before the advent of colonial rule in Punjab. The *Rahit Maryada* of the Shiromani Gurdwara Prabandhak Committee (SGPC) was based considerably on the Rahitnamas of the precolonial period. The *Bachittar Natak* gave rise to the form of literature called *Gurbilas*. Sainapat's *Sri Gur Sobha*, a contemporary work, complements the *Bachittar Natak*, covering the whole life of Guru Gobind Singh. The *Gurbilas Patshahi 10*, written by Koer Singh and Sukha Singh each during the eighteenth century, are more elaborate than the *Bachittar Natak* and the *Sri Gur Sobha*, and more focused on the life of Guru Gobind Singh.

It has been remarked recently that the eighteenth century served as a bridge between the Sikh tradition of the sixteenth and seventeenth centuries and the twentieth-century Sikhism, especially in terms of religious doctrines and institutions, political ideas and attitudes, social and ethical norms, rites and ceremonies, literary forms, and artistic conventions. All these developments of the eighteenth century converged on the crystallization and consciousness of a distinctive Sikh identity, which became a hallmark of the Sikh resurgence in colonial Punjab.[26] All these aspects of life of the Sikhs were influenced by what Guru Gobind Singh had said and done. The doctrines of the Guru Granth and the Guru Panth were at once the culmination of the old and the beginning of a new pattern of life. The former related more to ideology and the latter more to the Sikh social order.

Notes

1. See Karamjit K. Malhotra, 'Raj Karega Khalsa', in *The Eighteenth Century in Sikh History: Political Resurgence, Religious and Social Life, and Cultural Articulation* (New Delhi: Oxford University Press, 2016), pp.19–58.

2. The inscription in Persian reads: '*Sikkah zadd bar har do 'alam tegh-i Nanak wahib ast/Fateh Gobind (Singh) Shah-i Shahan fazl-i Sachcha Sahib ast.*'

3. The inscription in Persian reads as: '*Deg-o teg-o fateh-o nusrat be-diranj/Yaft az Nanak Guru Gobind Singh.*'

4. J. S. Grewal and Irfan Habib, eds, *Sikh History from Persian Sources* (New Delhi: Tulika/Indian History Congress, 2001), pp. 158–9.

5. *Sikh History from Persian Sources*, pp. 139–41.

6. Muzaffar Alam, *The Crisis of Empire in Mughal North India: Awadh and the Punjab, 1707–48* (New Delhi: Oxford University Press, 2013 [1986]), pp. 290, 293.

7. Kesar Singh Chhibber, 'Bansavalinama Dasan Patshahian Ka', edited by Ratan Singh Jaggi, in *Parkh*, vol. 2, (Chandigarh: Panjab University, 1972), pp. 157–99.

8. *Sikh History from Persian Sources*, pp. 193, 196.

9. Alam, *The Crisis of Empire in Mughal North India*, pp. 298–9.

10. B. N. Goswamy and J. S. Grewal, trans. and eds, *The Mughal and Sikh Rulers and the Vaishnavas of Pindori* (Shimla: India Institute of Advanced Study, 2010[1969]), document XVIII, pp. 205–8.

11. Goswamy and Grewal, *The Mughal and Sikh Rulers*, document XXV, pp. 230–3.

12. *Sikh History from Persian Sources*, pp. 174–7.

13. *Sikh History from Persian Sources*, pp.173–4, 176–7.

14. Ganda Singh, *Hukamname*, p. 233.

15. *Sikh History from Persian Sources*, p. 189.

16. *Sikh History from Persian Sources*, pp. 181–2.

17. *Sikh History from Persian Sources*, p. 190.

18. *Sikh History from Persian Sources*, pp. 190–1.

19. *Sikh History from Persian Sources*, p. 191.

20. *Sikh History from Persian Sources*, p. 192.

21. *Sikh History from Persian Sources*, p. 193.

22. *Sikh History from Persian Sources*, pp. 206–10.

23. 'Sakhi Rahit Patshahi Dasvin ki', in Padam, *Rahitname* (Amritsar: Singh Brothers, 2013), p. 61.

24. 'Rahitnama Bhai Daya Singh', in Padam, *Rahitname*, p. 74.

25. 'Sakhi Rahit Patshahi Dasvin ki', in Padam, *Rahitname*, p. 63.

26. Malhotra, *The Eighteenth Century in Sikh History*, p. 289.

Appendix 12A

Hanne Hanne Patshahi

It is interesting to note that 'Raj Karega Khalsa' was interpreted by the eighteenth-century Khalsa as the right of every Singh to carry arms, to fight, to conquer, and to rule.[1] The inscriptions on the coins struck in 1765 and 1780 could support this interpretation. Sovereignty was a gift received from the Gurus through the grace of God. By accepting the coin with either of the two inscriptions, a Khalsa ruler became sovereign. In principle, the Khalsa rulers had to respect one another's sovereignty, but they did not institutionalize political equality on a lasting basis.

Ratan Singh Bhangu hammers the point that under no circumstance were the Khalsa prepared to relinquish their claim to sovereignty.[2] They believed firmly that the Guru had assured them of nothing short of sovereign rule.[3] Bhangu uses the phrase '*hanne hanne patshahi*' (sovereignty for every saddle) to emphasize that every Khalsa could become a sovereign ruler.[4] Logically, the Sikh state was monarchical: all political power was held and exercised by one person.

The popular notion that the unit of Sikh government and administration in the late eighteenth century was the *misl*, and that there were 12 such units between the Indus and the Jamuna, is misleading. The Sikh writers of the eighteenth century use the term 'misl' for a fighting unit (as Sainapat does in his *Sri Gur Sobha* and Sukha Singh in his *Gurbilas Patshahi 10*). Bhangu, in the early nineteenth century, also talks of misls. A number of misls are mentioned during the Great Carnage (*Vadha Ghallughara*). Charhat Singh suggested that the Khalsa should have four misls at the centre and two on each wing; Charhat Singh was to provide support wherever it was needed. Jassa Singh Ahluwalia advised the leaders not to break up the misls in the midst of battle.[5] Elsewhere, a number of fighting units are mentioned without using the term misl.[6] The Ramgarhias and the Kanhiyas had one dera and used to divide their acquisitions equally among themselves. The land around the *amritsar* Gurdwara was kept as the common territory of all.[7] Bhangu talks of 10 misls, but the actual number of the fighting units he mentions is much larger. Bhangu presents the misl as a fighting unit under a particular leader. He does not talk of the misl as a territorial unit.

The orders issued by the Sikh rulers refer to them as independent individuals. In an order of Sahib Singh, dated 24 April 1781, he is referred to as *'Khalsa jio'*.[8] In an order of Jai Singh, dated 6 March 1788, he is referred to as *Sarkar-i Mu'alla* (the exalted government).[9] Ranjit Singh, in his order, is called 'Huzur Anwar' (the bright presence) or 'Sarkar A'la'.[10] On all these orders, the support of Akal (the immortal) is invoked. All the Sikh rulers seem to assume and convey the idea that they were not subordinate to any earthy ruler. Ranjit Singh was one of them during the last decade of the eighteenth century. In the early nineteenth century, he became the sole sovereign ruler of the former provinces of Lahore and Kashmir, and a large part of the province of Multan. This territorial expansion did not add anything to his sovereign status.

Notes

1. Karamjit K. Malhotra, 'Khalsa Raj', in *The Eighteenth Century in Sikh History: Political Resurgence, Religious and Social Life, and Cultural Articulation* (New Delhi: Oxford University Press, 2016), pp. 59–98.

2. Ratan Singh Bhangu, *Sri Gur Panth Parkash*, edited by Balwant Singh Dhillon (Amritsar: Singh Brothers, 2004), p. 134.

3. Bhangu, *Guru Panth Parkash*, p. 207.

4. Bhangu, *Guru Panth Parkash*, pp. 33, 194, 196, 207, 394.

5. Bhangu, *Guru Panth Parkash*, p. 341.

6. Bhangu, *Guru Panth Parkash*, pp. 344, 357.

7. Bhangu, *Guru Panth Parkash*, p. 385.

8. B. N. Goswamy and J. S. Grewal, trans. and eds, *The Mughal and Sikh Rulers and the Vaishnavas of Pindori* (Shimla: Indian Institute of Advanced Study, 2010 [1969]), document no. 32.

9. Goswamy and Grewal, *The Mughal and Sikh Rulers*, document no. 35.

10. Goswamy and Grewal, *The Mughal and Sikh Rulers*, document no. 37.

Chronology

22 December 1666: Birth of Gobind Das at Patna

March 1672: Gobind Das comes to Makhowal

11 November 1675: Martyrdom of Guru Tegh Bahadur

1677: Guru Gobind Das married Jito

1685: Guru Gobind Das married Sundari

April 1685: Guru Gobind Das at Paunta

1686: Meeting with Ram Rai at Dehra Dun; birth of Ajit Singh

18 September 1688: Battle of Bhangani

1689–90: Founded Anandpur; built fortresses

1690: Birth of Jujhar Singh

20 March 1691: Battle of Nadaun

19 February 1694: *Hukamnama* asking for a gun maker

November–December 1694: expedition of the Khanzada

1695: Husain's death in battle

2 August 1696: *Hukamnama* asking Bhai Taloka and Bhai Rama to come with horsemen

August–December 1696: Prince Mu'azzam's campaign

1697: Birth of Zorawar Singh

1698: Composition of the *Bachittar Natak* (*Apni Katha*)

30 March 1699: Institution of the Khalsa; birth of Fateh Singh

1701: Battle of Anandpur; temporary evacuation

6 February 1702: *Hukamnamas* asking several *sangats* to come fully armed; battles of Nirmoh, Basoli, and Kalmot; return to Anandpur

1704: *Hukamnama* to come with horsemen, foot soldiers, and musketeers; evacuation of Anandpur after a long siege; battle of Chamkaur, and the martyrdom of Sahibzada Ajit Singh and Sahibzada Jujhar Singh; martyrdom of Sahibzada Zorawar Singh and Sahibzada Fateh Singh; passing away of Mata Gujari

1705: Letter to Aurangzeb (*Zafarnama*)

1706: Stay at Talwandi Sabo (Damdama)

21 October 1706: Hukamnamas intimating departure for Ahmadnagar

20 February 1707: Death of Aurangzeb

8 June 1707: Bahadur Shah's victory in the battle of Jajau

23 July 1707: Meeting of Guru Gobind Singh with Bahadur Shah at Agra

2 October 1707: *Hukamnamas* sent by Guru Gobind Singh hoping to be back in Anandpur

November 1707: With Bahadur Shah in Rajasthan

1708: from Udaipur to Burhanpur

3 September 1708: Meeting with Banda at Nanded

7 October 1708: Passing away of Guru Gobind Singh

Glossary

Abchalnagar	eternal city; used especially for Nanded
Ād Purkh	The primal being, an epithet for God
Ādi Granth	the Sikh scripture, compiled by Guru Arjan in 1604 (containing the compositions of the first five Gurus and a number of *bhaktas*, *sants* and Sufis) and authenticated by Guru Gobind Singh with the compositions of Guru Tegh Bahadur. It is now known as *Guru Granth Sahib*
*Ahadī*s	individuals attending on the emperor for important duties
Akāl Purkh	Immortal Being
Akāl Takht	Immortal throne
Akhand Pāṭh	a continuous, unbroken, reading of Guru Granth Sahib
'amalguzār ('āmil)	revenue collector
amīn	revenue assessor
amrit	nectar, elixir of life; water prepared for initiation of the double-edged sword

amritsar	literally the pool of nectar; the term originally used for the tank constructed by Guru Ram Das; the usage was extended to the town of Ramdaspur (Amritsar) by the early nineteenth century
ardās	a prayer; the formal and collective prayer of the Sikhs, noticed by the author of the *Dabistan-i Mazahib* in the seventeenth century; far more elaborate, it is now called Ardas
ardāsia	one who performs *ardās*; a person employed for this purpose
bairāgī	a renunciate, usually Vaishnavite
ba'it	a rhyming couplet
bakhshī	an officer in charge of the army affairs in the Mughal times; he was directly responsible to the emperor
banda	a slave; a devotee
bandagī	devotion, dedication
Bāṇī	utterance; used for the utterance or the word of the Guru; generally equated with Gurbani
begam	a lady of rank
bhaddan (also *bhaddar*)	the rite of shaving the head, especially on the death of one's father
bhagautī	used in Sikh literature generally for the sword, and not the goddess 'Bhagavati'
bhākhā	spoken language
bhet	an offering; an offering to a deity; an offering made to the Guru or Guru Granth Sahib; land given in charity
bhujangī	from *bhujang*, literally a reptile, used as a metaphor for the Khalsa warrior, a young Khalsa

Bīr	used for a mythical being known for bravery
bhog	conclusion of the reading of Guru Granth Sahib, followed generally by singing of hymns, ardās, and distribution of sacred food
Bungā	a structure, a building; used for each of the many structures raised around the pool of nectar (amritsar) in Ramdaspur
chālihāā	a kind of rite on the fortieth day after death; an offering for the Guru on this account
Chandāl	one of the lowest categories of the outcastes; an untouchable
charan-pahul (charan-amrit)	water of the foot; the initiatory rite of drinking the water in which the toes of the Sikhs have been dipped, symbolizing humility and dedication on the part of the initiate; also called *charan-amrit*
chaudharī	the head of a group of villages for collecting revenues on behalf of the government; the office was generally hereditary
chaukī-shabad	kīrtan; kīrtan by turns for a fixed time called *chauki* at the Harmandar Sahib
chhand	a verse
Chhīpa	used for both a tailor and a calico-printer
Dal Khālsa	a term used for the combined forces of the Sikh leaders during the eighteenth century
dām	a coin, cash
dān	charity; to give away something from one's honest earnings for the use of others

darbār	court
dargāh	a holy place; the place of a pīr who is no longer alive, regarded as a place of pilgrimage
daroghā	a superintendent or head of any organization
darshan	the sight of a venerable person or place; used in the context of the Sikhs visiting the Guru as an act of merit
dasvandh	one-tenth; the share of annual income of a Sikh for the Guru's treasury, or expected to be spent for the welfare of others in the name of the Guru
deg	literally, a cauldron, signifying bounty
dehurā	a structure raised over a spot of cremation
derā	a camp; a unit of soldiers; a religious establishment
devī	a goddess or the Goddess as the supreme deity
Devīdwārā	a temple dedicated to a goddess
Dev	a god
dhādī	a singer who generally used a miniature drum (*dhad*) while singing of love or war for the entertainment of his patrons; used as a metaphor for the Guru as the singer of God's praises
dhādī darbār	a gathering in which a minstrel (dhādī) sings heroic poems called *Vārs*
dharam	the appropriate moral and religious obligations attached to any particular group; duty, moral obligation; a righteous cause

dharmarth	charitable grant; grant of revenue free land; also called *madad-i ma'ash* or *aima*
dharamsāl	the place for earning merit; Sikh sacred space or the Sikh place of worship in early Sikh history, now generally called Gurdwara
dharamsālā	a resting place for way-farers, like a *sarai*
dharamsāliā	one who looks after the Sikh sacred space called *dharamsal*
dharamyudh (dharamjudh)	a righteous war
Dhir Mallia	a follower of Dhir Mal, the elder grandson of Guru Hargobind, a descendant of Dhir Mal
dhukhdhukhī	a scarf studded with jewels
dīwān	used for a religious gathering in Sikh literature as a synonym for sangat; also used for the keeper of a treasury; the head of the finance department and also a title
dusht	a wicked person; an enemy
fateh-darshan	the slogan introduced by Banda Singh in place of '*Vāhegurūjī kā Khālsa, Vāhegurūjī kī fateh*'; used in his *hukamnama* of 1710, it appears to stand for the victory of a school or sect
faujdār	one who keeps troops; a military officer under the Mughals whose duty in peace time was to maintain law and order and to assist civil authorities in a Sarkār; the office survived into the early nineteenth century Punjab
fotadār	a treasurer
Gāyatrī	a *mantra* of the *Rig Veda* which is often recited by Brahmans as a prayer

Ghoṛiāṅ	verses meant to be sung when the bridegroom mounts the mare at the time of wedding
golak	treasury; a box to receive cash offerings; money saved in a home to be carried to the Guru
granth	a book
Granthī	a professional reader of *Granth Sahib*
Gurbāṇī	an utterance of the Guru; compositions of the Gurus included in *Guru Granth Sahib*
Gurbilās	a poetical work written in praise of a Guru
Gurdwāra	'the door of the Guru'; a Sikh place of worship, generally the centre of social activity too
Gurmat	the Guru's instruction, the Guru's wisdom; Sikh ideology as a whole
Gurmata	decision of a general congregation of Sikhs, generally taken in the presence of *Guru Granth Sahib*
Gurmukh	one who has turned to the Guru, a Sikh, a pious Sikh
Gurpūrab	celebration of an event associated with the Guru, like birth and death
Guru	preceptor; religious teacher; an epithet used for the founder of Sikhism and each one of his nine successors, and also for the *Granth Sahib* and the Panth
Guru Granth	the doctrine that the Sikh scripture authenticated by Guru Gobind Singh is the Guru, and not any individual other than the 10 Gurus from Guru Nanak to Guru Gobind Singh
Guru Panth or Guru Khalsa	the doctrine that the collective body of the Khalsa (Sikhs) is the

	Guru; the authority of this doctrine is next only to that of Guru Granth
halāl	the traditional Muslim mode of slaughtering animals for meat; anything lawful, as opposed to haram (unlawful)
Harmandar	'the temple of God'; the central Sikh Gurdwara in Amritsar popularly called the Golden Temple
hasb al-hukm	order issued by a minister in accordance with the emperor's instructions
haumai	the psyche of self-centredness, arising out of attributing to oneself what actually is due to God's will
havelī	a large mansion for residence
Hindvī	any Indian (regional) language from Punjab to Bengal
Holī	the festival of colours, sanctified by the belief in Lord Krishna's sportive practice
hom	fire sacrifice
hukam	an order; the divine order operative in the natural and the moral world as an expression of God's omnipotence
hukamnāma	'a written order'; used generally for the letters of the Sikh Gurus to their followers
hukkā	from the Arabic *huqqa*, a device for smoking tobacco
hundī	a bill of exchange
huzūrī	in the presence; in the presence of the Guru; used for Sikhs living in the Guru's presence; also for literary works prepared at the court of the Guru

jāgīr	an assignment of land revenue in lieu of salary for performing service for the state
jāgīrdār	the holder of a *jāgīr* who is entitled to collect revenues from a given piece of land in lieu of salary for service to the state
jāgīrdārī	the system of paying the servants of the state by alienating land-revenue in their favour in lieu of cash salary
jamdhar	a type of dagger
Janamsākhī	a collection of episodes associated with the life of Guru Nanak, meant primarily to depict his doctrines, ethics and his spiritual status; several traditions of this genre developed in the seventeenth and eighteenth centuries
jathā	a band; a fighting band
jātī	an occupational group placed within a larger category of caste, indicating its ritual status in the *varna* order
jhatkā	the mode of slaughtering an animal for meat with one stroke of the sword or some other weapon; the traditional mode of slaughtering animals in India. Unlike halal, it carried no religious signification
jīgha	an ornament or a jewel on the turban
jizya	toll tax, imposed on non-Muslims in a Muslim state
jog	pursuit of spirituality through asceticism
Jogī, jogī or yogī	one who practises *yoga*; a person belonging to any of the 12 orders of the followers of Gorakh Nath

Kabitt	a stanza of four rhyming lines
kachh (kachhehrā)	drawers of a special kind meant to be worn by those Sikhs who are initiated through pahul of the double-edged sword
kakār	words starting with the letter 'k', used for five symbols of the Khalsa *rahit*
kalāl	a vintner, a distiller of alcohol; a seller of alcoholic drinks; a person of the *jātī* called *kalāl*
kalgī (kalghī)	a plume, an aigrette
Kaliyuga	the fourth and the last of the cosmic ages traditionally regarded as the age of degeneration
kār	offering to the Guru, probably as a share from the profits or income
karhā parsād	sacramental food distributed in Gurdwaras to all persons present, generally prepared with equal quantities of wheat flour, sugar and ghee
kard	a short sword, a dagger
kārkhāna	a workshop, a manufactory
kārkun	a worker, an agent, an official
kathā	an exposition of the Guru's verses, generally in connection with the life of the Guru
kes	hair of the head, uncut hair
Kesdhārī	an initiated Singh who maintained long unshorn hair
Khālsa	the order instituted by Guru Gobind Singh; used for an individual as well as the collective body
Khālsa Panth	the collectivity of the Khalsa
khālisa	land under direct control of the ruler of a state
khandā	a double-edged sword

khande kī pahul	initiation of the double-edged sword introduced by Guru Gobind Singh as a rite for admission into the order of the Khalsa Singhs
khānqāh	a religious establishment under a Sufi Pir; a Sufi hospice
khil'at	a robe of honour
Khulāsā (Khalāsā)	a term used for the Sikhs not initiated through pahul of the double-edged sword and, consequently, not keeping unshorn hair, and not bearing arms or the epithet 'Singh'; also called 'Khalasa'
khidāwa	one who teaches children to play and entertains them
kīrtan	the singing of hymns in praise of God, especially from the sacred scriptures of the Sikhs; hence *kīrtan darbār* for an elaborate performance
kiryā (kiryā-karam)	performance of the traditional Brahmanical rituals on the occasion of death
kos	a measure of distance, about 3 kilometers
kurahit	a deviation from prescribed rules (*rahit*)
langar	the kitchen attached to a Gurdwara from which food is served to all regardless of caste or creed; a community meal
Lāvān	the four verses of Guru Ram Das meant to be sung for the marriage ceremony among the Sikhs, called 'Anand' marriage because the

	Anand of Guru Amar Das is recited or sung at the end
madad-i ma'āsh	grant of revenue from a specified area for charitable purposes
makara	five words beginning with the letter 'M', denoting wine, flesh, fish, parched grain, and sexual intercourse used in Left hand worship of the goddess
makbarā	from *maqbarah*, a tomb
'manjī' system	the system of appointing representatives, introduced by Guru Amar Das
mannat	an offering vowed for the fulfilment of a wish
mansab	a rank in administrative hierarchy
mansabdār	holder of a rank
mantar	magical formulae; verses or words regarded as sacred
maṛhī	a small structure raised on a spot of cremation, treated by some people as an object of worship
masand	a representative appointed by the Guru to look after the affairs of a local congregation of Sikhs, or a number of such congregations
masandiā	the follower of a masand
maṭṭh	a religious establishment, a monastery; generally associated with renunciates who remain celibate
māyā	the material world and the earthly attachments, treated in the Sikh tradition as 'false' in contrast with the eternal truth of God
mazār	a mausoleum; the tomb of a Sufi Shaikh regarded as a place of pilgrimage; the site of a *dargah*

Mazhabī	used for the out-caste *chūhrā* who accepts initiation of the double-edged sword
melī	an associate, a synonym for sahlang; a person initiated into the Sikh faith by a masand
Mīṇā	a derogatory epithet used for Prithi Chand, the elder brother of Guru Arjan, and also for the former's successors and their followers, broadly meaning a cunning and perfidious pretender
Mīrī-Pīrī	temporal and spiritual authority
Misal *(misl)*	a small unit or group of soldiers; also used for a combination of Sikh leaders in the eighteenth century for the purpose of defence and occupation of territories
Misaldārī *(misaldari)*	generally but misleadingly refers to the system of polity established by the Sikh leaders in the late eighteenth century
mlechh	impure; a derogatory term used for an outcaste or a foreigner, both were regarded as outside the four-tier *varna* order
muftī	a learned Muslim who expounds Islamic law
mukte	generally refers to the 40 Sikhs who had disowned the Guru at Anandpur but later died fighting on his behalf near the present Muktsar, regarded as 'the redeemed'
munshī	a writer or a scribe
muqaddam	a village headman
murīd	a disciple; also a devout Sikh
musaddī (from *mutassadi*)	a functionary of the government or an establishment

mutawallī	a superintendent or officer at pargana level who kept a check on the revenue grant
nagārchī	a drummer
Nāī	a barber
nām	the Name, the name of God; the transcendent and immanent God; the whole creation; the Guru's *shabad*, Gurbani
nām, dān, isnān	the phrase used by Guru Nanak for the essential features of the Sikh way of life, that is, meditation on God, charity, and both physical and moral purity
Nanak Panthīs	the followers of the path of Guru Nanak equated with Sikhs in general
Nāth	master; used for the *jogi* of an exalted status; one of the nine mythical Nāths
nāzim	the governor of a province; an administrator
naubat	arrangement for regular beating of the drum, regarded as a royal prerogative
Nihang	the militant followers of Guru Gobind Singh who regarded themselves to be the guardians of the faith
nirgun	without qualities, without attributes; the primal state of God before creation
Nirmalā	the ascetics and renunciates who propagated the Sikh faith
padārath	a thing, a blessing; one of the four *padaraths* of observance of religious duties, material wealth, fulfilment of desires and

liberation (*dharma, arth, kam* and *moksh*)

Pādhā (Pāndhā) a Brahman officiant at social ceremonies; a teacher of arithmetic; an astrologer

pahul water used for initiating a person as a Sikh (*charan pahul*) or a Singh (*khande ki pahul*)

paisa a copper coin worth 64th part of a rupee

pālakī palanquin

panch the five; one of the five; the member of a *panchayat*; the headman of a village or one of its subdivisions; also of a locality or trade in urban areas

Pandit a learned Brahman; a learned person

panj pyāre the 'five beloved' so called for offering their heads to Guru Gobind Singh; they were the first to be initiated all afresh through pahul of the double-edged sword and authorized to initiate others, starting with Guru Gobind Singh himself

Panth literally a path; the people following a particular path; collectively the followers of the Gurus; the Sikh community

pargana a small unit of administration in a province under the Mughals; remained in use in the Punjab till the mid-nineteenth century and became synonymous with the *ta'alluqa*

par-upkār something good done for others

patāsha a lump of sugar

path	reading of Gurbāṇī or Guru Granth Sahib
pātshāhī	rulership, sovereignty
pattah	document stating revenue demand
pattal	a tree leaf used as a plate
pattīdārū	share holding; a system by which a joint conquest was divided among partners, and each was authorized to collect revenues from his share in the conquered territory
patwārī	village accountant
peshkash	tribute
pind	a ball of rice for feeding Brahmans as a part of mortuary rites
pīr or Shaikh	among Muslim mystics the guide who leads on the path of union with God; believed to be a bestower of blessings after his death
pothī	a book, used interchangeably with *granth*
purohit	the Brahman who performs the priestly duties for a family, or a number of households
qānūngo	a hereditary keeper of the revenue records at the pargana or the *ta'alluqa* level
Qāzī	a Muslim judge
qila'dar	Commander of the garrison
Qur'ān	the scripture of Islam regarded as revealed by Allah to the prophet Muhammad through the angel Gabriel
rabābī	one who plays on the *rabab*, a kind of violin with three strings
rāgī	a singer, particularly of the hymns of the Sikh scripture
rahit	a way of life, used especially for the Sikh way of life in

accordance with the philosophic
and ethical principles advocated
by the Gurus

Rahitnāma a written code of belief and conduct;
norms laid down for the Sikh way of
life in accordance with the principles
of Sikhism, including 'penance' for
infringing those principles

ra'iyatī land under peasant rights

rāj-tilak formal installation of the head of
an institution

Ranghretā a Singh whose background is that
of an untouchable *chuhra*, also
called Mazhabi

sādh a religious and pious person

sadr Chief Justice, also looked after
charitable grants

sahaj state of liberation-in-life

Sahajdhārī a Sikh who is not initiated as
a Singh and does not adopt the
Khalsa symbols; initially used
for a non-Singh Khalsa, but later
extended to all non-Singhs

sahaj-jog the path through which *sahaj* is
pursued and attained; used for
the path of Guru Nanak and his
successors

sāhibzāda a son of the Master; used for the
sons of Guru Gobind Singh

sahlang an associate; a person admitted to
the Sikh faith by a representative of
the Guru on his behalf

sākhī an eyewitness; testimony; an
episode bearing witness to the
spiritual status of a religious guide;
a statement bearing witness to the
truth of God; used generally for an
episode in the life of a Guru

samādh	a structure raised over a spot of cremation in honour of an important person, whether secular or religious; the counterpart of a mausoleum
sanad (dastāwīz)	a voucher, document, note of hand or bond; a title deed; a written authority for holding land or an office
sangat	association, an assembly, a religious congregation; a congregation of Sikhs; the collective body of Sikhs at one place
sanyāsī	a renunciate, generally Shaivite
sarkar	subdivision of a province, containing a group of usually contiguous parganas
Sardār	a leader; a Sikh ruler
sarovar	a tank, a pool of water
satī	the practice in which the wife burnt herself on the funeral pyre of her husband as a mark of her devotion and fidelity to him
sevā	service; service of God; service of the Guru; service of the Sikhs; service of others
shabad	the word; a hymn; a verse in *Guru Granth Sahib*
Shahīd	one who bears witness to his faith; a martyr, especially in Islam and Sikhism
shahīdganj	a structure built in commemoration of a Sikh martyr or martyrs
Shaikh	a leader; the head of a Sufi order; a respectable Muslim
Shaikhzāda	the son of a guide on the Sufi path, or his descendant
shari'at	Islamic law

shastardhārī	an arms-wearing person, used for the Khalsa
shrāddh	the rite by which the dead ancestors are supposed to be fed through the mediacy of Brahmans
Siddh	a renunciate of great spiritual status; a mythical entity
siddhī	the supernatural powers
slok	a unit of verse, generally rather short, like a *doha* or a rhyming couplet
Sohilā	a composition of Guru Nanak recited especially at the end of a ceremony
sūbadār	the governor of a province
Sūfī	a mystic of Islam subscribing to devotional theism
sukhā	hashish
takht	a throne; one of the four or five Sikh religious centres of authority
tankhāh	ordinarily salary, but used by the compilers of the Rahitnamas (manuals for the Sikh way of life) for corrective penance prescribed for a Sikh who has infringed a particular norm
takā	a copper coin worth 2 pice
Taksāl	a mint; used for a particular school of Gurmat
Tantric	a religious rite involving a secret ritual
tarpan	offering water in ritual worship
teg (tegh)	the sword, signifying physical force
Thākurdwārā	a temple dedicated to Vishnu or one of his incarnations
thāṇāā	a place; a place where troops are posted for maintaining peace and order, and for assistance in the collection of revenues
thāṇedār	the commandant of a garrison or a fort

tilak	the sacred mark on the forehead, also called *tikka*
tīrath	a sacred place; a place of pilgrimage; one of the 68 sacred places in India
'Turk'	generally used for a Muslim, especially a Muslim associated with the state
Udāsī	a renunciate belonging to an order tracing its origin to Guru Nanak through his son Sri Chand but not through Guru Angad and his successors
Vāhegurū	praise be to the Guru; used for God
vakīl	an agent or a deputy; and envoy
Vār	a literary genre, generally used for heroic poetry; Guru Nanak used it for his religious compositions; the most famous Vars in Sikh literature were composed by Bhai Gurdas in the early seventeenth century for celebrating Sikh Gurus and the Sikh Panth
varna	literally colour, used for any one of the ideal four-fold social order
varnāshrama	the four-fold division of society into *varnas* or classes and of human life into *ashramas* or stages
waqi'a-navīs	official news-writer
wazīr	the first or the prime minister, next in authority and importance to the king; a minister
zamīndār	literally the holder of land; applied alike to the intermediary who collected revenue on behalf of the state, to a vassal chief, and to a peasant proprietor
zāt	personal rank of a mansabdār

Bibliography

Contemporary and Near-Contemporary Sources
Gurmukhi Sources

Bachittar Natak. In Dr Rattan Singh Jaggi and Dr Gursharan Kaur Jaggi, *Sri Dasam Granth Sahib*, vol. 1. New Delhi: Gobind Sadan, 1999.

Bhalla, Sarup Das. *Mahima Prakash*. Edited by Shamsher Singh Ashok and Gobind Singh Lamba. Part I. Patiala: Punjab Languages Department, 1970.

———. *Mahima Prakash*. Edited by Gobind Singh Lamba and Khazan Singh. Part II. Patiala: Punjab Languages Department, 1972.

Bhangu, Ratan Singh. *Prachin Panth Prakash*. Edited by Bhai Vir Singh. New Delhi: Bhai Vir Singh Sadan, 1993 (called 'new edition', but actually a reprint).

———. *Sri Gur Panth Prakash*. Edited by Balwant Singh Dhillon. Amritsar: Singh Brothers, 2004.

Chhibber, Kesar Singh. 'Bansavalinama Dasan Patshahian Ka'. In *Parkh*, vol. 2, edited by Ratan Singh Jaggi. Chandigarh: Panjab University, 1972.

Ganda Singh (ed.). *Hukamname Guru Sahiban, Mata Sahiban, Banda Singh ate Khalsa Ji De*. Patiala: Punjabi University, 1967.

Gurbilas Chhevin Patshahi. Patiala: Bhasha Vibhag Punjab, 1970.

Gurdas (Singh). *Var 41*. In *Varan Bhai Gurdas*, edited by Giani Hazara Singh. Amritsar: Khalsa Samachar, 1962 (1911).

Guru Khalse De Rahitname. Edited by Shamsher Singh Ashok. Amritsar: Sikh History Research Board, 1979.

Hukamnamas: Shri Guru Tegh Bahadur Sahib. Edited by Fauja Singh. Patiala: Punjabi University, 1976.

Hukamnamas of Guru Tegh Bahadur: A Historical Study. Edited by Sabinderjit Singh Sagar. Amritsar: Guru Nanak Dev University, 2002.

Hukamname: Guru Sahiban, Mata Sahiban, Banda Singh Ate Khalsa Ji De. Edited by Ganda Singh. Patiala: Punjabi University, 1967.

Janam Sakhi Sri Guru Nanak Dev Ji. 2 vols. Edited by Kirpal Singh and Shamsher Singh Ashok. Amritsar: Khalsa College, 1962, 1963.

Kankan Kavi. *Das Gur Katha*. In Sarwan Singh, 'Amritsar in Medieval Punjabi Literature: An Historical Analysis', Ph.D. Thesis, Guru Nanak Dev University, Amritsar, 1994.

Kaushish, Bhai Svarup Singh. *Guru Kian Sakhian*. Edited by Piara Singh Padam. Amritsar: Singh Brothers, 1999 (1986).

Nasihatnama. MS No. 770. Amritsar: Guru Nanak Dev University.

Nishan te Hukamname. Edited by Shamsher Singh Ashok. Amritsar: Shiromani Gurdwara Prabandhak Committee, 1967.

Prem Sumarag Granth arthat Khalsai Jivan Jach (Patshahi Dasvin). Edited by Randhir Singh. Jalandhar: New Book Company, 1965 (1953).

Prem Sumarag: The Testimony of a Sanatan Sikh. Translated by W.H. McLeod. New Delhi: Oxford University Press, 2006.

Rahitnama. In *Bhai Nand Lal Granthavali*, edited by Ganda Singh. Malacca (Malaysia): Sant Sohan Singh, 1968.

Rahitnama Bhai Daya Singh. In *Rahitname*, edited by Piara Singh Padam. Amritsar: Singh Brothers, 1995 (reprint).

Rahitnama Bhai Desa Singh. In *Rahitname*, edited by Padam.

Rahitnama Bhai Prahilad Singh. In *Rahitname*, edited by Padam.

Rahitnama Huzuri Bhai Chaupa Singh Chhibber. In *Rahitname*, edited by Padam.

Rai, Ani. *Jang Nama Sri Guru Gobind Singh Ji*. Edited by Shamsher Singh Ashok. Amritsar: Shiromani Gurdwara Prabandhak Committee, 1971 (1947).

Rao, Ram Sukh. *Jassa Singh Binod*. MS, M/772. Patiala: Punjab State Archives.

Sainapat. *Shri Gur Sobha*. Edited by Shamsher Singh Ashok. Amritsar: Shiromani Gurdwara Prabandhak Committee, 1967.

———. *Sri Gur Sobha*. Edited by Ganda Singh. Patiala: Punjabi University, 1967.

Sakhi Rahit Ki. In *Rahitname*, edited by Padam.

Sakhi Rahit Patisahi 10. In *The Chaupa Singh Rahit-Nama*, translated and edited by W. H. McLeod. Dunedin, New Zealand: University of Otago Press, 1987.

Sewadas. *Episodes from Lives of the Gurus: Parchian Sewadas*. Translated and edited by Kharak Singh and Gurtej Singh. Chandigarh: Institute of Sikh Studies, 1995.

Shabdarth Sri Guru Granth Sahib Ji. 4 vols. Amritsar: Shiromani Gurdwara Prabandhak Committee (standard pagination).

Sikhan di Bhagatmala. Edited by S. S. Padam. Amritsar: Singh Brothers, 2013.

Singh, Koer. *Gurbilas Patshahi 10*. Edited by Shamsher Singh Ashok. Patiala: Punjabi University, 1968.

Singh, Sewa. *Shahid Bilas* (Bhai Mani Singh). Edited by Giani Garja Singh. Ludhiana: Punjabi Sahit Akademi, 1961.

Singh, Sukha. *Gurbilas Patsahi 10.* Edited by Gursharan Kaur Jaggi. Patiala: Punjab Languages Department, 1989.

Sri Dasam Granth Sahib. 5 vols. Edited by Ratan Singh Jaggi and Gursharan Kaur Jaggi. New Delhi: Gobind Sadan, 1999.

Sri Dasam Granth Sahib Text and Translation. 2 vols. Translated by Jodh Singh and Dharam Singh. Patiala: Heritage Publications, 1999.

Tankhahnama. In *Bhai Nand Lal Granthavali*, edited by Ganda Singh. Malacca (Malaysia): Sant Sohan Singh, 1968.

The B40 Janam-Sakhi. Translated and edited by W. H. McLeod. Amritsar: Guru Nanak Dev University, 1980.

The Chaupa Singh Rahit-Nama. Translated and edited by W.H. McLeod. Dunedin, New Zealand: University of Otago Press, 1987.

Var Durga Ki. In *Punjabi Varan*, edited by Piara Singh Padam. Amritsar: Singh Brothers, 2008.

Var Sri Bhagauti ki (Chandi di Var). Edited by Kala Singh Bedi. New Delhi: Punjab Book Store, 1965.

Persian Sources

Anon. *Asrar-i Samadi*. Translated by Janak Singh. Patiala: Punjabi University, 1972.

Bute Shah. *Tarikh-i Punjab*. MS, 1288. Sikh History Research Department, Khalsa College, Amritsar.

Early Nineteenth Century Punjab: *From Ganesh Das's Char Bagh-i Panjab*. Translated and edited by J. S. Grewal and Indu Banga. Amritsar: Guru Nanak Dev University, 1975.

Husaini, Khwajah Kamgar. *Ma'asir-i Alamgiri*. Edited by Azra Alavi. Aligarh: Aligarh Muslim University, 1978.

Ibrat, Muhammad Qasim Lahauri. *Ibratnama*. Edited by Zuhuruddin Ahmad. Lahore: Panjab University, 1977.

In the By-Lanes of History: Some Persian Documents from a Punjab Town (belonging to the *Bhandari Collection*, Punjab State Archives, Patiala). Translated and edited by J. S. Grewal. Simla: Indian Institute of Advanced Study, 1975.

Khan, Khafi. *Muntakhab al-Lubāb*. Calcutta: 1984.

Khan, Muhammad Hadi Kamwar. *Tazkirat us-Salatin Chagta: A Mughal Chronicle of Post-Aurangzeb Period, 1707–1724*. Edited by Muzaffar Alam. Bombay: Asia Publishing House, 1980.

Khan, Saqi Must'ad. *Ma'asir-i Alamgiri*. Edited by Jadunath Sarkar. Calcutta: Royal Asiatic Society of Bengal, 1947.

Makhiz-i Tarikh-i Sikhan. Edited by Ganda Singh. Amritsar: History Society, 1949.

Nagar, Iswar Das. *Futuhat-i Alamgiri*. Edited by Raghubir Singh and Quazi Karametullah. Translated by M. R. Lokhandwala and Jadunath Sarkar. Vadodara: 1995.

Nath Mal. *Amarnamah*. Translated and edited by Ganda Singh. Amritsar: Sikh History Society, 1953.

Razi, Aqil Khan. *Waqiat-i-Alamgiri*. Aligarh: Aligarh Historical Institute, 1945.

Sikh History from Persian Sources: Translations of Major Texts. Edited by J. S. Grewal and Irfan Habib. New Delhi: Tulika/Indian History Congress, 2001.

The Mughals and the Jogis of Jakhbar: Some Madad-i Ma'ash and other Documents. Translated and edited by B. N. Goswamy and J. S. Grewal. Simla: Indian Institute of Advanced Study, 1967.

The Mughal and Sikh Rulers and the Vaishnavas of Pindori: A Historical Interpretation of 52 Persian Documents. Translated and edited by B. N. Goswamy and J. S. Grewal, Simla: Indian Institute of Advanced Study, 2010 [1969].

Zafarnama. In *Sri Dasam Granth Sahib*, vol. 5. Edited by Ratan Singh Jaggi and Gursharan Kaur Jaggi. New Delhi: Gobind Sadan, 1999.

Zafarnama. Edited by Piara Singh Padam. Amritsar: Singh Brothers, 1996 [1989].

English Sources

(Captain Matthews), An Officer of Bengal Army. 'A Tour to Lahore in 1808'. In *The Panjab Past and Present*, nos 1 and 2 (1967) [1809].

Early European Accounts of the Sikhs. Edited by Ganda Singh. Calcutta: Indian Studies, Past & Present, 1962.

Forster, George. *A Journey from Bengal to England through the Northern Part of India, Kashmire, Afghanistan and Persia and into Russia by the Caspian Sea*. 2 vols. Patiala: Punjab Languages Department, 1970 (1798).

Griffin, Lepel. H. *Rajas of the Punjab*. Patiala: Punjab Languages Department, 1970 (1870).

Hutchison, J. and J. P. Vogel. *History of the Punjab Hill States*. 2 vols. Simla: Department of Languages and Culture, Himachal Pradesh, 1982 (reprint).

Malcolm (John). *Sketch of the Sikhs*. New Delhi: Asian Educational Services, 1986 (1812).

Prinsep, Henry T. *Origin of the Sikh Power in the Punjab and Political Life of Maharaja Ranjit Singh with an Account of the Religion, Laws and Customs of the Sikhs*. Patiala: Punjab Languages Department, 1970 (1834).

'Sicques, Tigers, or Thieves': Eyewitness Accounts of the Sikhs (1606– 1809). Edited by Amandeep Singh Madra and Parmjit Singh. New York: Palgrave Macmillan, 2004.

Secondary Works

Books ·

Alam, Muzaffar. *The Crisis of Empire in Mughal North India: Awadh and the Punjab, 1707–48*. New Delhi: Oxford University Press, 2013 (1986).

Avtar Singh. *Ethics of the Sikhs*. Patiala: Punjabi University, 1996 (1970).

Baagha, Ajit Singh. *Banur Had Orders: A Critical Study of an Hitherto Unknown 'Hukamnamah' of Guru Gobind Singh*. Delhi: Ranjit Printers and Publishers, 1969.

Bajwa, Kulwinder Singh. Edited by *Mahima Prakash (Vartak)* (Punjabi). Amritsar: Singh Brothers, 2004.

Banga, Indu. *Agrarian System of the Sikhs: Late Eighteenth and Early Nineteenth Century*. New Delhi: Manohar, 1978.

Bhagat Singh. *Sikh Polity in the Eighteenth and Nineteenth Centuries*. New Delhi: Oriental Publishers and Distributors, 1978.

Cunningham, Joseph Davey. *History of the Sikhs: From the Origin of the Nation to the Battles of the Sutlej*. New Delhi: Rupa & Co., 2002 (1849).

Daljeet. *The Sikh Heritage: A Search for Totality*. New Delhi: Prakash Book Depot, 2004.

Dhavan, Purnima. *When Sparrows Became Hawks: The Making of the Sikh Warrior Tradition, 1699–1799*. New York: Oxford University Press, 2014 (2011).

Fenech, Louis E. *Martyrdom in the Sikh Tradition: Playing the 'Game of Love'*. New Delhi: Oxford University Press, 2000.

———. *The Darbar of the Sikh Gurus: The Court of God in the World of Men*. New Delhi: Oxford University Press, 2008.

———. *The Sikh Zafar-Namah of Guru Gobind Singh: A Discursive Blade in the Heart of the Mughal Empire*. New York: Oxford University Press, 2013.

Goswamy, B. N. *Piety and Splendour: Sikh Heritage in Art*. New Delhi: National Museum, 2000.

Goswamy, B. N. and Caron Smith. *I See No Stranger: Early Sikh Art and Devotion*. New York: Rubin Museum of Art, 2007.

Goswamy, B. N. and Eberhard Fishcher. *Pahari Masters: Court Painters of Norther India*. Zurich: Artibus Asiae Publishers, 1992.

Grewal, J. S. *Guru Tegh Bahadur and the Persian Chroniclers*. Amritsar: Guru Nanak Dev University, 1976.

———. *Guru Nanak and Patriarchy*. Shimla: Indian Institute of Advanced Study, 1993.

———. *Historical Perspectives on Sikh Identity*. Patiala: Punjabi University, 1997.

———. *Contesting Interpretations of the Sikh Tradition*. New Delhi: Manohar Publications, 1998.

———. *Guru Nanak in History*. Chandigarh: Panjab University, 1998 (1969).

———, ed. *The Khalsa: Sikh and Non-Sikh Perspectives*. New Delhi: Manohar, 2004.

———. *Sikh Ideology, Polity and Social Order: From Guru Nanak to Maharaja Ranjit Singh*. New Delhi: Manohar, 2007 (1996).

———. *Lectures on History, Society and Culture of the Punjab*. Vol. I. Patiala: Punjabi University, 2007.

———. *The Sikhs: Ideology, Institutions and Identity*. New Delhi: Oxford University Press, 2009.

———. *A Study of Guru Granth Sahib: Doctrine, Social Content, History, Structure and Status*. Amritsar: Singh Brothers, 2009.

———. *Recent Debates in Sikh Studies: An Assessment*. New Delhi: Manohar, 2011.

———. *Historical Writings on the Sikhs (1784–2011): Western Enterprise and Indian Response*. New Delhi: Manohar, 2012.

————. *Four Centuries of Sikh Tradition: History, Literature, and Identity*. New Delhi: Oxford University Press, 2013 (2011).

————. *The Sikhs of the Punjab* (The New Cambridge History of India, II. 3). Cambridge: Cambridge University Press, 2014 (1990).

Grewal, J. S. and S. S. Bal. *Guru Gobind Singh: A Biographical Study*. Chandigarh: Panjab University, 1987 (1967).

Gupta, Hari Ram. *History of the Sikhs 1739–1768 (Evolution of the Sikh Confederacies)*. Calcutta: S.N. Sarkar,1939.

Habib, Irfan. *The Agrarian System of Mughal India 1556–1707*. New Delhi: Oxford University Press, 1999 (1963).

Hans, Surjit. *A Reconstruction of Sikh History from Sikh Literature*. Patiala: Madaan Publications, 2005 (1987).

Herrli, Hans. *The Coins of the Sikhs*. New Delhi: Munshiram Manoharlal, 2004 (1993).

Jaggi, Ratan Singh. *Dasam Granth dā Kartritav*. New Delhi: Punjabi Sahit Sabha, 1966.

————. *Guru Granth Vishavkosh* (Punjabi). 2 Parts. Patiala: Punjabi University, 2002.

Jakobsh, Doris R. *Relocating Gender in Sikh History: Transformation, Meaning and Identity*. Delhi: Oxford University Press, 2003.

————, ed. *Sikhism and Women: History, Texts, and Experience*. New Delhi: Oxford University Press, 2010.

Khan, A. R. *Chieftains in the Mughal Empire During the Reign of Akbar*. Simla: Indian Institute of Advanced Study, 1977.

Lafont, Jean-Marie. *Maharaja Ranjit Singh: Lord of the Five Rivers*. New Delhi: Oxford University Press, 2003 (2002).

Loehlin, C. H. *The Granth of Guru Gobind Singh and The Khalsa Brotherhood*. Lucknow: Lucknow Publishing House, 1971.

Macauliffe, Max Arthur. *The Sikh Religion: Its Gurus, Sacred Writings, and Authors*. Vol. 5. New Delhi: Low Price Publications, 1995 (1909).

M'Gregor, W. L. *The History of the Sikhs*. 2 vols. Patiala: Punjab Languages Department, 1970 (1846).

Malhotra, Anshu and Farina Mir, eds. *Punjab Reconsidered: History, Culture and Practice*. New Delhi: Oxford University Press, 2012.

Malhotra, Karamjit K. *The Eighteenth Century in Sikh History: Political Resurgence, Religious and Social Life, and Cultural Articulation*. New Delhi: Oxford University Press, 2016.

————, ed. *The Punjab Revisited: Social Order, Economic Life, Cultural Articulation, Politics, and Partition (18th–20th Centuries)*. Patiala: Punjabi University, 2014.

Mann, Gurinder Singh. *The Goindval Pothis: The Earliest Extant Source* of the Sikh Canon. Cambridge, Massachusetts: Harvard University Press, 1996.

———. *The Making of the Sikh Scripture*. New Delhi: Oxford University Press, 2001.

McLeod, W. H. *The Evolution of the Sikh Community*. Delhi: Oxford University Press, 1975.

———, trans. and ed. *Textual Sources for the Study of Sikhism*. Manchester: Manchester University Press, 1984.

———. *The Sikhs: History, Religion, and Society*. New York: Columbia University Press, 1989.

———. *Sikhism*. London: Penguin Books, 1997.

———. *Sikhs of the Khalsa: A History of Khalsa Rahit*. New Delhi: Oxford University Press, 2003.

———. *Discovering the Sikhs: Autobiography of a Historian*. Delhi: Permanent Black, 2004.

Murphy, Anne. *The Materiality of the Past: History and Representation in Sikh Tradition*. New York: Oxford University Press, 2012.

Nabha, Bhai Kahn Singh. *Gurshabad Ratnakar Mahan Kosh* (Punjabi). Patiala: Punjab Languages Department, 1960 (1930).

———. *Guru Mahima Ratnavali*. Edited by Pritam Singh and Krishan Lal. Amritsar: Guru Nanak Dev University, 1984.

Nijhawan, Michael. *Dhadi Darbar: Religion, Violence, and the Performance of Sikh History*. New Delhi: Oxford University Press, 2006.

Oberoi, Harjot. *The Construction of Religious Boundaries: Culture, Identity and Diversity in Sikh Tradition*. New Delhi: Oxford University Press, 1994.

Padam, Piara Singh. *Sri Guru Gobind Singh Ji De Darbari Ratan*. Jalandhar: Hamdard Printing Press, 1994 (1974).

Randhawa, T. S. *The Sikhs: Images of a Heritage*. New Delhi: Prakash Book Depot, 2000.

Sarkar, Jadunath. *A Short History of Aurangzib (1618–1707)*. New Delhi: Orient Longman, 1979 (paperback).

———. *History of Aurangzib: Northern India, 1658–1681*. Vol. III. Calcutta: M.C. Sarkar & Sons, 1921 (2nd edn).

Sharma, Sri Ram. *The Religious Policy of the Mughal Emperor*. Bombay: Asia Publishing House, 1962 (2nd edn).

Singh, Bhagat Lakshman. *A Short Sketch of the Life and Work of Guru Gobind Singh*. Patiala: Punjab Languages Department, 2002 (1909).

Singh, Bhayee Sikandar and Rupinder Singh. *Sikh Heritage: Ethos & Relics*. New Delhi: Rupa Publications, 2012.

Singh, Chetan. *Region and Empire: Panjab in the Seventeenth Century*. Delhi: Oxford University Press, 1991.

Singh, Ganda. *Life of Banda Singh Bahadur*. Patiala: Punjabi University, 2006 (1935).

―――. *Guru Gobind Singh's Death at Nanded: An Examination of Succession Theories*. Patiala: Punjabi University, 2008 (1972).

―――. *Sardar Jassa Singh Ahluwalia*. Patiala: Punjabi University,1969 (Punjabi); 1990 (English).

Singh, Gurmukh. ed. *Gurbilas Patshahi 6*. Patiala: Punjabi University, 1997.

Singh, Harbans. *Guru Gobind Singh*. Chandigarh: Guru Gobind Singh Foundation, 1966.

Singh, Harbhajan. *Gurbani Sampadan Nirnay*. Chandigarh: Satnam Prakashan, 1982.

Singh, Kapur. *Parasharprasna or The Baisakhi of Guru Gobind Singh (An Exposition of Sikhism)*. Jullundur: Hind Publishers, 1959.

Singh, Kavita ed. *New Insights into Sikh Art*. Mumbai: Marg Publications 2003.

Singh, Nikky-Guninder Kaur. *The Feminine Principle in the Sikh Vision of the Transcendent*. Cambridge: Cambridge University Press, 1994.

Singh, Nripinder. *The Sikh Moral Tradition: Ethical Perceptions of the Sikhs in the Late Nineteenth/Early Twentieth Century*. Columbia Missouri: South Asia Publications, 1990.

Singh, Pashaura. *The Guru Granth Sahib*. New Delhi: Oxford University Press, 2001.

Singh, Pashaura and Louis E. Fenech, eds. *The Oxford Handbook of Sikh Studies*. Oxford: Oxford University Press, 2014.

Singh, Surinder. *Sikh Coinage: Symbol of Sikh Sovereignty*. New Delhi: Manohar, 2004.

Singh, Teja and Ganda Singh. *A Short History of the Sikhs (1465–1765)*. Patiala: Punjabi University, 1999 (1950).

Sinha, Narendra Krishna. *Rise of the Sikh Power*. Calcutta: A Mukherjee & Co., 1963 (1936).

Articles in Edited Volumes

Banga, Indu. 'Alha Singh: The Founder of Patiala State'. In *Punjab Past and Present: Essays in Honour of Dr Ganda Singh*, edited by Harbans Singh and N. Gerald Barrier. Patiala: Punjabi University, 1976.

―――. 'Formation of the Sikh State, 1765–1845'. In *Five Punjabi*

Centuries: Polity, Economy, Society, Culture, c.1500–1990, edited by Indu Banga. New Delhi: Manohar, 2000 (1997).

———. 'Gender Relations in Medieval India'. In *The State and Society in Medieval India,* vol. 7, part 1 of *History of Science, Philosophy and Culture in Indian Civilization,* edited by J. S. Grewal. New Delhi: Oxford University Press, 2005.

Banga, Indu, and J. S. Grewal, 'The Study of Regional History'. In *Different Types of History,* vol. XIV, part 4 of *History of Science, Philosophy and Culture in Indian Civilization,* edited by Bharati Ray. Delhi: Pearson Education, 2009.

Deol, Jeevan Singh. 'Eighteenth Century Khalsa Identity: Discourse, Praxis, and Narrative'. In *Sikh Religion, Culture, and Ethnicity,* edited by Christopher Shackle, Gurharpal Singh, and Arvind-Pal Singh Mandair. Surrey: Curzon, 2000.

———. 'Illustration and Illumination in Sikh Scriptural Manuscripts'. In *New Insights into Sikh Art,* edited by Kavita Singh. Mumbai: Marg Publications, 2003.

Dhillon, Dalbir Singh. 'Bipan Chandra's view About Guru Gobind Singh's Relations with Bahadur Shah – A Historical Analysis'. In *Guru Gobind Singh and Creation of the Khalsa,* edited by Madanjit Kaur. Amritsar: Guru Nanak Dev University, 2000.

Fenech, Louis E. 'The History of *Zafar-namah* of Guru Gobind Singh'. In *Punjab Reconsidered: History, Culture, and Practice,* edited by Anshu Malhotra and Farina Mir. New Delhi: Oxford University Press, 2012.

Goswamy, B. N. and J. S. Grewal. 'Sikh Patronage of Painting'. In *Five Centuries of Sikh Tradition: Ideology, Society, Politics and Culture,* edited by Reeta Grewal and Sheena Pall. New Delhi: Manohar, 2005.

———. 'Some Persian Documents from Nurpur'. In *Miscellaneous Articles,* edited by J. S. Grewal. Amritsar: Guru Nanak (Dev) University, 1974.

Grewal, J. S. 'The Zafarnama of Guru Gobind Singh'. In J. S. Grewal, *From Guru Nanak to Maharaja Ranjit Singh: Essays in Sikh History.* Amritsar: Guru Nanak (Dev) University, 1972.

———. 'The *Qazi* in the *Pargana*'. In *Miscellaneous Articles,* edited by J. S. Grewal. Amritsar: Guru Nanak (Dev) University, 1974.

———. 'Valorizing the Tradition: Bhangu's *Panth Prakash*'. In *The Khalsa: Sikh and Non-Sikh Perspectives,* edited by J. S. Grewal. New Delhi: Manohar, 2004.

———. 'The Gurdwara'. In *Religious Movements and Institutions in Medieval India,* vol. 7, part 2 of *History of Indian Science,*

Philosophy and Culture in Indian Civilization, edited by J. S. Grewal. New Delhi: Oxford University Press, 2006.

———. '*Bachittar Natak*: Proclamation of a Mission'. In J. S. Grewal, *Sikh Ideology, Polity and Social Order*. Delhi: Manohar Publishers and Distributors, 2007.

———. 'Celebrating Freedom: The Var of Gurdas'. In J. S. Grewal, Sikh Ideology, Polity and Social Order. Delhi: Manohar Publishers and Distributors, 2007.

———. 'Cleavage in the Panth'. In J. S. Grewal, *Sikh Ideology, Polity and Social Order*. Delhi: Manohar Publishers and Distributors, 2007.

———. '*Gursobha*: In Praise of the Khalsa'. In J. S. Grewal, *Sikh Ideology, Polity and Social Order*. Delhi: Manohar Publishers and Distributors, 2007.

———. 'In Defence of the Freedom of Conscience'. In J. S. Grewal, *Sikh Ideology, Polity and Social Order*. Delhi: Manohar Publishers and Distributors, 2007.

———. 'Insistence on Justice'. In J. S. Grewal, *Sikh Ideology, Polity and Social Order*. Delhi: Manohar Publishers and Distributors, 2007.

———. 'The *B40 Janamsakhi*'. In J. S. Grewal, *Lectures on History, Society and Culture of the Punjab*. Patiala: Punjabi University, 2007.

———. '*Zafarnama*: Declaration of Moral Victory'. In J. S. Grewal, *Sikh Ideology, Polity and Social Order*. Delhi: Manohar Publishers and Distributors, 2007.

———. 'An Eighteenth Century Janamsakhi'. In J. S. Grewal, *The Sikhs: Ideology, Institutions and Identity*. Delhi: Oxford University Press India, 2009.

———. 'Caste and the Sikh Social Order'. In J. S. Grewal, *The Sikhs: Ideology, Institutions and Identity*. Delhi: Oxford University Press India, 2009.

———. 'Sikhism and Gender'. In J. S. Grewal, *The Sikhs: Ideology, Institutions and Identity*. Delhi: Oxford University Press India, 2009.

———. 'The *Prem Sumarg*: A Sant Khalsa Vision of the Sikh Panth'. In J. S. Grewal, *The Sikhs: Ideology, Institutions and Identity*. Delhi: Oxford University Press India, 2009.

———. 'Bullhe Shah'. In J. S. Grewal, *Historical Studies in Punjabi Literature*. Patiala: Punjabi University, 2011.

———. 'Study of Sikhism, Sikh History and Sikh Literature'. In *Approaches to History: Essays in Indian Historiography*, edited by Sabyasachi Bhattacharya. Delhi: Indian Council Historical Research in association with Primus Books, 2011.

———. 'The Gurmukh Panth: Guru Nanak'. In J. S. Grewal, *History, Literature and Identity*. Delhi: Oxford University Press, 2011.

———. 'The Basic Significance of the *Mahima Prakash (Vartak)*'. In *The Punjab Revisited: Social Order, Economic Life, Cultural Articulation, Politics, and Partition (18th–20th Centuries)*, edited by Karamjit K. Malhotra. Patiala: Punjabi University, 2014.

———. 'From Guru Har Gobind to Guru Gobind Singh'. In *Brill's Encyclopedia of Sikhism: History, Literature, Society Beyond Punjab*. Vol. 1. Leiden, Boston: Brill, 2017.

Kaur, Madanjit. 'Koer Singh's *Gurbilas Patshahi 10:* An Eighteenth-Century Sikh Literature'. In *Sikhism*, edited by Jasbir Singh Mann and Kharak Singh. Patiala: Punjabi University, 1992.

Malhotra, Karamjit K. 'The Earliest Manual on the Sikh Way of Life'. In *Five Centuries of Sikh Tradition: Ideology, Society, Politics and Culture*, edited by Reeta Grewal and Sheena Pall. New Delhi: Manohar, 2005.

———. 'Religious Beliefs and Practices of the Eighteenth-Century Sikhs'. In *The Punjab Revisited: Social Order, Economic Life, Cultural Articulation, Politics, and Partition (18th–20th Centuries)* edited by Karamjit K. Malhotra. Patiala: Punjabi University, 2014.

Mann, Gurinder Singh, 'Five Hundred Years of Sikh Educational Heritage'. In *Five Centuries of Sikh Tradition*, edited by Reeta Grewal and Sheena Pall, New Delhi: Manohar, 2005.

McLeod, W. H. 'Gender and the Sikh Panth'. In W. H. McLeod, *Essays in Sikh History, Tradition, and Society*. New Delhi: Oxford University Press, 2007.

Murphy, Anne. 'An Idea of Religion: Identity, Difference, and Comparison in the *Gurbilas*'. In *Punjab Reconsidered: History, Culture, and Practice*, edited by Anshu Malhotra and Farina Mir, New Delhi: Oxford University Press, 2012.

Padam, Piara Singh. 'Ani Rai'. In *Encyclopedia of Sikhism*, vol. I, edited by Harbans Singh. Patiala: Punjabi University, 1992.

Rai, Gurmeet and Kavita Singh. 'Brick by Sacred Brick: Architectural Projects of Guru Arjan and Guru Hargobind'. In *New Insights into Sikh Art*, edited by Kavita Singh. Mumbai: Marg Publications, 2003.

Rinehart, Robin. 'The Dasam Granth'. In *The Oxford Handbook of Sikh Studies*, edited by Pashaura Singh and Louis E. Fenech. Oxford: Oxford University Press, 2014.

Shan, Harnam Singh. 'Guru Gobind Singh's Address to the Baisakhi Congregation of 1699 on the Occasion of the Creation of the

Khalsa'. In *Guru Gobind Singh and Creation of the Khalsa*, edited by Madanjit Kaur. Amritsar: Guru Nanak Dev University, 2000.

Singh, Avtar. 'Sikh Identity and Continuity: A Perspective from Ethics'. In *Philosophical Perspectives on Sikhism*, edited by Gurnam Kaur. Patiala: Punjabi University, 1998.

Singh, Gurtej. '*Amarnamah*, An Important Document of Sikh History'. In *Chakravyuh: Web of Indian Secularism*, edited by Gurtej Singh. Chandigarh: Institute of Sikhs Studies, 2000.

———. 'Compromising the Khalsa Tradition: Koer Singh's *Gurbilas*'. In *The Khalsa: Sikh and Non-Sikh Perspectives*, edited by J. S. Grewal. New Delhi: Manohar, 2004.

Singh, Jagjit. 'Caste System and the Sikhs'. In *Perspectives on the Sikh Tradition*, edited by Gurdev Singh. Patiala: Siddharth Publications, 1986.

Journal Articles

Banga, Indu. 'Raj-Khalsa: Ideology and Praxis'. *Journal of Punjab Studies* (Special Issue on Guru Gobind Singh) 15, nos 1 and 2 (Spring–Fall, 2008): 33–64.

Grewal, J. S. 'To Update Guru Gobind Singh: New Dimensions of Historical Scholarship'. *Journal of Regional History* 13–14 (2007–8): 39–74.

———. 'Guru Gobind Singh: Life and Mission'. *Journal of Punjab Studies* (Special Issue on Guru Gobind Singh) 15, nos 1 and 2 (Spring–Fall 2008): 3–31.

Grewal, J. S. and Indu Banga. 'The Sikh Prayer (*Ardas*). *Punjab Journal of Sikh Studies* I (2011): 9–23.

Grewal, Reeta. 'Anandpur: The City of Guru Gobind Singh'. *Journal of Punjab Studies* (Special Issue on Guru Gobind Singh) 15, nos 1 and 2 (Spring–Fall 2008): 65–93.

Malhotra, Karamjit K. 'History, Literature and Ideology: A Historiographical Perspective on the Rahitnamas'. *Journal of Regional History* 13–14 (2007–8): 75–96.

———. 'Contemporary Evidence on Sikh Rites and Rituals in the Eighteenth Century'. *Journal of Punjab Studies* 16, no. 2 (Fall 2009): 179–97.

———. 'Banda Singh Bahadur in the *Mahima Prakash*'. *Journal of Sikh Studies* 36 (2012): 99–110.

———. 'Banda Singh in Chhibber's *Bansavalinama*: Image, Idea and Reality'. *Panjab Journal of Sikh Studies* 2 (2012):111–22.

———. '*Guru Granth Sahib* in the Eighteenth Century'. *The Panjab Past and Present* 43, no. I (April 2012): 11–20.

———. 'Expanding Scope of Sikh Studies on the Eighteenth Century'. *Panjab Journal of Sikh Studies* 3 (2013): 33–71.

———. 'Issues of Gender among the Sikhs: Eighteenth-Century Literature'. *Journal of Punjab Studies* 20, nos 1 and 2 (Spring–Fall 2013): 53–76.

———. 'Situating Banda Singh in his Historical Context'. *The Calcutta Historical Journal*, 30, nos 1 and 2 (2014): 47–66.

———. 'Guru Gobind Singh's Legacy'. *The Panjab Past and Present* 47, no. 2 (October 2016).

Mann, Gurinder Singh. 'Sources for the Study of Guru Gobind Singh's Life and Times'. *Journal of Punjab Studies* 15, nos 1 and 2 (Spring–Fall 2008).

McLeod, W. H. 'Reflections on *Prem Sumarag*'. Review Article, *Journal of Punjab Studies* 14, no. 1 (Spring 2007): 123–32.

Randhawa, M. S. 'Paintings of the Sikh Gurus in the collection of Mahant of Gurdwara Ram Rai, Dehradun'. *Roopa-Lekha* 39, no. 1.

Shackle, Christopher. '*Zafarnama*'. *Journal of Punjab Studies* 15, nos 1 and 2 (Spring–Fall 2008).

Shah, Ami P. 'Liturgical Compositions in the *Dasam Granth*'. *Journal of Punjab Studies* 15, nos 1 and 2 (Spring–Fall 2008).

Proceedings of History Conferences

Banga, Indu. 'Ahmad Shah Abdali's Designs over the Punjab'. *Proceedings Indian History Conference*, 67th Session. Patiala, 1968.

Grewal, J. S. 'Gender Relations in the *Mahima Prakash (Vartak)*'. 44th Session. *Proceedings Punjab History Conference*. Patiala, 2013.

Malhotra, Karamjit K. 'Equality and Caste among Eighteenth-Century Sikhs'. *Proceedings Indian History Congress*, 72nd Session. Patiala, 2012.

Singh, Gurtej. 'Bhai Mani Singh: in Historical Perspective'. *Proceedings Punjab History Conference*, Patiala: Punjabi University, 1968.

Dissertations

Goswamy, B. N. 'The Social Background of Kangra Valley Painting'. PhD diss., Panjab University, Chandigarh, 1961.

Sarwan Singh. 'Sant Das Chhibber, *Ustat Sri Amritsar Ji Ki*'. MPhil diss., Guru Nanak Dev University, Amritsar, 1988.

———. 'Amritsar in Medieval Punjabi Literature: An Historical Analysis'. PhD diss., Guru Nanak Dev University, Amritsar, 1994.

Shah, Ami P. 'In Praise of the Guru: A Study and Translation of Sainapati's *Gursobha*'. PhD diss., University of California, Santa Barbara, 2010.

Index

294 Index

About the Author

J.S. Grewal, formerly professor and vice chancellor, Guru Nanak Dev University, Amritsar, India, and director and later chairman, Indian Institute of Advanced Study, Shimla, India, has published extensively on the historiography of medieval India and Punjab and Sikh history. His most recent books published by Oxford University Press are *The Sikhs: Ideology, Institutions and Identity* (2009), *History, Literature, and Identity* (2014), *Master Tara Singh in Indian History* (2017), and *A Political Biography of Maharaja Ripudaman Singh of Nabha (1883–1942)* (2018).